ORGANIZING
THE PRESIDENCY

ORGANIZING
THE PRESIDENCY

Stephen Hess

☆ ☆ ☆ ☆ ☆ ☆ ☆ ☆ ☆ ☆ ☆ ☆

THE BROOKINGS INSTITUTION
WASHINGTON, D.C.

Copyright © 1976 by
THE BROOKINGS INSTITUTION
1775 Massachusetts Avenue, N.W.
Washington, D.C. 20036

Library of Congress Cataloging in Publication Data:

Hess, Stephen.
  Organizing the Presidency.

  Includes bibliographical references and index.
  1. Presidents—United States—Staff. 2. United
States—Politics and government—1933–1945.   3. United
States—Politics and government—1945– I. Title.
JK518.H46   353   76–28668
ISBN 0-8157-3588-x
ISBN 0-8157-3587-1 pbk.

1 2 3 4 5 6 7 8 9

THE BROOKINGS INSTITUTION is an independent organization devoted to nonpartisan research, education, and publication in economics, government, foreign policy, and the social sciences generally. Its principal purposes are to aid in the development of sound public policies and to promote public understanding of issues of national importance.

The Institution was founded on December 8, 1927, to merge the activities of the Institute for Government Research, founded in 1916, the Institute of Economics, founded in 1922, and the Robert Brookings Graduate School of Economics and Government, founded in 1924.

The Board of Trustees is responsible for the general administration of the Institution, while the immediate direction of the policies, program, and staff is vested in the President, assisted by an advisory committee of the officers and staff. The bylaws of the Institution state: "It is the function of the Trustees to make possible the conduct of scientific research, and publication, under the most favorable conditions, and to safeguard the independence of the research staff in the pursuit of their studies and in the publication of the results of such studies. It is not a part of their function to determine, control, or influence the conduct of particular investigations or the conclusions reached."

The President bears final responsibility for the decision to publish a manuscript as a Brookings book. In reaching his judgment on the competence, accuracy, and objectivity of each study, the President is advised by the director of the appropriate research program and weighs the views of a panel of expert outside readers who report to him in confidence on the quality of the work. Publication of a work signifies that it is deemed a competent treatment worthy of public consideration but does not imply endorsement of conclusions or recommendations.

The Institution maintains its position of neutrality on issues of public policy in order to safeguard the intellectual freedom of the staff. Hence interpretations or conclusions in Brookings publications should be understood to be solely those of the authors and should not be attributed to the Institution, to its trustees, officers, or other staff members, or to the organizations that support its research.

Foreword

THE PRESIDENCY has provided a rich field of inquiry for social scientists and historians, but its organization has remained largely unexamined. Partly, one suspects, this is because the inner workings of the White House have been hidden from public scrutiny by some former presidential assistants and mythologized by others. It may also be that scholars have been little attracted to what seemed to be questions of mechanics. But the organization of the presidential office can influence events and policy, and an understanding of how the White House has been—and might be—organized is a desirable complement to recent studies of the effect that presidential character has on presidential behavior.

Stephen Hess, a Brookings senior fellow and former White House staff member, uses the history of the White House staffs during the administrations of Franklin Roosevelt through Richard Nixon as the background for prescriptive conclusions on how the presidency could be organized so as to improve policy formulation, delivery of services, and fidelity to democratic principles. His proposals are meant to correct what he sees as serious imbalances that have developed over past decades in the presidential system. Most specifically, he believes the relation between the White House and the Cabinet agencies has become distorted, and that the distortion has consequences not intended forty years ago when scholars and public officials first made the case for a "strong" presidency.

Mr. Hess is grateful to his Brookings colleagues Martha Derthick, I. M. Destler, Chester E. Finn, Jr., Hugh Heclo, Herbert Kaufman, Richard P. Nathan, Judith H. Parris, Gilbert Y. Steiner, and James L. Sundquist for their comments on the manuscript. He is equally grateful to the following readers outside Brookings: Benjamin V. Cohen, Andrew J. Goodpaster, Jr., Fred Greenstein, Erwin C. Hargrove, and Richard E. Neustadt. For making unpublished material available to him, he thanks Joel Aberbach, Thomas E. Cronin, Harrison W. Fox, Stephen Horn,

John Kessel, Fordyce Luikart, James Pfiffner, and Richard Rose. He also appreciates the services of Tadd Fisher, editorial associate, and of Florence Robinson, indexer, and the secretarial assistance of Gloria Jimenez, Radmila Reinhart, and Donna D. Verdier.

The views expressed in this book are those of the author and should not be ascribed to the trustees, officers, or other staff members of the Brookings Institution.

GILBERT Y. STEINER
Acting President

July 1976
Washington, D.C.

Contents

☆ ☆ ☆ ☆ ☆ ☆ ☆ ☆ ☆ ☆ ☆ ☆ ☆

INTRODUCTION

The Ultimate
Modern Presidency

☆ ☆ ☆ ☆ ☆ ☆ ☆ ☆ ☆ ☆ ☆ ☆ ☆

DURING the period from 1933 through 1964, when the majority view
was that social progress is best achieved through a strong presidency,
social scientists and others concentrated on finding ways to support a
President's natural instincts for doing good. This involved identifying
the forces that were frustrating presidential efforts, devising mechanisms to overcome those frustrations, and providing a President with
the means—people and money—to do his job. Thus the battle cry of
the famous 1937 Brownlow Report: "The President needs help."[1] Later,
given Vietnam and Watergate, Lyndon Johnson and Richard Nixon,
attention turned to how to inhibit a President from doing what he
wished to do. In either case—helping or hindering—the answer was often
sought in adjusting the way the presidency is organized.

Presidents had been given vast emergency powers before the New
Deal, always in anticipation of war or during its conduct. But the concept of the powerful Chief Executive was otherwise alien to the American ethic. According to the White House Chief Usher, before World
War I Woodrow Wilson "worked but three or four hours a day and
spent much of his time happily and quietly, sitting around with his
family." Calvin Coolidge is reported to have "slept on an average of
eleven hours per day."[2] The pace of the White House was reflected

1. President's Committee on Administrative Management, *Administrative Management in the Government of the United States* (Government Printing Office, 1937),
p. 5. The chairman of the committee was Louis Brownlow. (Hereafter referred to
as the Brownlow Report.)

2. Irvin H. Hoover, *Forty-two Years in the White House* (Houghton Mifflin, 1934),
pp. 266, 268.

1

in the modest size of its staff when Franklin Roosevelt took office. It soon became obvious, however, that the existing arrangements were inadequate to meet both the new responsibilities that Congress had given the President and the people's rising expectations of what they wished the federal government to do.

There were three possibilities for reorganization. A "fourth branch" could be created to fill the gap between the executive and the rest of government, a solution that had been tried without great success since the 1870s through congressionally sanctioned and presidentially appointed commissions and agencies. The executive departments could be restructured by subdividing the departments into smaller units or by consolidating them into fewer and larger units, with the hope in either case that they would be more efficient and responsive. Or the presidential office could be enlarged.

With Roosevelt's blessing, the President's Committee on Administrative Management, chaired by Louis Brownlow, chose the third option, urging the creation of an Executive Office of the President and additional all-purpose White House aides. Subsequent bodies of distinguished citizens proposed other ways to help the President. The first Hoover Commission (1949) proposed a White House office for personnel management and a staff secretariat. The President's Advisory Committee on Government Organization (1953) proposed a strengthened National Security Council staff with a presidential assistant as its executive officer. The Commission on Intergovernmental Relations (1955) proposed a presidential office to monitor federal-state relations. The President's Task Force on Government Organization (1967) proposed stationing "presidential representatives" around the country. The Advisory Council on Executive Organization (1970) proposed a Domestic Council.

World War II and its aftermath, the country's new role as a world leader, and national fears of economic dislocation, thrust additional burdens on the President and accelerated the trend toward White House centralization. Congress passed laws creating the President's Council of Economic Advisers (1946) and the National Security Council (1947). Later, Congress enlarged the Executive Office with the addition of an Office of Special Representative for Trade Negotiations (1963), a Council on Environmental Quality (1970), and a White House Office of Science and Technology Policy (1976).

Thus the growth of the White House establishment reflects a conscious effort over four decades to impose a presidential presence on an

executive conglomerate, which today is too vast for personal supervision. It also is a manifestation of the multiple roles that have been
given to or assumed by Presidents: Commander in Chief, primary pro-
poser of legislation and chief lobbyist, top executive in the executive
branch, guardian of the economy, negotiator with other nations, head
of state, party leader, and moral leader.[3]

A President allots his time and organizes his administration along
the lines of the diverse functions he must perform, hires different people
to support him in his different duties, and organizes those around him
to accommodate his perceptions of his task. Roosevelt constructed a
circle with himself at the hub. Eisenhower designed a pyramid with
himself at the apex. A President chooses the degree of tidiness or chaos
that best supports his work habits. He chooses the amount of advice
he wants to get from within government and how much he wants to
receive from outside. He decides to give competing assignments and
overlapping jurisdictions or to rely on aides with specific and tightly
defined responsibilities. He selects between formal lines of command
and informal arrangements. He chooses between the advice of specialists
and generalists.

Each President receives advice in the way he finds most congenial.
Big meetings. Small meetings. No meetings. Long reports. Short memos.
Each picks his own advice systems. He convenes conferences, commissions, task forces, and committees. He turns to Cabinet members, cronies,
family, and staff. Each picks his own immediate subordinates, relying
on lawyers and businessmen, generals and diplomats, scholars, union
leaders, and party leaders. He seeks advice that is agreeable and advice
that is representative. From blacks, westerners, Catholics, bankers. He
seeks assistants who are loyal yet independent, free thinkers yet team
players.

And each President expects his way to make a difference.

The United States is a nation of organizations and organizers. Americans care about efficiency and effectiveness. They are troubled by waste,
duplication, incompetence, and corruption. In a nation that knows
a great deal about corporate management, surely there must be methods
and techniques of organization that can be successfully transplanted
to government.

3. This list is only meant to be illustrative. In "What Makes a 'Strong' President?"
New York Times Magazine, December 13, 1953, Sidney Hyman lists Chief of State
and fourteen other "chiefships."

"Organization cannot make a genius out of an incompetent," Eisenhower thought. "On the other hand, disorganization can scarcely fail to result in inefficiency and can easily lead to disaster."[4]

When a President makes a bad decision, Americans expect him and others in government to try to figure out what went wrong with "the system." After the Bay of Pigs, President Kennedy had a better understanding of whose advice to trust, but he also thought he had learned some things about what sort of a system he should rely on for advice. Perhaps reflecting on President Johnson's escalation of the war in Vietnam, Johnson's former Press Secretary, George Reedy, wondered what is wrong with a system in which no one ever invites a President to go soak his head?[5]

The Watergate scandals raised a series of troubling questions about how President Nixon organized his administration. Had he delegated too much responsibility? Had he given too much power to others? Had his staff grown beyond control? Why did he pick the wrong advisers? Was Watergate related to the centralizing of administration in the White House and the downgrading of the Cabinet and permanent government?[6]

The organization of the presidency, with few exceptions, is not rooted in statute and has changed so many times, often so substantially, as to suggest that it will continue to change in response to needs, whims, pressures, the desires of incumbents, and even new information. Most Americans assume that there is an inevitable relationship between policy content, implementation, and organization, and that therefore adjustments in organization can produce better policy and better delivery. This postulate deserves more skepticism than it usually receives. Still, it is a hopeful way of proceeding, premised as it is on the belief that how things are done makes a difference.

THIS STUDY is about how modern Presidents have organized themselves. Primarily it concerns the White House staff and secondarily those other

4. Dwight D. Eisenhower, *The White House Years: Mandate for Change, 1953–1956* (Doubleday, 1963), p. 114.

5. George E. Reedy, *The Twilight of the Presidency* (New American Library, 1970), p. 18.

6. See *Watergate: Its Implications for Responsible Government*, A report by a Panel of the National Academy of Public Administration at the request of the Senate Select Committee on Presidential Campaign Activities (Government Printing Office, March 1974), especially pp. 27–42.

avenues of advice—the Executive Office, the Cabinet, the Vice President, outsiders—on whom Presidents rely in order to perform their duties. The first chapter is devoted to the context in which Presidents work and is a view of the presidency from the vantage point of those who have attained it during the past four decades. It provides a frame of reference for the subsequent discussion of recent presidential administrations and why Presidents act the way they do in handling such common problems as personnel selection; congressional relations; press relations; speechwriting; gathering economic, domestic, and national security information; and relations with their Cabinets and between their department heads and White House assistants.

Presidents before Roosevelt did not "run" or "manage" the executive branch from the White House, at least not in the sense of a corporation being run or managed by its chief operating officer. During Roosevelt's first two terms the White House staff was structured to serve his personal needs. It was considerably bigger, though not significantly different from that of past Presidents. Since Roosevelt conceived of the presidency as a "bully pulpit," in the manner of his cousin Theodore, his assistants were largely engaged in helping him in his efforts to shape public opinion.

There was no National Security Council or Domestic Council with responsibilities for departmental oversight. There was no congressional relations office in the White House. Presidential assistants were considered utility infielders who moved from one position to another as needed or as the President's fancy dictated.

While Roosevelt did not seek collective counsel from his Cabinet, the Cabinet officers still had the major responsibility for running their departments, drafting legislation, and lobbying it through Congress. At the same time, however, Roosevelt created a myriad of new agencies, reporting directly to him, that impinged on the jurisdictions of the Cabinet departments.

During Roosevelt's third term some independent power bases were established on the White House staff. Subtly, the direction of decision-making changed; certain major policies began to take form in the White House offices of intimate advisers who frequently assumed the prerogatives of the department heads.

The new Executive Office of the President, created in 1939, vastly expanded Roosevelt's outreach and, like the Brownlow Committee, he began to see his task as President as being that of chief manager of the executive branch. The Bureau of the Budget, meant to serve the institutional presidency, was gradually being pulled into the stronger magnetic field of the personal presidency. It is of special importance that Roosevelt lived in the White House for over twelve years and that during that period the United States fought a great depression and a great war. The unprecedented duration of his tenure as President meant that to an unusual degree his style shaped the concept of the office, and great events shaped the magnitude of government. Thus by the time of Roosevelt's death in 1945 most of the elements of the modern presidency were in place, even if in embryonic form. The President, rather than Congress, had clearly become the center of federal attention.

Under Harry Truman, the atomization of the White House—the separation of staff by function—assumed modest momentum. While his assistants, like Roosevelt's, were generalists for the most part, some now handled specific subject assignments. John Steelman, for example, dealt with labor-management relations; others were charged with minority group relations and congressional relations. A hierarchical form also started to take shape as top presidential aides began to build supporting staffs. Steelman, Clark Clifford, and Charles Murphy had assistants of their own—precedent for the fiefdoms that later distinguished the White House.

The distinction between Cabinet officers as policy advocates and White House staff as personal service aides had narrowed somewhat in the late Roosevelt period, given the powers bestowed on Harry Hopkins and Samuel Rosenman. But Clifford, as the chief architect of Truman's Fair Deal, virtually erased the boundary between Cabinet and White House in this regard. Moreover, Clifford's success illustrated that proximity to the President was a blessing of no small value.

The theoretical line between the institutional and personal presidencies that separated the Executive Office from the White House also became more blurred as the Budget Bureau provided staff and services for presidential assistants. At the same time, two major units joined the White House complex, the Council of Economic Advisers and the National Security Council, each giving the President a capacity for surveillance of important government activities that was not totally dependent on the departments.

Dwight Eisenhower, having spent most of his life in the military, organized the White House along different lines that he found more familiar and congenial. He surrounded himself with structure, including a staff secretariat in charge of the flow of papers to and from the Oval Office and a secretariat in charge of the machinery of Cabinet meetings. Experts, rather than generalists, advised on a variety of questions that he felt were inadequately handled by the departments. An elaborate apparatus was invented for national security affairs, although the chief foreign policy adviser continued to be the Secretary of State. A full-scale congressional relations office was added to the White House and acted as a buffer between the President and Congress. Eisenhower's Press Secretary devised more sophisticated techniques for controlling the flow of news. A Chief of Staff, notably Sherman Adams, was responsible for the proper functioning of all these new offices—which had increased the size of the White House but not its operational capacity. Eisenhower still expected Cabinet officers to run their departments with a minimum of second-guessing from his staff.

John Kennedy and Lyndon Johnson scuttled much of the machinery they found in the White House because they were told it was unsuited to the needs of an activist liberal administration and because it made them uncomfortable. Yet even without the paraphernalia of staff and Cabinet secretariats, a Chief of Staff's office, and an overblown National Security Council, the total size of the presidency (personal staff, executive office units, presidential councils) continued to grow. Kennedy and Johnson wanted government to do more faster, and as a result agencies such as the Office of Economic Opportunity were placed directly under the presidential umbrella.

A consequence of the trend toward more direct White House involvement in department operations was that presidential aides sometimes issued instructions to Cabinet officers' subordinates. This reflected Kennedy's disinterest in organizational maintenance, the energy and impatience of his White House staff, and the President's conception of the presidential office as the moving force of government. By the Johnson administration "the White House was no longer an antiseptic shrine where high policy was formulated and promulgated in dignity" and had become, for the first time, "the operational center" of the executive branch.[7]

The Rooseveltian model, as adapted by Kennedy, attracted some superior persons to Washington, raised the level of debate on certain issues, and produced several government initiatives. Kennedy also took

7. William D. Carey, "Presidential Staffing in the Sixties and Seventies," *Public Administration Review*, vol. 39 (September-October 1969), p. 454.

the nation on a roller coaster ride of successes and failures—the Bay of Pigs and the Cuban missile crisis—and when the presidency was inherited by Johnson, who retained most of Kennedy's advisers and who shared Kennedy's faith in the Rooseveltian model, the end result was a string of stunning legislative enactments and massive involvement in Vietnam.

By Johnson's time, the advantages of the personalized and centralized presidency had been well documented by a generation of commentators; its liabilities first came under serious questioning after he took office. The personalized presidency largely depends on the leader's ability to mobilize public opinion to put pressure on the government to perform as he desires and to support what he believes is right. If the President lacks this skill, he cannot compensate in the long run by relying on the inherent strength of the office. The centralized presidency largely depends on the leader's ability to keep lines open to those outside his immediate circle and to resist minutiae. If the President is suspicious of Cabinet members and relies too heavily on overworked assistants, he is apt to lose perspective and even his sense of reality.

When Richard Nixon succeeded Johnson in 1969 he became the first activist conservative President. In the White House, party and ideology changed, but not the direction of the personalized and centralized presidency. There was, however, an essential difference in style, which ultimately had a major impact on governance. Johnson, even when the Vietnam protest limited his mobility, quested for contacts beyond the confines of the White House; Nixon, on the contrary, sought isolation. He structured his White House staff to limit his associates to those with whom he felt most comfortable, his most loyal aides over whom he had greatest control. In the end, a Greta Garbo conception of the presidency was unsuited to democratic leadership, which must depend on keeping in touch with the other actors in the governing process.

But even putting aside the character of Richard Nixon and the question of how presidential precedents, when pushed beyond the limits of legality, contributed importantly to Watergate and the resignation of a President, Nixon's mode of operating illustrates the inadequacy of running the government through an overly personalized, centralized White House command post.

DURING THE COURSE of the six chapters on the administrations of Roosevelt through Nixon, the development of four characteristics that contribute to the malfunctioning of the modern presidency will be traced.

The first is the prodigious growth of the presidency. By the time Nixon left office the number of people employed by the White House and the Executive Office had nearly doubled from its size under Johnson, just as Johnson's staff had nearly doubled from its size at the time of FDR's death. Over the course of forty years the White House staff had grown from 37 to 600, the Executive Office staff from zero to many thousands.[8] With the bureaucratizing of the presidency, it is hardly surprising that the White House fell heir to all the problems of a bureaucracy, including the distorting of information as it passes up the chain of command and frustrating delays in decisionmaking.

The second characteristic of the modern presidency is the steadily rising influence of White House staff members as presidential advisers, with a corresponding decline in Cabinet influence. (The Eisenhower administration was the only exception.) Under Nixon virtually all policy, domestic and foreign, was initiated at the White House. This has meant a serious separation of policy formulation from its implementation. It also may have created more idiosyncratic policy, since White House aides often operate with fewer constraints and less feel for what can be achieved.

A third characteristic of the modern presidency that has gradually come into focus is the President's increasing suspicion of the permanent government, leading to a vast proliferation of functional offices within the White House and to the White House doing things because the President does not trust the bureaucracy to do them, including spying on government officials and journalists. Blaming the bureaucracy is an easy way to gloss over the failures of government, yet running a government without the support of the bureaucracy is like running a train without an engine.

The fourth characteristic is that presidential assistants increasingly become "special pleaders." This trend began benignly enough when Truman gave an aide responsibility for minority group affairs, in a sense creating a presidential spokesman for those who were otherwise underrepresented in the councils of government. Then each successive President added other "representatives" until under Nixon there were White House assistants for the aged, youth, women, blacks, Jews, labor,

8. See "The Development of the White House Staff," a report prepared by the Congressional Research Service, Library of Congress, May 25, 1972, in *Congressional Record* (daily ed., June 20, 1972), pp. H5818–20.

Hispanic-Americans, the business community, Governors and Mayors, artists, and citizens of the District of Columbia, as well as such concerns as drug abuse, energy, environment, physical fitness, volunteerism, telecommunications, and national goals.[9] Where once the White House had been a mediator of interests, it now had become a collection of interests.

So by the early 1970s the Ultimate Modern Presidency was attempting to create all policy at the White House, to oversee the operations of government from the White House, to use White House staff to operate programs of high presidential priority, and to represent in the White House all interests that are demographically separable. This attempt could never have succeeded. The White House staff—even at its overblown size—was simply too inadequate a fulcrum to move the weight of the executive branch, which employed nearly 5 million people and spent over $300 billion annually.

In the final four chapters of this study I return to the riddle left by Roosevelt—has the growth of government outstripped a highly personalized presidency that has to rely on the involvement of the Chief Executive and his staff surrogates?—and argue on behalf of creating a more collegial form of presidential establishment.

I propose a redefinition of the tasks of Presidents, those activities that they must perform and that cannot be performed by others. The corollary is that the many other tasks currently performed badly by Presidents must be performed elsewhere.

My contention is that Presidents have made a serious mistake, starting with Roosevelt, in asserting that they are the chief managers of the federal government. It is hard to find firm evidence for the chief manager proposition in the Constitution. Congress, in fact, except in the case of the Secretary of State and in certain emergency legislation, gives the authority to run programs directly to department heads, not to the President to be redelegated to department heads.

This suggests that a trend of forty years must be reversed. Presidents must rely on their department and agency heads to run the departments and agencies, must hold these executives strictly accountable, and must rely on them as principal advisers.

Rather than chief manager, the President is chief political officer

9. See Thomas E. Cronin, "The Swelling of the Presidency and its Impact on Congress," *Working Papers on House Committee Organization and Operation*, House Select Committee on Committees, 93 Cong. (Government Printing Office, 1973).

of the United States. His major responsibility, in my judgment, is to annually make a relatively small number of highly significant political decisions—among them, setting national priorities, which he does through the budget and his legislative proposals, and devising policy to ensure the security of the country, with special attention to those situations that could involve the nation in war.

Agreed, this is a considerably more modest definition of the presidency than national leaders and some scholars have led Americans to expect, and it does not guarantee that U.S. leaders will always make wise decisions. It is also a definition that may warrant rethinking at some future time and under different circumstances. For now, however, it is a definition for presidential conduct that is apt to provide more effective government services, fewer unfulfilled promises, and less alienation in our society.

To the degree that Presidents undermine confidence in the presidency by overloading the White House staff beyond its capacity to effect change and deliver services, the solution lies in a different set of reciprocal relationships between Presidents, presidential staffs, and Cabinet members. The prescriptive section of this study suggests criteria and strategies to support such a reorganization. These proposals do not relate to ideology; a liberal or a conservative President could operate equally well within this framework with markedly different results. My task is to make the case that these arrangements are both necessary and feasible.

Evolution
☆ 1933-1974 ☆

☆ ☆ ☆ ☆ ☆ ☆ ☆ ☆ ☆ ☆ ☆ ☆ ☆

The Presidential
Context

☆ ☆ ☆ ☆ ☆ ☆ ☆ ☆ ☆ ☆ ☆ ☆ ☆

ALTHOUGH my experiences are not a part of this study, in one sense
they reinforce a premise of this chapter. Twice I have served on White
House staffs—at the end of one administration (1959–61) and at the
beginning of another (1969). All presidencies, of course, are different.
But one could hardly fail to observe differences that were exclusively
a product of time. *Beginnings* and *endings* are different. There are differences of pace, attitude, objectives, and response, not only between
administrations but also within each one.

This point would be readily apparent in a detailed year-by-year
description of the presidency since 1933. For the purposes of this study,
however, I have chosen to base my conclusions on relatively short, sometimes impressionistic, accounts of six modern presidencies. Still, it is
useful to keep in mind the plastic qualities of each administration.

This, then, is a composite portrait of a President over the course of
his years in office. (Exceptions to generalities are noted.) I attempt to
see the presidency as it appears to a President, in the "presidential context." The emphasis may seem strange to many who have not had an
opportunity to glimpse a President up close, especially since much of
the current literature focuses on the powerfulness of the office. My conclusion is not that the office is unpowerful. Rather, the accent is on
presidential constraints. Often in the following pages the President will
seem a hapless giant, surrounded by enemies, hemmed in by competing
power centers, responding to events that he did not create and cannot
control. This is how the presidency increasingly looks to the man who
occupies it. The vantage point may help to explain why Presidents act
the way they do.

EVERY FOURTH even-numbered year, on a Tuesday between the second and eighth of November, a President is elected. If he is not the incumbent, he has a period of grace until January 20 during which he can organize his administration without having to assume the responsibilities of office. He brings to this task certain knowledge and experience, obligations and commitments.

If he is like most of his predecessors, he probably has a background as a legislator or a Governor. If the nation has recently fought in a popular war, he may be a military man. It is possible that he has served as Vice President. The odds, however, are great that he has not held an executive position in the federal government.[1] He may, in fact, never have been an executive. Some of his experiences will be of considerable value; for example, Lyndon Johnson's understanding of the workings of Congress and Dwight Eisenhower's understanding of the workings of the Pentagon. By the act of running for the presidency, all elected Presidents should have gained some useful understanding of public opinion. But no matter how much he may have thought and read about the presidency, the most startling fact about a new President is the depth of his ignorance about the *job* to which he has just been elected. At least two recent Presidents have commented on this phenomenon. The learning period for a new President has been estimated by one scholar as taking about eighteen months.[2] One consequence is that a new President makes some of his most important decisions at a time when he is least capable of deciding wisely.

The White House staff will consist largely of those who have surrounded the candidate during the campaign and who have his trust. They bring to their jobs an understanding of the President, loyalty, and in some cases a set of skills that are transferable from the campaign, such as press relations and scheduling. Their primary interests, however, usually have been in the art of politics, not governance. While they are apt to begin their White House duties in a personal services relationship with the President, they will eventually acquire more and more governmental responsibilities, for Presidents have a habit of giving the jobs at hand to the persons at hand. Some of these former campaign workers may be qualified to assume operational assignments,

1. Of the modern Presidents, Franklin Roosevelt through Gerald Ford, only FDR had ever served as a political executive in Washington, having been Assistant Secretary of the Navy during World War I.

2. John H. Kessel, *The Domestic Presidency* (Duxbury, 1975), p. 10.

but not because they were campaign workers. One need only look at why they were in the campaign. Often their chief qualification—and an important one in a campaign—was availability; their chief motivations may have been the expectation of excitement, an excess of zeal, or hero worship.

The policy commitments of a new President are found in his campaign speeches, in the party platform, and to a lesser degree in the promises of other members of his party. These commitments are usually vague, given the tendencies of elective politics. In no sense can they be considered a presidential program. A program has a price tag and relates to available resources. One consequence is that at the time Congress is inclined to be most responsive to the wishes of a President, he is least able to make his wishes known in concrete terms.

On the morning after his victory, a President-elect is consumed with thoughts of Cabinet-making and other matters of personnel selection. No shadow Cabinet waits in the wings. A new President suddenly discovers how few people he knows who are qualified to assume major posts in government. "People, people, people!" John Kennedy exclaimed three weeks after his election, "I don't know any people. I only know voters."[3] A President-elect has obligations and political debts, but they are not necessarily to those with the backgrounds he now needs. Sometimes he picks incompetents. Often he turns to strangers. With each appointment, a President makes a contract to share his responsibilities. If it turns out that the appointee and the President disagree, the appointee can quit or the President can fire him. Either action is a tacit admission of failure on the part of the President. More likely, the President and the appointee split their differences and the President loses some part of the direction of his administration.

The problems of the presidential transition may be exacerbated by animosities between the incoming and outgoing Presidents and by tensions between the incoming President and the civil service.[4] If the newly elected President is from the party out of power, he probably campaigned against "bureaucracy," "red tape," and the "failures" of government programs. Almost all Presidents-to-be ascribe an alien political

3. Arthur M. Schlesinger, Jr., *A Thousand Days* (Fawcett, 1967), p. 124.

4. The problems are naturally greatest when the President-elect has defeated the incumbent President (FDR and Hoover in 1932) and least when both are of the same party, although problems can still exist in the latter case (Theodore Roosevelt and William Howard Taft in 1908), but they are apt to be caused by bruised egos rather than lack of cooperation.

coloration to the permanent government. Franklin Roosevelt considered it too conservative; Richard Nixon considered it too liberal. Nor is the new President necessarily paranoid. He is committed to change and perhaps even to reductions in programs and personnel; the permanent government may well see its interests as threatened.

Moreover, the next President is exhausted from the campaign. He will undoubtedly devote some of his precious transition days to recuperating, and if he holds another position, such as Governor, he will also have to wind up that business. Other chores must be attended to— planning for the inauguration, writing an inaugural address, possibly drafting a State of the Union message, making budget revisions, and getting ready for the opening of Congress.

On taking office, the new President finds he is confronted with a backlog of decisions that need to be made. Government has a way of treading water during presidential campaigns as it waits to see who will be its next leader. And decisions postponed build pressure for resolution. Thus the President at first is presented with great opportunities and great dangers.

The dangers are compounded by the arrogance of the incoming administration. For two years or more the candidate and his closest advisers have been working toward a single goal. The goal has been incredibly difficult and complex to achieve. Gaining it has been a rare achievement that comes to few. They have a right to believe that they succeeded because of their skill, intelligence, political understanding, and hard work. It is not surprising that some of the greatest presidential disasters—even to second-term Presidents—have come in the immediate afterglow of election victories.[5] Indeed the bigger the victory, it would seem, the greater the opportunity for disaster.

The new President also finds he has inherited a variety of organizational arrangements that were created to deal with his predecessor's problems. Each administration over time invents a variety of offices that reflect the special talents or deficiencies of appointees, rivalries between advisers, pet projects of the President, and constituent pressures. Sometimes new Presidents will overreact to this legacy, as when Kennedy quickly jettisoned the National Security Council machinery of the Eisenhower administration so that he was left without an appropriate

5. Among the disasters that followed election victories have been the Roosevelt court-packing plan (1937), the Bay of Pigs (1961), and the decision to escalate the Vietnam war (1965).

evaluative capacity at the White House when an early foreign policy crisis arose.

Each President soon comes to agree with Woodrow Wilson: "Governments grow piecemeal, both in their tasks and in the means by which those tasks are to be performed, and very few governments are organized as wise and experienced men would organize them if they had a clean sheet of paper to write upon."[6] Yet no matter how inefficiently or illogically the government is organized, there are those who like it that way. Congress, special-interest groups, and bureaucrats have grown comfortable with existing arrangements and have a vested interest in their continuation. The public is not usually much concerned and hence is hard to mobilize for such bloodless matters as structural change. Presidents fret a lot about the ill-fitting shape of government, but generally they conclude that serious attempts at restructuring are no-win propositions. Neither the voters nor the annals of history reward them for such efforts. So (with the exception of Roosevelt and Nixon) they propose only marginal reforms. They add boxes to the organizational chart as needs arise, rarely erase existing offices unless they are glaringly obsolete, and thus leave government even more cumbersome than they found it.

Much of the tone of the new administration is a response or reaction to the outgoing administration. Eisenhower felt strongly the necessity of establishing a sense of calm after what he considered the divisiveness of Harry Truman's government. In the wake of Kennedy's assassination, Johnson stressed the need for continuity. Gerald Ford's open behavior was meant as an antidote to the dark side of the Nixon presidency.

Other elements of a President's inheritance start to come into focus. He finds that it will not be until his third year in office that he will be able to operate under a budget that his own appointees have initiated. Even then much federal spending will be in "uncontrollables" and not subject to his influence. His power to appoint only extends to some 3,000 people out of a government civilian work force of over 2 million. Some officials have term appointments and cannot be removed before their time is up. The new President must abide by laws and treaties that were not of his making. There are traditions that he cannot ignore except at great risk. He begins to realize that government is like a con-

6. Ray S. Baker and William F. Dodd, eds., *The Public Papers of Woodrow Wilson* (Harper, 1926), vol. 1, p. 222.

tinuously moving conveyor belt. He jumps on while it is in motion. It cannot be stopped in order for him to engineer change.

His ability to act, he finds, is also limited by external considerations: whether the nation is in the midst of war or peace, whether the gross national product is rising or falling, the rate of inflation, the balance of payments, the composition of the Supreme Court and Congress, and the size of his electoral mandate. Once in office, President Kennedy was fond of quoting Thomas Jefferson's dictum, "Great innovations should not be forced on slender majorities."[7]

Yet the new administration begins in a state of euphoria. Reporters are inclined to be kind. Congress is quiescent. There is not yet a record to defend. The President, for the only time, takes a broad-gauged look at existing policies. His popularity ratings in the polls will never again be as high.[8]

An adviser to Presidents summed up the importance of an administration's early months:

Everything depends on what you do in program formulation during the first six or seven months. I have watched three presidencies and I am increasingly convinced of that. Time goes by so fast. During the first six months or so, the White House staff is not hated by the cabinet, there is a period of friendship and cooperation and excitement. There is some animal energy going for you in those first six to eight months, especially if people perceive things in the same light. If that exists and so long as that exists you can get a lot done. You only have a year at the most for new initiatives, a time when you can establish some programs as your own, in contrast to what has gone on before.[9]

Then the administration has its first foreign crisis and its first domestic scandal. Weaknesses in personnel begin to appear. The novelty of new personalities wears off for the press. The President introduces his legislative program. The process known as "the coalition-of-minorities" takes hold. Every presidential action will alienate someone. The longer he is in office, the more actions he must take, and collectively, the more sizable the body of those in opposition will be. Groups that would not attack him when his popularity was high now become vocal.

7. Theodore C. Sorensen, *Decision-Making in the White House* (Columbia University Press, paperback ed., 1964), p. 48.
8. See John E. Mueller, *War, Presidents and Public Opinion* (Wiley, 1973), p. 206.
9. Unidentified adviser quoted in Thomas E. Cronin, *The State of the Presidency* (Little, Brown, 1975), p. 184.

His poll ratings start to drop at a rate of some six percentage points a year.[10]

By the end of his first year the President should have learned two important lessons: first, that the unexpected is likely to happen; second, that his plans are unlikely to work out as he had hoped. The Soviet Union launches Sputnik. A U-2 is shot down. There is an uprising in Hungary, a riot in Watts, a demonstration at Berkeley. U.S. missiles that he thought had been removed from Turkey were not removed. The Chinese explode a nuclear device earlier than his intelligence forecasts had predicted. The President finds that much of his time is spent reacting to events over which he has no control or trying to correct the errors of others.

Presidents start to turn inward, some sooner than others, the rate depending on personality factors and the ratio of successes to failures. Reading the morning newspapers becomes less satisfying. They bring bad news. They never seem to get their stories straight. Editorials and columns note only the things that go wrong. The President holds fewer news conferences. He looks for ways to go over the heads of the press corps, such as televised speeches. He grants exclusive interviews to friendly reporters.

Some members of his Cabinet, he feels, have "gone native." They badger him on behalf of their departments' clients. Others he finds long-winded or not very bright. There are now longer intervals between Cabinet meetings. He tells his Appointments Secretary to make it difficult for certain department heads to get in to see him alone.

Time is running out on his first term. Things are not getting done, or not fast enough. He begins to feel that if he wants action he will have to initiate it himself—meaning through his own staff. The White House grows bigger, despite his early promises to reduce its size. Types of decisions that used to be made in the departments now need White House clearance. Bottlenecks develop as too many agencies are funneled through too few presidential assistants. Programs that the President wishes to give high priority are placed directly within the Executive Office.

The midterm congressional elections approach, and the President

10. Mueller, *War, Presidents and Public Opinion*, pp. 220, 223. The only exception is Eisenhower, whose popularity *increased* by some two and one-half percentage points a year in his first term.

tries to restore his luster at the polls. He always fails.[11] His party loses seats. The new Congress is less receptive to the President's wishes. This process was described by Lyndon Johnson late in his administration:

> You've got to give it all you can that first year. Doesn't matter what kind of majority you come in with. You've got just one year when they treat you right, and before they start worrying about themselves. The third year, you lose votes. . . . The fourth year's all politics. You can't put anything through when half of the Congress is thinking how to beat you. So you've got one year. That's why I tried. Well, we gave it a hell of a lick, didn't we?[12]

The President now devotes a larger part of his time to foreign policy, perhaps as much as two-thirds. This is true even if his pre-presidential interests had been mainly in the domestic area. He takes trips abroad, attends summit meetings, hosts heads of state at the White House. Like Kennedy, he believes that "the big difference" between domestic and foreign policy "is that between a bill being defeated and the country [being] wiped out."[13] But he also turns to foreign policy because it is the area in which he has the most authority to act and, until recently, the least public and congressional restraint on his actions. Moreover, history usually rewards the foreign policy President, and the longer a President stays in office, the larger looms his "place in history."

The third year the exodus from government begins and the problems of replacing personnel assume some importance. Many of those who were attracted to the glitter of a new administration find that they cannot spare any more time away from their "real" careers, especially if they come from the highly competitive corporate world; others find that their government experience has created nongovernment offers they cannot refuse; some realize they made a mistake in coming to Washington, or their families are urging them to return home. "Fatigue becomes a factor," Henry Kissinger noted in 1972. "I always thought my mind would develop in a high position." But he found that the "mind is always working so hard that you learn little. Instead, you tend to work with what you learned in previous years."[14] The lure of

11. The only modern President to have his party gain seats in both houses of Congress in a midterm election was Franklin Roosevelt in 1934. See Louis H. Bean, *How to Predict the 1972 Election* (Quadrangle, 1972), pp. 228–30.

12. Quoted in Harry McPherson, *A Political Education* (Atlantic Monthly Press, 1972), p. 268.

13. Quoted in Theodore C. Sorensen, *Kennedy* (Bantam Books, 1966), p. 573.

14. Quoted in Norman Mailer, *St. George and the Godfather* (New American Library, 1972), p. 120.

a waning administration is not great and so the President often turns to careerists, promoting from within.

Personal alliances and rivalries by now have had full opportunity to develop within the administration. Remembering his experiences on the Truman staff, Clark Clifford recalled how "you develop areas of resistance. You come up with an idea, and you could guarantee in advance those men in government who would take the opposite position, just because you favored something."[15] The President's needs change, too. Milton Eisenhower noted how in the beginning of Roosevelt's presidency "he needed ideas" (and turned to Raymond Moley, Rexford Tugwell, A. A. Berle, and others); later he needed "legislative and political skills" (Thomas Corcoran); and finally his "greatest need was for administrative trouble shooters" (Harry Hopkins and Samuel Rosenman).[16] Rarely are all three types of abilities found in the same person.

The President may have taken office with only the most limited notions of what he wanted to do, but by the second half of his term he has accumulated a long list of his positions, which must be promoted and defended and which will determine whether he is reelected or not. He now has strong feelings about what is in the national interest and what must be done—regardless of the popularity of his actions. He has come to see the national interest as uniquely his to uphold. When announcing the decision to send troops into Cambodia in the spring of 1970, President Nixon told the American people, "I would rather be a one-term President and do what I believe is right than to be a two-term President at the cost of seeing America become a second-rate power and to see this Nation accept the first defeat in its proud 190-year history."[17] There may have been some posturing in his statement, yet his is a posture that is eventually assumed by all Presidents. The lines harden.

As the administration enters its fourth year, the President's attention snaps back to domestic considerations.[18] The political quotient that enters into each presidential act becomes more determining. Appointments are made with an eye to mending fences in his party. Program-

15. Quoted in Joseph C. Goulden, *The Superlawyers* (Dell, 1973), pp. 87–88.

16. Milton S. Eisenhower, *The President is Calling* (Doubleday, 1974), p. 155.

17. *Public Papers of the Presidents, Richard Nixon, 1970* (Government Printing Office, 1971), p. 410.

18. See John H. Kessel, "The Parameters of Presidential Politics" (paper delivered at the Annual Meeting of the American Political Science Association, Washington, D.C., September 5–9, 1972; processed).

matic decisions of high risk may be deferred. "Wait until next year, Henry," Roosevelt told Treasury Secretary Morganthau in May 1936. "I am going to be really radical." [19] Some members of the administration join the campaign staff, others continue to perform their duties with an eye to the election payoff of actions taken. The President finds excuses to make "nonpolitical" speeches around the country. By summer he is nominated for a second term and begins active campaigning.

If the President is reelected, it is largely on the basis of the past—the state of the nation during his incumbency—rather than his promises for the future. What is unspoken is that his next four years will be less productive than the previous four years. There are some exceptions. Wilson in 1917 and Roosevelt in 1941 had opportunities to preside over "just" wars. Generally, however, at least since Jefferson, the second term is downhill.[20]

But first the newly reelected President will make an effort to recast his administration by bringing in new people or by giving new assignments, as Nixon did in 1973. He will take advantage of his renewed popularity by pushing his legislative program, as Johnson did in 1965. He will unveil pet schemes that he had previously kept to himself, as Roosevelt did in 1937. In the President's fifth and sixth years—as in his third—there is considerable maneuvering room to shape events. (Although deaths and a resignation have meant that some Presidents did not get their full allotment of years in office.)

Then, as Harold Laski noted as far back as 1940, the two-term tradition (now the two-term limitation) "operates decisively to weaken his influence in the last two years of his reign. Few Presidents have had substantial results to show during that period."[21] The President's party again loses seats in the midterm election—a signal for potential presidential candidates to start increasing their visibility. One way to make news is to attack the incumbent. The attention of the press gradually shifts to these new men. Some of the President's executives resign to enter the embryonic campaigns. The personnel pattern of the first term repeats itself, only it is now even more difficult to recruit from outside

19. Quoted in Arthur M. Schlesinger, Jr., *The Age of Roosevelt*, vol. 3: *The Politics of Upheaval* (Sentry, 1966), p. 513.

20. See John Pierson, "Is a Second Term Always Downhill?" *Wall Street Journal*, January 4, 1973. He claimed that Theodore Roosevelt's second term was "uphill" and that the second terms of Coolidge and Eisenhower were no worse than their first terms.

21. Harold J. Laski, *The American Presidency* (Harper, 1940), p. 65.

government. The President will continue to hold the nation's attention if there is a serious international crisis; otherwise, he must try to manufacture interest through summit meetings, foreign travel (the more exotic the better), and by attaching himself to major events, such as space exploits, disaster relief, or even athletic achievements that involve his countrymen. Foreign powers may prefer to stall various negotiations until a new President is installed. The last year of his administration is also an election year for the House of Representatives and a third of the Senate, with the predictable consequences for the President's legislative program.

In the final July or August, the national conventions nominate two other men to run for President. The President will campaign for the nominee of his party, but fairly casually; he does not see it as his battle.

After the new man is elected there is no longer any vital force in the administration. There is some rush to tidy loose ends. Most appointees are looking forward to new jobs or retirement. The President collects his papers and ships his files so as to be able to get a quick start on his memoirs. There are farewell parties and a farewell address. The incoming people arrive for routine briefings, but except for mechanical advice, they are not really interested in the wisdom of those they will succeed.

At noon on January 20 the President watches his successor being sworn in. He is now an instant elder statesman.

THIS ACCOUNT stresses the institutional forces that press in upon a President. But, of course, being President need not be a grim experience. Depending on his personality, a President may have a very good time. Social scientists are beginning to become more aware of the importance of personality on presidential performance. In a heroic stab at identifying "healthy" presidential character, James David Barber used "positive-negative effect" as one measurement. The "positive" character "gives forth the feeling that he has *fun* in political life."[22] Roosevelt and Kennedy immediately come to mind as men who displayed a special enjoyment in being President.

And being President need not be an unproductive experience. Each President does realize some of his legislative goals and prevents by veto the enactment of other laws that he feels are not in the nation's best interests. His authority in the conduct of war and peace is sub-

22. James David Barber, *The Presidential Character* (Prentice-Hall, 1972), p. 11.

stantial. He uses his unique position to preach doctrines that have a better chance of entering the public consciousness than the competing ideas of other politicians. His power and influence may be limited, but they are also greater than those of any other individual.

Still, the experience of being President was different from what he thought it would be or from what he learned in his civics textbooks. Four years or eight years seemed like a very long time from the outside, a very short time when he was in office. Never long enough to do any real planning—to think about where the country ought to be even in the next decade and to design programs to get from here to there. His time was largely consumed by crises and the demands of others, bargaining with Congressmen, feuds, small symbolic acts, worrying about getting reelected, finding people for jobs and getting rid of them (usually by "kicking them upstairs"), approving budgets that he could only change around the edges. He never really "ran" the government as he had expected. Rather, the President found that his job was to try to keep the social fabric intact; to keep the peace if possible; to defend the nation from aggressors; to maintain the nation's place in the world, even by force; to attempt to balance economic growth and stability; and at best to make some new initiatives that the history books would record as his.

☆ ☆ ☆ ☆ ☆ ☆ ☆ ☆ ☆ ☆ ☆ ☆ ☆

CHAPTER TWO

Franklin D. Roosevelt
☆ 1933-1945 ☆

☆ ☆ ☆ ☆ ☆ ☆ ☆ ☆ ☆ ☆ ☆ ☆ ☆

THAT PART of the government over which Franklin Delano Roosevelt assumed command in March 1933 consisted of a thirty-seven-person White House staff, nine of professional rank, with those in the three key positions, known as Secretaries to the President, assigned to handle appointments, press, and correspondence; a career Executive Clerk in charge of mail and files; the Bureau of the Budget, located in the Treasury but otherwise an arm of the presidency, employing thirty-five persons; and ten Cabinet departments.[1] A number of commissions, although within the executive establishment, were beyond the range of presidential control, except for the power to appoint members for fixed terms.

There were 578,231 executive branch employees, of whom 467,161 were in the classified civil service. "A considerable proportion of them," in the opinion of a Roosevelt adviser, "had been appointed during the preceding twelve years of Republican rule. . . . What we called the Civil Service was, in the main, merely a mass of Republican political appointees frozen into office by act of Congress."[2]

In the year of Roosevelt's election 273,000 families were evicted from their homes. Yet government had neither the structure nor the personnel to deal with the most serious economic crisis in the nation's history.

1. State, War, Treasury, Post Office, Justice, Navy, Interior, Agriculture, Commerce, and Labor. There had been no change in departmental structure since the dividing of Commerce and Labor into separate departments in 1913.

2. Raymond Moley, *After Seven Years* (Harper, 1939), p. 128.

While the next years were to coincide with a worldwide trend toward centralized executive government, it was hardly without effect that Roosevelt was the first person to be the presiding officer of the modern presidency. Despite having been Governor of the most populous state, he was not much interested in the traditional forms of administration. "The Presidency is not merely an administrative office," he told Anne O'Hare McCormick in 1932. "That's the least of it. It is more than an engineering job, efficient or inefficient. It is pre-eminently a place of moral leadership."[3] Moreover, he was to stay in office long enough to give special weight to his view of the presidency. His administrative predilections were to stay flexible, to work informally, often outside the normal chain of command, to give competing assignments, to keep shifting the composition of his inner circle, to marshal support through adroit appeals to the public, and to maintain himself at the center of the action. A generation of political scientists would make of this style a virtue by which to measure future Presidents.

In staffing the administration, some appointments were the result of the usual vagaries, but in general Roosevelt relied on five (often overlapping) sources of talent:

—The friends and colleagues of his young years, his contemporaries in Washington under Woodrow Wilson (Daniel Roper, William Phillips, Breckinridge Long, William Bullitt); and more important, the small band of supporters who had recognized Roosevelt's political potential, in some cases as early as during his pre–World War tenure in the New York state legislature (Louis McHenry Howe, Stephen Early, and Marvin McIntyre).

—Those who had been in his state administration (Frances Perkins, Henry Morgenthau, Jr., Harry Hopkins, Samuel Rosenman).

—The 1932 campaigners, particularly those for Roosevelt before Chicago: professional politicians (James Farley); money men (Joseph Kennedy); and the Brain Trust, that body largely of Columbia University professors (Raymond Moley, Rexford Tugwell, Adolf Berle) who had provided the position papers and otherwise sought to educate the candidate on policy.

—The Old Boy Networks, people-who-knew-people-who-knew Roosevelt, the most fertile network being united through a connection with Professor Felix Frankfurter and the Harvard Law School.

3. Anne O'Hare McCormick, "Roosevelt's View of the Big Job," *New York Times Magazine*, September 11, 1932.

—The rank and file of the Democratic party, the foot troops of politics whose just rewards would be the more lowly jobs in Washington and around the country.

Roosevelt's staffing practices were primarily a haphazard blend of fortuity, friendship, obligation, and pressure, as were those of the Presidents who followed him. He was luckier than most and his network of acquaintances was larger than most. But it was not until much later that Presidents began to make tentative efforts to systematically assess the qualities needed in appointive office, and even now staffing remains an underdeveloped field of public administration.

When selecting the Cabinet, at least as it appeared to Moley, "there was neither a well-defined purpose nor an underlying principle" that guided Roosevelt.[4] Perkins was picked for Labor in part because Roosevelt wanted a woman in the Cabinet, although she was only tolerated by the unions. Harold Ickes at Interior was a Bull Mooser and not personally known to the President-elect. The choice of Claude Swanson for Navy may have been made for no better reason than to create a place in the Senate for Governor Harry Byrd of Virginia, and anyway, Roosevelt as an old Navy man would want to make key decisions himself. Henry Wallace, while a distinguished agricultural economist, was, like Ickes, a nominal Republican. Roper added no weight of any sort, but Commerce was no longer to be treated as a first-line department. Homer Cummings at Justice was a last-minute substitution, again like Ickes, reflecting the fact that four U.S. Senators had declined to enter the Cabinet. The practice of appointing the national committee chairman of the President's party to the position of Postmaster General was continued: Farley was put in charge of routine patronage, and by July 1934 he had located jobs for about 100,000 deserving Democrats—mostly in the new emergency agencies.

The one appointee of national stature was the Secretary of State, Senator Cordell Hull of Tennessee. Rosenman was to comment that "Hull was the one man in public life who could give the President substantial concern by threatening . . . to resign."[5] Later, men of greater distinction, such as Henry Stimson and Frank Knox, would join the Cabinet on the eve of World War II when FDR wished to give a bipartisan cast to national defense. Others, of course, would acquire distinction in office. But Rosenman's comment hinted at an "underlying

4. Moley, *After Seven Years*, p. 110.
5. Samuel I. Rosenman, *Working with Roosevelt* (Harper, 1952), p. 205.

principle": Roosevelt sought Cabinet subordinates who would not prove overshadowing or politically threatening—his administration was designed to be distinctly Rooseveltian.

A second underlying principle (although it is hazardous to attribute too much theorizing to Roosevelt, who operated largely on instinct) was the balancing of opposites. William Woodin, the first Secretary of the Treasury, was a conservative financier, as was Budget Director Lewis Douglas; others were clearly in the "spender" category, such as Hopkins, the Federal Emergency Relief Administrator and later Secretary of Commerce. "A little rivalry is stimulating, you know," the President was to explain to Perkins. "It keeps everybody going to prove he is a better fellow than the next man. It keeps them honest too."[6] In practice, the balancing of opposites sharpened the decisionmaking process, but the price paid was that frictions often carried over into program implementation.

Appointments to the sub-Cabinet—Under Secretaries, Assistant Secretaries, General Counsels—were of superior quality. Dean Acheson, Jerome Frank, Charles Wyzanski, James Landis, and many others, generally in their late thirties and early forties, usually were more ideological, technicians and academicians who, in the opinion of Vice President John Nance Garner, had never worked a precinct. Roosevelt, as the supreme mixmaster of his administration, made the secondary selections himself. His Cabinet members acquiesced with forbearance or veiled distaste. Observing the blend of disparate ingredients from within the Agriculture Department, Russell Lord reported "national figures using the same washroom, shoulder to shoulder, and pretending not to see each other."[7]

The presidential staff, those on the White House payroll, were noted primarily for the duration of their dedication to Roosevelt. "Those who were closest to him for the longest time," thought Tugwell, "were kept there because they did not probe or try to understand but rather because they gave an unquestioning service."[8] McIntyre, Early, Marvin (Pa) Watson, Missy LeHand, and Grace Tully provided the President with a comfortable, good-humored core around which the New Deal revolved. That the core did not develop into a cocoon was due mostly to Roosevelt's insatiable appetite for information and his immediate

6. Quoted in Louis W. Koenig, *The Invisible Presidency* (Rinehart, 1960), p. 308.
7. Russell Lord, *The Wallaces of Iowa* (Houghton Mifflin, 1947), p. 358.
8. Rexford G. Tugwell, *The Democratic Roosevelt* (Doubleday, 1957), p. 333.

staff's recognition of its own role and limitations. Primus inter pares of this original group was Howe, also little interested in policy questions other than for their political ramifications. He was more hair shirt than comforter to the President, however. Wrote Ickes, "Howe was the only one who dared to talk to him frankly and fearlessly. He not only could tell him what he believed to be the truth, but he could hang on like a pup to the root until he got results."[9] After Howe's death, there was never to be another intimate with the same willingness to tell the President to "go to hell," as Howe was known to have done.

Roosevelt placed other essentially personal aides in the departments. Moley and Tugwell were made Assistant Secretaries of State and of Agriculture, respectively, although they were involved in a variety of presidential chores. The schizophrenic nature of their responsibilities, especially in Moley's case, eventually caused substantial problems for the Cabinet officers to whom they supposedly reported and ultimately ended their usefulness to the President. This was not the case with those persons whose departmental employment was at more modest levels and whose work at the White House did not bring them into conflict with their nominal bosses; Thomas Corcoran and Benjamin Cohen, for example, were never on the White House staff proper.

The President also relied heavily on volunteers outside government to perform duties that would later become routinized White House operations. This was often true of speechwriting. A problem was that the outsiders could not always be available when needed. Rosenman was a Justice of the New York State Supreme Court and could be in Washington only on weekends and during summer recesses. The physical strain finally led to his resignation from the court in 1943 at which time he was given the title of Counsel to the President.

Dividing the Roosevelt staff into those on the White House payroll, political appointees with special presidential assignments, those in the departments who were loaned to the White House, and outside volunteers, still leaves out one important member of the President's professional establishment. Eleanor Roosevelt was "essentially a presidential aide."[10] Her special responsibilities were two-fold: she was an experienced fact finder who traveled widely and reported to her husband, and

9. Quoted in Arthur M. Schlesinger, Jr., *The Coming of the New Deal* (Sentry, 1958), p. 515.

10. James MacGregor Burns, *Roosevelt: The Soldier of Freedom* (Harcourt Brace Jovanovich, 1970), p. 60.

she was an in-house advocate for liberal causes, social welfare programs, minority groups, and youth. In tracing the organization of the modern presidency, it is apparent that those chief executives who can rely on members of their families (usually wives or brothers) for advice and even for carrying out formal assignments are uniquely blessed.

Although there was never anyone resembling a Chief of Staff to the President, Roosevelt played favorites at least to the degree that the press was constantly bestowing the title of Assistant President on someone or other. Over the course of three terms those who received this type of appellation included Moley, Donald Richberg, Tugwell, Corcoran, Hopkins, and James Byrnes. All save Byrnes worked on presidential speeches, none exclusively; Tugwell and Moley were involved in different fields of economics; Corcoran, more than the others, in bill-drafting and congressional relations; Richberg and Byrnes were "coordinators"; and Hopkins was given a broad but fairly random variety of assignments, including diplomatic missions. None of them performed duties similar to those later given to such men as Sherman Adams and H. R. Haldeman.

The White House staff's relations with Roosevelt were very informal. There were no staff meetings with the President. Staff members, singly or in combination, would appear while the President was having breakfast to discuss the day's work. They could then see him in his office if necessary—if not by going through the office of Appointments Secretary McIntyre, then through the more accessible door of Missy LeHand, the President's personal secretary. The cocktail hour also was a time when Roosevelt was usually available. And the evenings were reserved for drafting sessions with his speechwriters.

The official members of Roosevelt's government formed only the first line of the President's information network. Unlike some Presidents whose careers have been on a single track, often legislative or military, Roosevelt's various pre–White House years in national politics, state and federal government, and simply as a Roosevelt, had given him broad and diverse acquaintances throughout the country whose opinions and observations he now used to supplement or challenge the advice he received from his subordinates. He also sought ancillary information by expanding the device known as the presidential commission. One study covering the Roosevelt years through 1940 mentions more than 100 advisory bodies.[11]

11. See Carl Marcy, *Presidential Commissions* (New York: King's Crown, 1945).

The pattern of the President's week, always subject to change, eventually revolved around three events—sessions with the congressional leadership on Mondays or Tuesdays, press conferences on Tuesday afternoons and Friday mornings, and Cabinet meetings on Friday afternoons.

There was no organized congressional liaison office in the White House. Roosevelt handled this chore himself with the assistance of ad hoc troubleshooters such as Corcoran. The President's dealings with Capitol Hill were conducted almost exclusively with the House Speaker, majority leaders, and committee chairmen. This system created some dissatisfaction among the less privileged legislators. "There is a group of aggressive progressive Democrats who have stuck by you through thick and thin, about seventy-five in number, as well as a number of other progressives, not classed as Democrats," wrote Representative Kent Keller of Illinois in 1938, "and I do not believe that you have ever called in a single one of this group in consultation as to administration policies." [12]

The twice-weekly press conferences were held in the Oval Office with the reporters crowded around the President's desk. The frequency of these sessions meant that Roosevelt, rather than his Press Secretary, was the chief White House spokesman. Roosevelt, who prided himself on his detailed mastery of government operations, needed little advance preparation; as a rule, Steve Early merely reminded Roosevelt of topics on which inquiries were expected. The President broke with tradition by abolishing written questions, but he established three ground rules: no reporters could directly quote the President unless granted permission, presidential answers could be given for "background" (meaning that the reporters must not identify their source), and the President could speak off the record (strictly for information). Nearly half the meetings began with a statement by the President, assuring in these cases that Roosevelt controlled at least part of the session's substance. On occasion, moreover, the presidential Press Secretary planted questions with friendly reporters.

Thus Roosevelt tailored the format of the press conference into an instrument of considerable utility. The flexibility of responding without quotation or sometimes even without attribution allowed him to meet the press with hardly any fear of error—politically, sub-

12. Quoted in Richard Polenberg, *Reorganizing Roosevelt's Government* (Harvard University Press, 1966), pp. 179–80.

stantively, or grammatically—a luxury that rules out comparison with later Presidents.

But it was also Roosevelt's keen knowledge of the mechanics of journalism and the elements of newsworthiness that assured proper attention would be paid to what he wanted accented. The White House press corps liked him (Leo Rosten found that 64 percent of its members favored his reelection in 1936)—in part because he was good copy, in part because they were sympathetic to his programs, and in part because he liked the reporters, who were often invited to Sunday suppers at which the "Missus" scrambled eggs. Then, too, he was a masterful performer. After observing a Roosevelt press conference, John Gunther wrote:

In twenty minutes Mr. Roosevelt's features had expressed amazement, curiosity, mock alarm, genuine interest, worry, rhetorical playing for suspense, decision, playfulness, dignity, and surpassing charm. Yet he *said* almost nothing. Questions were deflected, diverted, diluted. Answers—when they did come—were concise and clear.[13]

Not that the Roosevelt-reporter relations could have continued at their initial level of mutual admiration, the interests of press and President often being contradictory. Rosten wrote in 1937 that the press corps' enthusiasm for Roosevelt was based on "a will-to-believe which, because it ignored future possibilities and past experiences, would end by tearing down the myth it was creating." While the situation never reached this point, FDR's press relations did deteriorate over time.[14]

Speeches were the other primary way in which the President reached the public. As Governor, Roosevelt had grasped the potential of radio as a way to break through "the paper curtain of the publishers and appeal directly to the voters."[15] His calm and reassuring voice was ideally suited to the medium. Yet his celebrated "fireside chats" averaged only two or three a year; as he explained, "individual psychology cannot . . . be attuned for long periods of time to a constant repetition of the highest note in the scale."[16]

13. John Gunther, *Roosevelt in Retrospect* (Harper, 1950), p. 22.

14. Leo C. Rosten, "President Roosevelt and the Washington Correspondents," *Public Opinion Quarterly*, vol. 1 (January 1937), p. 39. See also Edward S. Corwin, *The President: Office and Powers, 1787–1957* (New York University Press, 1957), p. 470.

15. Frank Freidel, *Franklin D. Roosevelt: The Triumph* (Little, Brown, 1956), p. 31.

16. Quoted in Elmer E. Cornwell, Jr., *Presidential Leadership of Public Opinion* (Indiana University Press, 1965), p. 261.

Given the consistent style of Roosevelt's rhetoric, it is startling that so many hands were involved in the crafting of his messages. Speech drafts were prepared by teams or by one writer gathering submissions from a number of sources. During 1933 Moley was the chief gatherer; drafts were prepared in 1933 and 1934 by Richberg, Howe, Bullitt, Frankfurter, Hugh Johnson, Tugwell, Cohen, and Corcoran. The team of Cohen and Corcoran played a more important role after Moley broke with the administration. Rosenman, who had been FDR's draftsman in Albany, again emerged as chief speechwriter in 1936; Stanley High was active in the second presidential campaign; and Roosevelt's last team, from 1940 until his death, consisted of Rosenman, Hopkins, and Robert Sherwood, with occasional help from Archibald MacLeish. A high style, such as Roosevelt's, lends itself to imitation by speechwriters, but that words from so many sources could have taken on one distinct character can be explained only by Roosevelt's personal involvement in the process. In the end, as Sherwood wrote of FDR's martinis, the President "mixed the ingredients with the deliberation of an alchemist."[17]

The speechwriting operation often also served as a decision-forcing mechanism. Rosenman explained, for example, how in preparing a 1942 congressional message on economic stabilization he first arranged a conference of the Vice President, Secretary of the Treasury, Chairman of the Federal Reserve Board, Director of the Budget, and Price Administrator, whose suggestions and disagreements were presented to the President in a memorandum, then fought out in various forums, and eventually resolved by Roosevelt under deadline pressure.[18]

"Our Cabinet meetings are pleasant affairs," Ickes wrote in his diary, "but we only skim the surface of routine affairs." Roosevelt did not consider his department secretaries as a collegial body whose collective wisdom should be applied to the formulation of high government policy. The chief value of the Friday sessions, Stimson felt, was their usefulness "as a way in which to get into the White House to have a word with the President in private after the meetings were over."[19]

In relating to the Cabinet members as individuals, Roosevelt had little respect for jurisdictional boundaries. Treasury Secretary Morgen-

17. Robert E. Sherwood, *Roosevelt and Hopkins* (Harper, 1948), p. 214.

18. Rosenman, *Working with Roosevelt*, pp. 333–40.

19. Ickes and Stimson quoted in Richard F. Fenno, Jr., *The President's Cabinet: An Analysis in the Period from Wilson to Eisenhower* (Vintage Books, 1959), pp. 125 and 138.

thau was given assignments that rightly belonged to Secretary of State Hull and Secretary of War Harry Woodring. Cabinet members survived as best they could in this laissez-faire atmosphere, if not by contract with their fellow department heads, then by conquest. Ickes was tenacious in his quest for additional responsibilities, as when he attempted to snatch the Forest Service from the Department of Agriculture. Hull, on the other hand, drew a narrow line around the State Department, even allowing himself to be excluded from wartime summit meetings on the grounds that they dealt with military planning and were not of diplomatic concern. The President tried to stay above the interdepartmental battles. Typical of this approach was a memorandum he sent to Rosenman: "Get [Budget Director] Harold Smith, usually known as 'Battling Smith,' into a room with the Secretary of the Treasury, usually known as 'Sailor Morgenthau,' lock them in and let the survivor out."[20] Yet despite the President's seemingly cold-blooded practice of management by combat, he was almost incapable of firing anyone, either for incompetence or even disloyalty. Rather, he devised ways to go around them, as when he chose to conduct War Department business with Assistant Secretary Louis Johnson instead of Woodring.

When the President felt most strongly that a job was important, however, he often simply ignored the departments and created a new agency. Topsy was the patron saint of Roosevelt's administrative theory. As a deliberate policy, this implied one or more of the following: that a new function was to be undertaken for which there was no niche in the existing structure; that the costs of giving new duties to an ongoing agency were too high in terms of disrupting existing programs or in disturbing the ecology between departments; that a new agency indicated a symbolically higher level of concern; that existing agencies either lacked capable personnel or were unable to move quickly enough; or that a new agency could circumvent existing regulations. James Rowe, a Roosevelt aide, thought one reason the President frequently employed this device was that it was the best way to deliver on his patronage obligations.[21] The end result was an administrative monstrosity, proliferating the number of executives who had the right and obligation to report directly to the President.

20. Rosenman, *Working with Roosevelt*, p. 357.
21. Martin and Susan Tolchin, *To the Victor . . . Political Patronage from the Clubhouse to the White House* (Random House, 1971), p. 257.

He made a short-lived attempt to coordinate the work of the new agencies with the old-line departments through the creation of an Emergency Council. At one time the coordinating involved 124 interdepartmental committees and 224 subsidiary subcommittees. The enterprise ultimately collapsed under the weight of its apparatus, the unwieldy size of its meetings, the pro forma reading of mimeographed reports, and the President's disenchantment with its director, Richberg. General confusion may have been somewhat lessened by government's ability to attract experienced managers during a time of decreased employment opportunities in the private sector.

By the time Roosevelt stood for reelection in 1936 his methods of running the government had become as controversial in some quarters as his goals. He therefore set up a Committee on Administrative Management, with Louis Brownlow as chairman and Charles Merriam and Luther Gulick as the other members. Their report, which Roosevelt enthusiastically forwarded to Congress in January 1937, accepted as its premise that "the American Executive must be regarded as one of the very greatest contributions by our Nation to the development of modern democracy." The need for reorganization was not based on potential savings to the taxpayers, as in past reports, but because "the President needs help."[22] The committee's solution, as George Graham put it, was "a plan of salvation by staff."[23] The White House Office should be augmented by six administrative assistants, "possessed of high competence, great physical vigor, and a passion for anonymity."[24] In addition, there should be an Executive Office of the President consisting of "managerial arms" for personnel, fiscal affairs, and planning.

The reorganization bill became entwined in Roosevelt's attempt to alter the composition of the Supreme Court and did not become law until 1939. But eventually he got just about what he asked for with the exception of transferring the functions of the Civil Service Commission to the White House. The Executive Office was physically located next door to the White House.[25] Into it was placed the Bureau of the Budget

22. Brownlow Report, pp. 2, 5. For a useful summary of federal reorganization, see Harvey C. Mansfield, "Federal Executive Reorganization: Thirty Years of Experience," *Public Administration Review*, vol. 29 (July-August 1969), p. 234.

23. George A. Graham, "The Presidency and the Executive Office of the President," *The Journal of Politics*, vol. 12 (November 1950), p. 600.

24. Brownlow Report, p. 5.

25. See Herbert Emmerich, *Essays on Federal Reorganization* (University of Alabama Press, 1950), pp. 26–27.

and the National Resources Committee, renamed the National Resources Planning Board (NRPB). Thus the President had two managerial arms, fiscal and planning.[26]

Actually, the reorganization act did not measurably increase the size of Roosevelt's White House staff operation. The more significant personnel expansion had taken place in 1933–34 through the process of borrowing from the departments. Although authorized to have six administrative assistants, the President chose to appoint only three in 1939. The new aides—William McReynolds, James Rowe, and Lauchlin Currie—while performing largely as generalists, standing ready for whatever assignments were uppermost on the President's mind, also developed areas of special interest. McReynolds became liaison officer for personnel management, Rowe's particular involvements were in politics and patronage, and Currie was concerned with economics.[27] The importance of the Brownlow Report was in legitimating what Roosevelt had been doing all along. It was a ringing manifesto for presidential supremacy, which had not been an accepted fact before the New Deal.

The President's new planning unit did not fare well and was eventually abolished by a 1943 action of Congress that stipulated that the NRPB functions could not be transferred to any other agency. The three-member board of part-time advisers had been charged with preparing long-range plans for public works, with helping state and local planning bodies, and with informing the President of trends in the economy. Sherwood claimed that "the N.R.P.B. was dear to Roosevelt's heart, but to the conservative majority on Capitol Hill the very word 'plan' was considered a Communist invention and any planning must be part of a plot to disrupt the capitalist system of free enterprise."[28] At least one academic observer, however, could not find evidence "to support a claim that the research product of the Board ever influenced

26. Executive Order 8248 (September 8, 1939) also included in the President's Executive Office an Office of Government Reports to serve as a central clearinghouse for the collection and distribution of public information. This was consolidated into the Office of War Information in 1942. Two other short-lived additions to the Executive Office were the Committee for Congested Production Areas (1943–44) and the War Refugees Board (1944–45).

27. Alex B. Lacy, Jr., "The Development of the White House Office, 1939–1967" (paper delivered at the annual meeting of the American Political Science Association, Chicago, September 5–9, 1967; processed).

28. Sherwood, *Roosevelt and Hopkins*, p. 741.

vital decisions of the President."[29] Without underestimating the strong feelings of Congress, Sherwood failed to note that the legislators feared a long-term planning operation in the White House as an assault on their prerogatives. (They had no objections when the Senate created a Special Committee on Post-War Planning shortly after cutting off funds to the NRPB.) The collapse of the NRPB was the first of a series of unsuccessful attempts to graft a long-range planning capacity onto the White House. Ultimately they have failed because of the character of Presidents and the demands of the presidential office. The politicians who generally become Presidents have had little experience with and patience for extended planning, and once in the White House it becomes increasingly difficult for them to focus on projections beyond their terms of office.

The Bureau of the Budget, on the other hand, blossomed in the Executive Office, and under the directorship of Harold Smith (1939–45) rapidly expanded from a staff of about 40 to over 500. The bureau retained its position as the central budget review agency and vastly increased its powers in the areas of legislative clearance and administrative management. Previously the departments had had to clear legislative requests only if they had fiscal implications; now all proposed legislation went through the bureau's clearance process. A similar system was instituted for the preparation of executive orders and proclamations. Recommendations for presidential vetoes were centralized and funneled through the Budget Bureau. It became the coordinator of statistical services and drafted reorganization plans. Survey teams recommended management improvements in the departments, and as particularly competent young professionals were attracted to the bureau in the early 1940s, the President relied more and more on it to represent him on interdepartmental committees and to perform other odd jobs. In short, the augmented Bureau of the Budget provided a significant presidential presence throughout the executive branch.

So now Roosevelt had two types of staffs: those in the White House whose services were to the President and were of a personal, public relations, and political nature; and those in the Executive Office whose responsibilities were to the presidency and were institutional in nature. But policy and program initiatives still flowed up to the President through the departments and agencies. The President's men were not

29. Edward H. Hobbs, *Behind the President* (Public Affairs Press, 1954), p. 79.

operational; as the Brownlow Report recommended, they issued no orders. The pressures of World War II, however, brought measurable changes to this system. Except for sporadic periods in the past, Presidents had spent the bulk of their time concerned with domestic matters. The ushering in of world responsibility meant that from the 1940s forward Presidents would become more and more consumed by international affairs.

During the war, Harry Hopkins, who lived at the White House, often acted as a direct link between Roosevelt and allied governments; the State Department was informed after the fact of arrangements that had been concluded. Admiral William Leahy, also operating out of the White House, presided over meetings of the Joint Chiefs of Staff as Roosevelt's personal representative and daily briefed Roosevelt on military matters. Rosenman, now a full-time drafter of presidential messages and public documents, assumed a major role in the creation of domestic policy. The addition of these three White House advisers— with special involvements in diplomacy, military affairs, and domestic concerns—markedly altered the direction of decisionmaking. In particular, the domestic duties of Rosenman were expanded to fill the void left by the President's preoccupation with the war. Policies of the utmost importance began the formulation process in Rosenman's office at the White House and moved out from there, thus reversing the traditional flow. Moreover, as Roosevelt's health declined, responsibilities shifted to his aides.

The President mobilized the civilian side of the government for war in much the same manner as he had earlier organized for the economic emergency, through the creation of numerous ad hoc agencies in response to problems as they arose or were called to his attention.

While Roosevelt was given to picking the leadership of the New Deal agencies from a free-floating body of professionals (lawyers, professors, social workers, state and local administrators), the new war agencies were apt to be headed by economic group representatives (corporate executives, union leaders, and farm organization officials). The Office of Production Management, for example, was placed under the joint direction of William Knudsen of General Motors and Sidney Hillman of the Amalgamated Clothing Workers Union. Trade association officials, however, were generally excluded from the war agencies. Scientists, recruited by Vannevar Bush, began to play an important role in government for the first time.

Roosevelt also became the first President to give major responsibilities in the mainstream of the executive branch to the Vice President. Henry Wallace was made chairman of the Economic Defense Board, the Supply Priorities and Allocation Board, and the Board of Economic Warfare. This was in sharp contrast to the job description for the vice presidency under John Nance Garner, whose primary assistance to the Chief Executive had been as a bridge to Congress, at least until the ideological gulf between the President and the Vice President became unbridgeable. The liabilities of giving operational duties to a Vice President became apparent when Wallace and Commerce Secretary Jesse Jones clashed over policy and jurisdictional questions, exchanged public insults, and had to be relieved of their assignments by the President. Less controversial was Roosevelt's novel use of the Vice President as an envoy extraordinary on missions to South America, China, and the Soviet Union.

Roosevelt's war government has been described as a collection of *action agencies* (dealing with such matters as rubber, selective service, and prices) and *coordinating agencies* ("to keep the action agencies from getting in each other's way").[30] The coordinating was arranged in a series of layers with first-step coordinators (National Housing Agency), regional coordinators (Plant Site Board), second-step coordinators (Office of War Information), and at the White House, the supercoordinator of them all, the Office of War Mobilization (OWM).[31]

To head the OWM, the President lured James Byrnes from the Supreme Court. It was undoubtedly a difficult decision for Roosevelt to give one person so much authority to act in his name. But in picking Byrnes there was little cause for concern. A cautious southern politician, long comfortable in the folkways of Washington, Byrnes was not about to handle hot coals if he could help it. Byrnes deliberately was not an empire builder; he worked out of tiny, cluttered offices in the east wing of the White House, with a staff never exceeding ten and the unassuming Ben Cohen as his chief deputy. The OWM chose to

30. Luther Gulick, "War Organization of the Federal Government," *American Political Science Review*, vol. 38 (December 1944), p. 1174.

31. The authority for creating the OWM was contained in Roosevelt's landmark Executive Order of September 8, 1939, which stated that "in the event of a national emergency, or threat of a national emergency, such office for emergency management as the President shall determine" was to be set up in the Executive Office.

deal with issues only if they could not be resolved at lower levels and interpreted its role narrowly as adjudicating controversies rather than planning and commanding the home front from its elevated perch.

But Roosevelt's management techniques were better suited to the needs of the depression thirties than the wartime forties. When the New Deal groped its way toward economic solutions that had never before been considered within government's province, the heady clash of ideas and the heavy emphasis on experimentation proved to be highly productive. The needs of massive warfare were not as well served by improvisation and redundancy.

FRANKLIN ROOSEVELT's methods of organizing the presidency illustrate the intensely personal nature of the office. Even before the 1939 Reorganization Act gave him congressional sanction, he had reshaped his staff to suit his style and needs.

Despite Roosevelt's domination of the government, the White House staff during his first two terms was primarily a personal services unit, considerably bigger but not essentially different from that of past Presidents. His strong desire to mold public opinion called for aides who could assist him in his symbolic and informational duties, such as speechwriting and press relations.

Only during Roosevelt's last years did new powers begin to shift to the staff. This coincided with the war and the President's failing health. A vigorous Roosevelt, one suspects, would have been much more hesitant to delegate duties that he considered presidential. Hopkins's diplomacy impinged on the prerogatives of the Secretary of State; Rosenman moved into policy areas that had been the exclusive domain of the departments and agencies.

The accretion of White House staff functions was not part of a deliberate plan. The creation of the Executive Office of the President, however, had a theoretical base in the Brownlow Report. In effect, this produced a quantum jump in staff available to a President. Roosevelt was relatively meticulous in using the Bureau of the Budget for institutional purposes. Still, there were signs by the end of the administration that it was slipping into a more personal role. Late in the war Harold Smith is reported to have told a friend, "Roger, I am afraid I am becoming Mr. Fixit for the President, and this is bad for the Bureau of the Budget."[32]

32. Roger Jones, "Preliminary Papers, Conference on the Institutional Presi-

While the Cabinet failed to serve Roosevelt as a mechanism of collective advice—as it had failed previous Presidents—Cabinet officers continued to have the major responsibility for running their departments and proposing legislation. However, Roosevelt's habit of proliferating agencies outside the departmental framework diffused power throughout the executive branch, contributed to a diminution of some department heads' standing, and increased the number of officials reporting directly to the President. Within limits, this served the purpose of keeping subordinates dependent on the President.

The Rooseveltian legacy was to expand the reach of the presidency and to change the people's expectations of what government could and should do. Whether the growth of government would outstrip a President's ability to oversee its activities was a conundrum that Roosevelt left to his successors.

---

dency" (National Academy of Public Administration, March 1974; manuscript), p. 53.

☆ ☆ ☆ ☆ ☆ ☆ ☆ ☆ ☆ ☆ ☆ ☆ ☆

CHAPTER THREE

Harry S. Truman
☆ 1945-1953 ☆

☆ ☆ ☆ ☆ ☆ ☆ ☆ ☆ ☆ ☆ ☆ ☆ ☆

HARRY S. TRUMAN was a tidy man. He was offended by Roosevelt's style as an administrator. He believed that government should be orderly. He did not believe in promoting rivalries between members of his administration. He believed intensely in the importance of loyalty as a unifying principle. And he believed that the Cabinet was "the principal medium through which the President controls his administration."[1]

Harry S. Truman was also a man who had spent most of his adult life in Missouri organization politics and in the U.S. Senate. His circle of acquaintances was limited. His knowledge of power relationships within the bureaucracy was modest,[2] and his presidency was confronted with a series of crises produced by circumstances outside the boundaries of the United States.

His theories of organization, presented as accomplished fact in his memoirs, were in reality considerably modified by events, personalities, and habits. Thus Richard Neustadt, who was there, commented that "Truman's White House rather resembled a senatorial establishment, writ large."[3] His appointments resulted in a blending of stunningly capable patricians, unimaginative professionals, and incompetent cronies. His reliance on the Cabinet ultimately sorted itself out in accordance with the skills of its members and the immediate problems that

1. Harry S. Truman, *Memoirs*, vol. 1: *Years of Decision* (Doubleday, 1955), pp. 12–13, 329, 546.
2. See Richard E. Neustadt, *Presidential Power* (Wiley, 1960), pp. 171–79.
3. Richard E. Neustadt, "The Presidency at Mid-Century," *Law and Contemporary Problems*, vol. 21 (Autumn 1956), p. 641.

faced him. The result was that Truman's method of running the government was at almost midpoint between the designed chaos of his predecessor and the structural purity of his successor.

On suddenly assuming office in 1945, Truman invited his inherited Cabinet to remain in their posts, but it did not take long for the new President to realize that he must have his own team. Within three months he had replaced six of the ten Roosevelt department heads. Ultimately, twenty-four men would serve as his Cabinet officers. Four of the first half-dozen appointees were or had been members of Congress (only three had been during Roosevelt's three-plus terms). Treasury Secretary Fred Vinson, a former Congressman from Kentucky, proved to be a pillar of strength to Truman during the first year. When Vinson was moved to the Supreme Court, the President replaced him in the Cabinet with John Snyder, an orthodox banker without Vinson's breadth or perception. Snyder and Postmaster General Robert Hannegan were old friends of Truman from Missouri. Continuing the tradition, Hannegan doubled as Chairman of the Democratic National Committee; a subsequent National Chairman, J. Howard McGrath, was appointed Attorney General in 1949, beginning a new tradition that suggested that perhaps a more desirable kind of patronage was available through the Justice Department than through the postal system. Secretary of State James Byrnes and holdover Secretary of Commerce Henry Wallace had been Truman's rivals for the vice presidential nomination in 1944; both proved to be disloyal to the President according to his definition of loyalty, and both were eventually asked to resign. For his second- and third-wave Cabinet appointments, Truman generally sought people with long experience in the departments and even chose a careerist to supervise the Post Office. Under Secretaries and Assistant Secretaries—such as Oscar Chapman at Interior and Charles Brannan at Agriculture—were promoted to the Cabinet. By and large the later appointees were an improvement in quality.

Generally Truman picked superb people for the important jobs and ordinary or even unqualified people for the less important jobs. There were exceptions on both sides of the ledger. Truman never had a top-flight Attorney General, and one of his Secretaries of Defense, Louis Johnson, was not an outstanding success. Most often, however, the key posts in foreign policy and national security went to such luminaries as George Marshall, Dean Acheson, James Forrestal, Robert Patterson, Robert Lovett, Will Clayton, Paul Hoffman, David Lilienthal, and

Averell Harriman. Many of these appointees were part of the American aristocracy, products of elite schools and long-held wealth, having little in common socially with the former haberdasher who was President. Their relations with Truman were highly formal, but it was clear that they held him in affection and were deeply devoted to their President. The contrast with the performance of some Truman friends in the administration, those with whom he shared a comfortable intimacy, was striking.

At first Truman believed that the Cabinet should be analogous to "a board of directors." He sometimes even asked the Cabinet to vote on major issues. Cabinet meetings dealt with more substantive questions than they had during the Roosevelt era. Yet collective advice proved primarily useful on matters of tactics and political strategy. For example, Truman announced to the Cabinet that he planned to send aid to Greece—he requested their opinion, not on his decision, but "on the best method to apprise the American people of the issues involved." (They suggested a presidential address to a joint session of Congress.)[4] Over the years he drew back from the board of directors concept; powers delegated could be powers lost, and Truman, while modest about himself as President, was zealous in protecting those prerogatives that he felt were inherent in the presidency. Moreover, after the outbreak of the Korean war he began to hold weekly meetings of the new National Security Council, in effect a Cabinet subcommittee, thus further lessening the utility of full Cabinet sessions.

At first Truman intended to return the White House staff to its prewar size—secretaries for press, correspondence, and appointments, plus a handful of general assistants. But under the pressures of an increasing work load, the President reversed himself so that within a year the White House—in addition to the three traditional secretaries—began to take on the following configuration:

Assistant to the President (John R. Steelman). The appointment of this former head of the Federal Mediation and Conciliation Service reflected the seriousness with which the President viewed labor-management relations as a national problem (116 million man-days of work were lost because of strikes in 1945) and the ineffectuality of his Secretary of Labor (Lewis Schwellenbach, an ex-Senator from the state of Washington). Negotiations in major disputes—such as in the railroad

4. Truman, *Years of Decision*, pp. 328, 546; and Harry S. Truman, *Memoirs*, vol. 2: *Years of Trial and Hope* (Doubleday, 1956), pp. 104–05.

and steel industries—were conducted in Steelman's White House office. Steelman also acted as coordinator of federal agency programs and policies, which meant that he concerned himself with those Cabinet-level problems that were beneath presidential attention and served as the route to the President for the minor agencies that were without direct access to the Oval Office.

Special Counsel (Clark Clifford). The office remained as defined by Rosenman: the key position on the White House staff for domestic policy formulation by virtue of control over the speechwriting process and responsibility for reviewing congressional bills and executive orders. In addition to his other duties, Clifford, who first joined the Truman White House as a naval officer, handled liaison with the Pentagon and the State Department.

Administrative Assistant (Charles Murphy). Unlike Roosevelt's system of using troubleshooters to deal with Congress on an ad hoc basis, Truman gradually looked to Murphy as his coordinator of congressional messages. When he replaced Clifford as Special Counsel in 1950, Murphy continued his congressional liaison work, but did not assume Clifford's responsibility for national security coordination. Some duties were a function of the office and others a function of the officeholder.

Administrative Assistant (Donald S. Dawson). As staff coordinator for personnel and patronage, Dawson maintained the files from which Truman made most of his appointments except for those in the customs houses and the federal courts system. He also handled the arrangements for the President's trips and political appearances.

Administrative Assistant (David Niles). A holdover from the Roosevelt staff, he had special responsibility for liaison with minority groups.

Other administrative assistants had more generalized assignments and usually served as assistants to Steelman, Clifford, or Murphy. The presence on the White House staff of such men as David Lloyd, David Bell, George Elsey, Richard Neustadt, and David Stowe was in itself a development of some note—the beginning of a cadre of supporting staff for senior presidential aides.

Categorizing the duties of key staff members somewhat downplays the degree to which Truman parceled out assignments "on the basis of who was available" (as Lloyd recalled the system).[5] Nevertheless, in tracing the evolution of the presidential office, it is apparent that functional divisions were now emerging in sharper form. No one on Roose-

5. Quoted in Cabell Phillips, *The Truman Presidency* (Penguin, 1969), p. 133.

velt's staff had had either labor-management responsibilities similar to
Steelman's or such a continuing involvement in congressional relations
as Murphy. Equally important, the bloodless description of White
House assignments veils the dynamics of what Clifford has called "two
forces fighting for the mind of the President."[6] The fight over what was
to become known as the Fair Deal developed along classic liberal-
conservative lines. The chief conservative advocates were Steelman
and Treasury Secretary Snyder. The liberals, led by Clifford, included
Murphy, Leon Keyserling of the Council of Economic Advisers, and
several members of the sub-Cabinet, such as Oscar (Jack) Ewing, Director of the Federal Security Agency, Under Secretary of the Interior
Chapman, and David Morse, Assistant Secretary of Labor.

Here is the way Clifford told what happened:

> I think it was Jack Ewing who first suggested the idea that a few of us
> get together from time to time to try to plot a coherent political course for
> the administration. Our interest was to be exclusively on domestic affairs, not
> foreign. . . . We wanted to create a set of goals that truly met the deepest and
> greatest needs of the people, and we wanted to build a liberal, forward-moving
> program around those goals that could be recognized as a *Truman* program.
>
> The idea was that the six or eight of us [meeting each Monday evening
> in Ewing's apartment] would try to come to an understanding among our-
> selves on what direction we would like the President to take on any given
> issue. And then, quietly and unobtrusively each in his own way, we would
> try to steer the President in that direction.
>
> Naturally, we were up against tough competition. Most of the Cabinet and
> the congressional leaders were urging Mr. Truman to go slow, to veer a little
> closer to the conservative line. . . .
>
> Well, it was two forces fighting for the mind of the President, that's really
> what it was. It was completely unpublicized, and I don't think Mr. Truman
> ever realized it was going on. But it was an unceasing struggle during those
> two years [1946–48], and it got to the point where no quarter was asked and
> none was given.[7]

Of his own role, Clifford said:

> If I rendered any service to President Truman . . . it was as the representa-
> tive of the liberal forces. I think our forces were generally successful. We had
> something of an advantage in the liberal-conservative fight because I was there
> all the time. I saw the President often, and if he wanted to discuss an issue,
> I was at hand.[8]

6. Ibid., p. 164.
7. Quoted in ibid., pp. 163–64.
8. Quoted in Patrick Anderson, *The Presidents' Men* (Doubleday, 1968), p. 115.

The liberal forces prevailed. For example, Truman vetoed a weak price control bill and the Taft-Hartley bill, both actions urged by Clifford and opposed by almost the entire Cabinet. Clifford's skills—vastly greater than his opponents'—well may have been a factor. But also he was pushing the President in a direction that was clearly in keeping with the President's instincts.

There is nothing unusual, of course, about intra-administration struggles. They are inherent in a structure of government built on the separation of departments along interest-group lines. Roosevelt had designed his whole theory of management on conflict. Yet as a rule of thumb, there always had been a distinction between Cabinet officers (policy advocates and managers) and White House aides (facilitators, mediators, and performers of personal and political services). This changed somewhat in the closing years of the Roosevelt administration when the President, preoccupied with the war and in ill health, allowed Rosenman and others greater leeway in shaping domestic programs. But Clifford's performance during five years under Truman was of a different magnitude; since he acted primarily as a programmatic *adviser* to the President, the theoretical line between Cabinet and White House staff began to be less clearly drawn. And as Clifford's experiences illustrate, in any conflict between the two the law of propinquity is apt to be governing.

Besides Steelman, Clifford, and their assistants, there was another type, distinctly different and largely nonsubstantive, at the Truman White House. Ithiel de Sola Pool would later write, "Every President has felt the need to surround himself with a small group of mediocre men whose main qualification is loyalty. . . . In every administration they have gotten the President into trouble by their lack of moral perspective. . . . The President needs loyal personal assistants, yet they are dangerous." [9] While Clark Clifford, as much as anyone except Harry Truman, may have been responsible for creating the Fair Deal, it was Harry Vaughan, as much as anyone except Dwight Eisenhower, who may have been responsible for the defeat of the Democratic Party in 1952.

Truman had known Vaughan, his military aide, since they had served together in the National Guard during the 1920s. Patrick Anderson described Vaughan as

9. Ithiel de Sola Pool, "Inquiries Beyond Watergate," *Society*, September-October 1973, p. 25.

part George Babbitt and part Willie Loman, a man whose sunny smile and hearty handshake can any day be found in countless Elks Clubs and National Guard armories from coast to coast. Harry Vaughan is a loud, jovial, boastful, crude, cunning, not-too-bright, rather likable buffoon. He is a denizen of poker-parlors and a dabbler in local politics, a drinker of bourbon and a teller of tales. He is everybody's bachelor uncle, the one who turns up for Christmas dinner each year three sheets to the wind, the one whose off-color tales draw blushes from the ladies and guffaws from the men. . . .[10]

Vaughan, Appointments Secretary Matthew Connelly, Dawson and George Schoeneman of the patronage operation, and Dr. Wallace Graham, the President's physician, were people Truman liked to have around. They were comfortable. They were fun. Some of them also were accepters of petty graft, mink coats, deep freezers, and free hotel rooms and were friends of fixers. That Harry Truman of unexcelled personal integrity could have tolerated their presence says something about his background in machine politics, about his sense of loyalty and sentimentality, and also about man's deep-seated need for companionship. A President, even more than most, needs friends. The post of Court Jester has a long history. Indeed, the persistence with which Court Jesters have been found in the company of Presidents seems to attest to some useful service that they perform. "Yet they are dangerous." Recent Presidents have protected themselves by either "appointing" outsiders (such as George Allen in the case of Eisenhower) or making sure that they had no governmental duties (in the case of Dave Powers at the Kennedy White House). Truman's problems resulted from giving assignments of state to his Court Jesters.

There were definite patterns to the way Truman spent his days.[11] Mornings generally were devoted to what he called "customers"—often legislators; afternoons were spent on the more "serious" business of government—meetings of the Cabinet and National Security Council and sessions with the Budget Director. Time was measured out in small chunks; meetings rarely lasted more than a half hour, individual appointments often less than ten minutes. The only times the President was alone were early in the morning and late at night, before and after "working hours," when he could study or merely catch up with the constantly moving conveyor belt that deposited papers on his desk. Almost everyone who came into his office was a supplicant, someone

10. Anderson, *The Presidents' Men*, p. 97.

11. See John Hersey, "Mr. President," a five-part series in the *New Yorker*, April 14, 1951, through May 5, 1951.

who wanted something. His days were predetermined by other people—VIPs who asked for time with the President, officials who needed decisions—or by the cycles of government. (In January he saw a great deal of the Budget Director because the budget cycle was reaching its climax.) Private meetings were scheduled twice a week with the Secretary of State and once a week with the Defense Secretary, but none were scheduled on a regular basis with any member of the domestic departments. All Cabinet members may have been equal, but some were more equal than others.

The frequency of press conferences was only half that of Roosevelt's administration—down to one a week. Truman lacked his predecessor's skill in dealing with reporters; his maladroit handling of some questions, such as at one point leaving the impression that he was considering the use of the atomic bomb in Korea, created special problems for his Press Secretaries. (It is probably only coincidence that two of them died in office.) In time Truman came to regard the press as "often unfair to him and his administration." When a reporter prefaced a question by saying that he was puzzled, Truman snapped, "You're easily puzzled. You're always speculating about something you don't know anything about."[12] As self-protection, Truman developed a pre-conference staff briefing process, which toward the end of his presidency included the preparation of a notebook containing possible questions and answers, a practice continued by subsequent Presidents. Press conferences were no longer an informal give-and-take around the President's desk as in the Roosevelt period. The press corps had grown too big and the conferences were moved across the street to the Indian Treaty Room of the Executive Office Building. For the first time, too, the conferences were recorded and portions released for radio use.

In addition to Truman's own accessibility to members of Congress, after the 1948 election he assigned two low-level White House aides—one for the Senate, one for the House—to handle the servicing of Capitol Hill requests for "favors." They served under Appointments Secretary Connelly and did not deal with substantive legislation. The operation was rated "relatively ineffectual" by other Truman staff members.[13]

12. James F. Pollard, *The Presidents and the Press: Truman to Johnson* (Public Affairs Press, 1964), pp. 43, 48.
13. See Abraham Holtzman, *Legislative Liaison* (Rand McNally, 1970), pp. 232–33.

The period from 1947 through 1949 is considered by some as the golden age of the Bureau of the Budget. The close involvement of the bureau in shaping and directing administration policy was a product of Truman's interests and Budget Director James E. Webb's predilections. The President would later write, "The federal budget was one of my most serious hobbies, but it was also much more than that. In fact, I regarded it as one of the most serious of the responsibilities of the President—a responsibility that never failed to prove thoroughly fascinating."[14] Truman claimed that he spent "twice as much time on the preparation of the budget as any former President ever did."[15] Most Presidents soon become bored with the tedious juggling of figures that Truman found so fascinating. They then delegate these responsibilities, and in so doing, they let up on an important lever for fine-tuning policy priorities. It is beyond coincidence that the two Presidents who had served on congressional appropriations committees, Truman and Ford, have had the greatest personal involvement in preparing the budgets during recent years.

As the relations between Truman and his Budget Director became more intimate, Webb emerged as a principal adviser to the President (as distinct from adviser to the presidency, the prime role assumed by past directors). Neustadt reported that Webb "broke precedent by making his subordinates freely available to White House aides, on their terms, for their purpose."[16] The Clifford-Murphy axis in particular used Budget Bureau people as its personal backup staff. The interchange of personnel was such that Neustadt calculated that "in 1953 fully a third of the outgoing Truman assistants had come to the White House staff from the career service in the Budget Bureau."[17] Starting in 1948 the bureau's legislative clearance operation moved from "negative protection of President and agencies to positive development and drafting of Administration measures."[18] Policy often was formulated by "working teams" with the bureau's Legislative Reference Office functioning as secretariat. Only the advent of the Korean war and the usual loss of energy that afflicts an administration whose days in office

14. Truman, *Years of Trial and Hope*, pp. 36–37.
15. Ibid., pp. 33–34.
16. Richard E. Neustadt, "Presidency and Legislation: The Growth of Central Clearance," *American Political Science Review*, vol. 48 (September 1954), p. 659.
17. Ibid., p. 660.
18. Ibid., p. 661.

are numbered caused some diminution of the Budget Bureau's influence.

Congress sought to shape the institutional presidency for the first time while Truman was in the White House. The Employment Act of 1946 added the Council of Economic Advisers (CEA) to the Executive Office and the National Security Act of 1947 added the National Security Council (NSC).[19] Both were attempts to structure in statute the President's information systems. Congress could mandate advice, but could a President be forced to listen?

At least one economist has called Harry Truman "indifferent to the complexities of economics."[20] In this regard he was no different from his predecessor—or for that matter, from the five Presidents who have come after him. No professional economist has ever run for President. Tugwell proposed that Roosevelt create a "Federal Economic Council attached to the Executive."[21] Roosevelt declined the suggestion and instead gathered economic advice from his constantly shifting inner circle, some of whose members were economists. His several

19. Other additions to the Executive Office during the Truman administration:

(1) Telecommunications Adviser to the President, created by Executive Order 10297 (October 9, 1951); functions transferred to the Office of Defense Mobilization by Executive Order 10460 (June 16, 1953).

(2) Office of Defense Mobilization, created by Executive Order 10193 (December 16, 1950) and charged with the direction and coordination of federal agency activities during the Korean war; functions transferred to the new Office of Defense Mobilization (ODM) by Reorganization Plan 3 of 1953. The ODM, first under the direction of Charles E. Wilson of General Electric, was given broader powers than Byrnes had had during World War II. Steelman and an associate later wrote, "Possibly no other legal act of either the Congress or the President ever came so close to the actual creation of an Assistant President." (John R. Steelman and H. Dewayne Kreager, "The Executive Office as Administrative Coordinator," Law and Contemporary Problems, vol. 21 [Autumn 1956], p. 704.) The ODM's authority extended to assigning functions, issuing directives, and requiring reports from any agency, including the Cabinet departments, on mobilization matters.

(3) Office of Director for Mutual Security, established by the Mutual Security Act of 1951 and of 1952, for the purpose of furnishing military, economic, and technical assistance to other nations; functions transferred to the Foreign Operations Administration (August 1, 1953). This was an outgrowth of Truman's appointing Averell Harriman as his senior adviser on foreign and military policy at the beginning of the Korean war. Harriman's office grew so large and became so enmeshed in operations that Congress eventually "institutionalized" it.

20. E. Ray Canterbery, Economics on a New Frontier (Belmont, California: Wadsworth, 1968), p. 130.

21. Rexford G. Tugwell, The Brains Trust (Viking, 1968), pp. 525–28.

changes in economic policy may be attributed to changes in advisers. As a posthumous reaction to Roosevelt's ways of conducting the affairs of state, Congress decreed in 1946 that Presidents, starting with Truman, would have to have a pride of professional economists in the Executive Office. A President's economic advice would come from a *council*, not a solitary adviser; the three members of the CEA would be confirmed by the Senate, a provision that had never before been attached to presidential aides; and a new Joint Committee of the Congress would monitor the CEA's recommendations. Senator Joseph C. O'Mahoney, a principal supporter of the measure, made his intention clear. "This ... is a bill to restore the functions of Congress."[22]

For the first Chairman of the CEA, Truman chose Edwin G. Nourse, Vice President of the Brookings Institution and generally regarded as a moderate conservative. The other two members, John D. Clark and Leon Keyserling, were liberals. Nourse reported:

After the lapse of a little more than a year, it can be said that there has been no single case when he [Truman] has called upon us in any specific situation for counsel in his study of any matter of national economic policy. While he has accepted the material which we have presented to him for use in the Economic Report and passed it on without material change and with only minor omissions, there is no clear evidence that at any juncture we had any tangible influence on the formation of policy or the adoption of any course of action or feature of a program.[23]

This situation had at least three causes. Nourse was not in sympathy with the policy tendencies of the administration; at the same time, he believed presidential economic advisers could and should be "scientifically objective," somehow outside the political implications of their data; and there was an unfortunate chemistry between Chairman and President. Keyserling would later contend:

Dr. Nourse was simply unable to adjust himself to the nature and the problems of the Presidency. He could never understand that the President of the United States has too many things to do to engage in long bull sessions on economics of the kind that take place at The Brookings Institution.[24]

22. Quoted in Lester G. Seligman, "Presidential Leadership: The Inner Circle and Institutionalization," *Journal of Politics*, vol. 18 (August 1956), p. 419.

23. Edwin G. Nourse, *Economics in the Public Service* (Harcourt, Brace, 1953), p. 380.

24. Quoted in Edward S. Flash, Jr., *Economic Advice and Presidential Leadership* (Columbia University Press, 1965), p. 25.

Viewing the relationship from the President's perspective, Gerhard Colm, a member of the initial CEA staff, thought that perhaps Truman kept his distance because "he did not feel equal to discussing economics with a man whom he respected as a great scholar and authority."[25]

After Nourse resigned in 1949 and the chairmanship was assumed by Keyserling, whose views of the White House operation were more realistic and whose views of policy were more in tune with the President's, the council became a serious contending force in the formulation of administration policy. Unlike the Budget Bureau, which had a monopoly in its primary area of concern, the CEA still had to negotiate with the Treasury, Commerce, and Labor Departments and the other elements of government that took strong stands about the direction of the economy. However, freed of operating responsibility (with the exception of preparing the Economic Report) and located in close proximity to the President, the CEA had ample opportunity to develop and to expound its judgments within the higher reaches of the administration. Moreover, the CEA was given a small and competent staff, eight professionals at first. Mostly drawn from the ranks of government economists, their networks of friendships were invaluable in keeping the CEA in touch with the agencies and in avoiding the type of insensitivity that could have hampered a new entry in a crowded field. Harold Smith, for example, expected bad blood to develop between his Budget Bureau and the new council; this did not happen and it was not insignificant that two of the early CEA staff members had come from the bureau.

Congress was wrong in its belief that it could direct the President to accept economic advice; the experience under Nourse graphically proved otherwise. But it was right in believing that the quantity and quality of economic advice might be force-fed. The presence of a group of professional economists in the White House resulted in additional sources of information and analysis, which the President absorbed, often through his personal staff, sometimes by osmosis. The question of the place of professional advice in the White House would be fought again, with different results, in the scientific field. The lesson of the CEA, however, was that a President could be aided in policy-making by this type of expertise *if* his experts were congenial enough to

25. Gerhard Colm, "The Executive Office and Fiscal and Economic Policy," *Law and Contemporary Problems*, vol. 21 (Autumn 1956), p. 716.

gain entrance—this could not be taken for granted—and *if* they could provide him with information that was immediately and politically useful. Keyserling's stewardship was considered overly political by many and would lead to a reassessment of the CEA under Eisenhower. But it was judged a success by Truman, and in that it proved not to limit a President's flexibility, as Congress had intended, it survived and remained intact for each future President to adjust to his needs. Ironically, it was Nourse who correctly summed up the proper role of the CEA: "The success of the Council as an institution, the importance of the place it occupies and the value of its work will be just what the President makes them."[26]

The National Security Act of 1947 and its 1949 amendments were meant to unify the military establishment and to create a new system for advising the President—the National Security Council. The original members of the NSC were the President Chairman), the Secretary of State, the Secretary of Defense, the three military service secretaries (who were at the same time removed from the Cabinet), the Chairman of a new National Security Resources Board (a standby mobilization body, which was later merged into the Office of Defense Mobilization), and such other department or agency heads as the President might choose to give membership. The 1949 amendments dropped the service secretaries and added the Vice President. The Central Intelligence Agency was placed under the NSC (but has never really been regarded as part of the Executive Office of the President). In theory, the NSC would help the President to define broad national policy: the State Department would then know what policy to implement in its conduct of foreign relations; the military would know the policy for which it must devise strategic and logistic plans; and the National Security Resources Board would know the policy for which it must prepare industrial, manpower, and raw material mobilization plans.

Truman at first viewed the NSC with appropriate suspicion. There were some, particularly in the Defense Department, who hoped to use the NSC as a vehicle for committing the President to departmentally negotiated positions. The President had to make sure that the NSC would not make decisions but would be limited to giving advice. He chose to accomplish this in part by not attending council meetings: if he was not there, he could make no instant commitments, although he justified his absence by contending that council members would

26. Nourse, *Economics in the Public Service*, p. 378.

speak more freely if he was not in the room. He rejected a proposal to give the Executive Secretary the authority to see that NSC decisions were carried out. The staff, he felt, should not be insinuated between him and his principal advisers, the Secretary of State and the Secretary of Defense. The momentous decision to intervene in Korea was made without the President formally consulting with the NSC. (He did, of course, meet with his key officials, some of whom were NSC members.)

The war, however, convinced him that the NSC could be put to greater advantage. The council began to meet weekly with the President in the chair. A senior staff of eight persons drawn from the departments was assembled—a precursor of Eisenhower's Planning Board. The first Executive Secretary had been largely a briefing officer; the second now became a staff director as well. NSC papers began to be developed in the Executive Office, rather than in the departments. Truman was not prepared to turn the NSC into a comprehensive policy system, but he did discover that when molded to his terms it could serve him as a convenient staffing mechanism. Without fulfilling the original expectation of defining broad national policy, it nonetheless had its uses. It provided the excuse for Truman to regroup his advisers into a sort of War Cabinet with its own secretariat. Again Congress failed to bind a President to its intent; again a President chose to use or not use a body that Congress had unilaterally imposed on the institutional presidency; again, perhaps serendipitously, a President found functions for a staff to perform after it had been given to him.

THE SHAPE of the modern presidential organization—beginning to be defined yet still hazy at the end of the Roosevelt administration—started to come into sharper focus under Truman: the greater differentiation of staff functions—aides assigned such duties as labor-management relations and minority group relations; the building of staff in support of chief presidential assistants; policy advocacy moved into the White House; a blurring of the distinction between Executive Office and White House Office in the use of Budget Bureau personnel by White House aides; the grafting onto the White House of two major new units, the CEA and the NSC; and most important, the majority acceptance of the President as the locus of federal responsibility.

In 1947 a Republican Congress, looking forward to the election of a Republican President the next year, approved a bill to set up a Commission on the Organization of the Executive Branch of the Government. One of its stated objectives was "defining and *limiting* executive functions."[27] Truman, while he might have viewed himself as the commission's target, was enthusiastic about the undertaking, promised and delivered the full cooperation of his administration, and in a master stroke appointed Herbert Hoover as its Chairman. Hoover threw his prodigious energy into the assignment, serving even as his own staff director, and placing his personal imprint on all the commission's work. The first of the nineteen reports of the Hoover Commission appeared in 1949, and its first recommendation was to give the President continuing reorganization powers unrestricted by limitations or exemptions. The Executive Office of the President should be strengthened. The President should have stronger staff services, including a staff secretariat in the White House.[28] Newspapers, such as the *New York Herald Tribune* and the *Chicago Daily News*, which had greeted Roosevelt's efforts to implement the Brownlow Report as a "dictator bill" and an "aggrandizement of the President's constitutional powers," now hailed the Hoover Commission recommendations and wrote of a strong, unified executive as "a prime requisite of republican institutions."[29] Herbert Hoover, the last person to have been President before the modern era, had come out of retirement to legitimate the Rooseveltian concept of the presidency. It was symbolism of some potency.

27. *The Hoover Commission Report* (McGraw-Hill, n.d.), p. xiii.

28. The first Hoover Commission Report recommended that what it called "the President's Office" should contain six elements: the White House Office, Office of the Economic Adviser, Office of Personnel, Office of the Budget, National Security Council, and National Security Resources Board. The Office of Personnel should be headed by the Chairman of the Civil Service Commission; the Office of the Economic Adviser should replace the CEA and have a single head; the membership of the NSC should be determined by the President rather than frozen into law by Congress. See Edward H. Hobbs, "An Historical Review of Plans for Presidential Staffing," *Law and Contemporary Problems*, vol. 21 (Autumn 1956), pp. 683–84.

29. See Herbert Emmerich, *Essays on Federal Reorganization* (University of Alabama Press, 1950), p. 101.

☆ ☆ ☆ ☆ ☆ ☆ ☆ ☆ ☆ ☆ ☆ ☆ ☆

CHAPTER FOUR

Dwight D. Eisenhower
☆ 1953-1961 ☆

☆ ☆ ☆ ☆ ☆ ☆ ☆ ☆ ☆ ☆ ☆ ☆

IF A NEW administration appears as a tabula rasa, it is not because the tablet is blank but because the writing is invisible. It is there. But it can best be discerned later, after the fact, when it becomes possible to distinguish between those traits and experiences in a President's background that are casual and those that are causal in that they predetermined the shape and the organization of his presidency.

Dwight D. Eisenhower, elected to the presidency in 1952, was a genial, shrewd, optimistic, confident, successful small-town American of sixty-two years. He had devoted his life to government service in the military. A newcomer to partisan politics, he was not unfamiliar with bureaucratic politics. He had spent much time abroad, which gave a somewhat anomalous internationalist cast to his otherwise conventional beliefs. He was also the best-liked man of his era. (A good slogan can tell a great deal; Eisenhower's was "We Like Ike.")

His aspirations as President were limited to two overriding objectives: peace abroad and a balanced budget at home. In keeping with his aspirations, his view of the presidential role was circumscribed. Like many professional military men, he had a high regard for Congress, though not for Congressmen.

Eisenhower followed the pattern characteristic of the modern presidency by reacting to the style of the President who preceded him. As Roosevelt, the disorganization man, would be followed by tidy Harry Truman, so Eisenhower would see the purpose of his presidency as trying "to create an atmosphere of greater serenity and mutual confidence" in the wake of the cocky controversialist whose legacy, Eisen-

59

hower felt, was "an unhappy state . . . bitterness . . . quarreling."[1]
(Truman, of course, would have argued that presidential prestige is
meant to be used to force desirable actions, not to be hoarded as a
national asset.) Later, the youthful, liberal Kennedy would react to the
aging, conservative Eisenhower, and so on, back and forth in the nation's quadrennial attempt to achieve an unrealizable golden mean in
presidential leadership.

Confronted with the immediate problem of putting together a government—the first controlled by the Republican party in twenty years—
Eisenhower turned not to his party's leaders (they were not his friends),
but to his old friend General Lucius Clay, Chairman of the Board of
the Continental Can Company, and a new friend, New York attorney
Herbert Brownell. To them was left the initial screening of the Cabinet.
The Cabinet then made the initial selection of the sub-Cabinet. Other
matters of personnel were handled by Eisenhower's Chief of Staff,
Sherman Adams. An assistant to Adams estimated that "the Governor"
(as Adams was called inside the administration) made 75 percent of the
final decisions on personnel; the rest were made by the President from
lists of candidates prepared by Adams.[2] Eisenhower's noninvolvement
was partly an application of his theory of delegation; partly an expres-
sion of his distaste for the process of patronage; and partly a reflection
of his limited circle of acquaintances outside the military, coupled with
his strong belief in not appointing military people to civilian jobs if
equally capable civilians were available.

The result was that Eisenhower picked a Cabinet of strangers. There
was not one person in the Cabinet who could have been considered an
old friend; most were barely known or not known at all. Only two of
the ten initial department heads, Attorney General Brownell and Postmaster General Arthur Summerfield, had played major roles in the
campaign. (Some others had more minor parts and several had been
opposed to Eisenhower's nomination.) Yet if some of Eisenhower's
choices were unknown to him, he was well known to all of them. No one
declined an invitation from the great World War II leader—a statistic
unique in the modern presidency.

The construction of the Cabinet was not totally without attempts
at "balance." The Interior post followed tradition and went to a

1. Quoted in Emmet John Hughes, *The Ordeal of Power* (Atheneum, 1963),
p. 331.
2. Robert Keith Gray, *Eighteen Acres Under Glass* (Doubleday, 1962), pp. 62–63.

westerner. (Representatives of California and Arizona were ruled out because these states were involved in a bitter water dispute that came under Interior's jurisdiction; the Governor of Washington had just been reelected, which left, by a process of elimination, the retiring Governor of Oregon, Douglas McKay.) Eisenhower wanted a woman in the Cabinet, and Oveta Culp Hobby was made Director of the Federal Security Agency with the promise that the operation would be quickly transformed into a Department of Health, Education, and Welfare. (Hobby's appointment also gave the Cabinet a southerner and a registered Democrat.) And in the President's only eyebrow-raising selection, he named a trade unionist as his Secretary of Labor.

Picking Martin Durkin, head of the AFL Plumbers and Pipe Fitters Union, had two justifications in Eisenhower's mind. He was trying to rectify what he felt was Truman's unwise practice of drawing the presidency into labor-management relations. If the unions had their own man at Labor, presumably they would not go over his head to the White House.[3] More conventionally, Eisenhower was seeking to broaden the perspective of the Cabinet—"to help round out any debate," as he put it. In choosing Durkin, the President unrealistically believed he could get "an impartial adviser," not a "special pleader for labor."[4] On the other hand, he did not look upon his Secretary of Commerce, businessman Sinclair Weeks, as also being a special pleader. Totally out of phase with the administration, Durkin resigned after nine months. Eisenhower then got the type of Labor Secretary he wanted by going outside the union ranks. In replacing Durkin with James Mitchell, a respected specialist in industrial relations, he was able to keep labor disputes away from the White House and add a more liberal voice to his Cabinet. Mitchell remained in the post until the administration left office in 1961.

More than any other President, Eisenhower was looking for types rather than merely weighing the competing merits of individuals. "Eight millionaires and one plumber" was how the New Republic described his Cabinet.[5] But Eisenhower was not impressed by money per se. Truman's administration had more men to the manor born. What impressed Eisenhower was the ability to be *successful*. (Money

3. Sherman Adams, *Firsthand Report* (Harper, 1961), p. 302.

4. Dwight D. Eisenhower, *The White House Years: Mandate for Change, 1953–1956* (Doubleday, 1963), p. 197.

5. "Washington Wire," *New Republic*, December 15, 1952, p. 3.

was simply the unit in which success was measured.) Eisenhower believed that a successful person, someone who had already proved that he could run something big, would be best able to tame a government department. It was a view shaped by Eisenhower's conception of what a government department does (namely manage something) and honed by the nature of his election campaign and the philosophy of his party. The only two members of the Cabinet (save Durkin, the general exception) who did not have backgrounds in management—attorneys John Foster Dulles and Brownell—were put in charge of departments (State and Justice) that from the presidential perspective can be considered more analytical than operational.

He had led a "crusade" to clean up "the mess in Washington." In thinking about key appointments, Eisenhower wrote in his diary (January 5, 1953) that to seek a government position is "clear evidence of unsuitability. I feel that anyone who can, without great personal sacrifice, come to Washington to accept an important governmental post, is not fit to hold that post."[6] He would hire people who were above—or not in need of—chiseling. Moreover, as the representative of a party that placed its faith in the private enterprise system, who better than a businessman could ferret out "waste" and recognize "reckless spending"?

Nor did the administration seek a contrasting type for Under Secretaries. The standard practice had been to divide the work in a department between the two top political appointees along "inside" and "outside" lines—with the Secretary being the spokesman to the outer world. Yet most of the Republican Under Secretaries were carbon copies of their superiors. Eisenhower's businessmen joined the government in the spirit that one contributes to the Community Chest, not joyously but because it is what civic-minded citizens ought to do. What was remarkable is that they stayed—held by the magnetism of Ike's personality more than by any other force. Seven of his original Cabinet members were still in place at the end of the first term; most stayed much longer. One died in office, one left because he failed of Senate confirmation, and two lasted the full eight years. Replacements with one exception came from the ranks of the sub-Cabinet or the White House staff.

The kind of man the President chose was the kind of man he was. Dwight D. Eisenhower of Denison, Texas, and Abilene, Kansas, born October 14, 1890, surrounded himself with persons of similar background. Only Dulles was older—by two years; George Humphrey and

6. Eisenhower, *Mandate for Change*, p. 98.

Defense Secretary Charles E. Wilson were born in 1890; twelve of his twenty-one Cabinet officers were within a decade of the President's age and another missed this cutoff date by a month. Their places of birth read like a gazeteer of small-town America—Killeen and Burleson, Texas; McRae, Georgia; Whitney, Idaho; Minerva and Berea, Ohio; Pinconning and Grand Rapids, Michigan; Charleston, West Virginia; Kingston, New York. Their personalities also matched the President's. Cheerful and confident, these were not the dour conservatives buried in the stuffed chairs of the Union League Club. While Ezra Taft Benson and Dulles could not be mistaken for the life of the party, they were the exceptions that Eisenhower made in the name of expertise. "Foster has been in training for this job all his life," Eisenhower often said.[7]

They were decidedly not politicians. All three Cabinet members who had been in the U.S. Senate—Dulles, Weeks, and Eisenhower's second Secretary of the Interior, Fred Seaton—had held interim *appointments*. The only elected Senator to whom the President gave Cabinet status was UN Ambassador Henry Cabot Lodge, his earliest supporter. Legislator-politicians were difficult for Eisenhower to fathom. They seemed to be consumed with concerns that did not concern him, such as headlines and patronage. He was much more comfortable with executive-politicians, and five ex-Governors were to serve on his White House staff.

Under the Eisenhower system the Cabinet officers were expected to run the daily operations of their departments without presidential interference. They had the right to come to Eisenhower when their problems were big enough, which was left for them to decide. But the President was impatient if they too often sought his counsel on matters that he felt were strictly operational. Defense Secretary Wilson infuriated him by constantly wanting to discuss the internal workings of the Pentagon, problems that the President considered unpresidential. Cabinet officers were also to come to the White House—meaning Sherman Adams—when they disagreed among themselves. For example, Adams reported that he "spent many hours" with Commerce Secretary Weeks and Labor Secretary Mitchell "sitting across the table from each other while they ironed out their differences."[8] It was hard for the press to accept the fact that someone as powerful as Adams was not making policy, but he saw his role otherwise and largely resisted the temptation

7. Adams, *Firsthand Report*, p. 89.
8. Ibid., p. 304.

to overrule the department heads (although he was equally willing to take the blame for doing so when the decision really had been made by the President).

Of course, the basic differences within the Cabinet were minimal, at least by the standards set by the preceding administrations. The like-mindedness of the department heads assured that this would be the case. Nevertheless, the Eisenhower Cabinet was composed of very strong personalities. A body that included Dulles, Wilson, Humphrey, Benson, and Harold Stassen must rate high for sheer tenacity. The feuds smoldered, but they rarely surfaced, and Eisenhower effectively used his weekly Cabinet meetings to preach teamwork.

His conception of the Cabinet differed markedly from those of the other White House occupants during the modern era. Efforts were made to convert the Cabinet into a major deliberative mechanism. Eisenhower expanded the Cabinet meetings beyond the traditional heads of departments to include such key aides as the UN Ambassador, the Budget Director, the Director of Defense Mobilization, the Mutual Security Administrator, and the White House Chief of Staff. It was not his habit, as it had been Truman's, to read voraciously. He did not follow Roosevelt's technique of playing off his Cabinet members against each other. Nor was he a solitary brooder in the Nixon manner. Unlike Kennedy, he thought it useful to gather the views of all Cabinet members even if their departments were not directly involved. This practice did not mean that all Cabinet members were equal. George Humphrey and his successor, Robert B. Anderson, were the more-than-equal voices in domestic affairs, the predictable role of Treasury in a conservative government; and Dulles jealously guarded his position as chief adviser on foreign policy. Eisenhower got his information from listening; he formed his opinions by talking with others. This preference, perhaps more than theory, accounted for the heightened role of such groups as the Cabinet and the National Security Council. He concentrated on discussion around the table, and then if he had reached a conclusion he would announce it on the spot, thus assuring that all his subordinates heard what he had decided. This was not collective government, any more than it had been with other Presidents; Eisenhower accepted the fact that the decisions were his alone to make. The job of the White House staff was to ensure that important matters were placed on the Cabinet agenda, that department heads were prepared to state their positions, and that they were periodically reminded of their responsibilities in implementing decisions that the President had made. That department heads, competing as they must for scarce resources and answerable to constituents beyond the administration, would freely put their most cherished proposals up for grabs was not an entirely workable notion. Despite the prodding of the Cabinet secretariat in the White House, the trivial was often a substitute for the controversial on many Cabinet meeting agendas. Under Secretary of State Douglas Dillon later recalled one Cabinet meeting: "We sat around looking at the plans for Dulles Airport. They had a model and everything, and we would say why don't you put a door there, and they would explain why they didn't."[9]

Eisenhower's doctrine of extreme delegation had a number of consequences. It may have helped to keep his appointees on the job for longer than they planned to stay in Washington. It contributed to their comfort (some said complacency), for they knew the outer limits of their assignments and had no fear of poachers. It removed burdens from the President, which added to an impression that he was not on top of his job. (He would have argued that no presidential decisions were made by anyone save the President and as few as possible nonpresidential decisions were made by the President.) And according to the power equations by which Presidents are often measured, Eisenhower gave himself considerable freedom of action by giving his subordinates considerable latitude to act.

What Eisenhower artfully constructed was an elaborate maze of buffer zones. James Hagerty, his Press Secretary, later recalled:

President Eisenhower would say, "Do it this way." I would say, "If I go to that press conference and say what you want me to say, I would get hell." With that, he would smile, get up and walk around the desk, pat me on the back and say, "My boy, better you than me."[10]

The Republican loss in the 1954 midterm elections was blamed on Benson, not Eisenhower. A farmer's poll gave Benson a "poor" rating of 33 percent, while Eisenhower's negative vote was only 8 percent.[11] It was as if the President and the Secretary of Agriculture worked for different administrations. In foreign relations (especially with the British), the Secretary of State was as unpopular as the President was popu-

9. Quoted in Arthur M. Schlesinger, Jr., *A Thousand Days* (Fawcett, 1967), p. 132.

10. R. Gordon Hoxie, ed., *The White House: Organization and Operations* (New York: Center for the Study of the Presidency, 1971), p. 4.

11. Herbert S. Parmet, *Eisenhower and the American Crusades* (Macmillan, 1972), p. 320.

lar. If a Cabinet officer could not get to see the President, he blamed Adams, not Eisenhower. And when the time came to fire Adams, the job was given to Nixon. Nixon was to call Eisenhower "a more complex and devious man than most people realized," and then quickly add, "in the best sense of those words."[12] In one important instance, however, Eisenhower chose not to employ a buffer. When the shooting down of the U-2 over the Soviet Union threatened to cancel the Paris summit meeting in 1960, Allen Dulles, Director of the Central Intelligence Agency (CIA), volunteered to take full responsibility and resign. Khrushchev seemed to invite this approach by stating, "I am quite willing to grant that the President knew nothing."[13] But for Eisenhower to have denied knowledge of the U-2, he felt, would have been an unconscionable admission that he did not control the country's national security apparatus. He took the blame and the summit collapsed.

Another part of Eisenhower's buffer system was the use of Vice President Nixon as his political surrogate, an arrangement that also reflected the President's strong distaste for party politics. Nixon assumed the burdens of campaigning during the midterm elections of 1954 and 1958. This was Eisenhower's contribution to resolving the apparent conflict between the presidential roles of "chief magistrate" and "chief party leader," and it became standard operating procedure in subsequent administrations.

Because Eisenhower came from a career outside politics and often expressed his aversion to partisanship, some were led to conclude that he lacked the political skill to maneuver the machinery of government to his ends. Marquis Childs presented the conventional wisdom in 1958: "He brought to the office so little preparation."[14] What may have been overlooked was that Eisenhower had spent a lifetime in the Byzantium of military politics and had come out on top. Richard Neustadt's often quoted comment that "the Presidency is no place for amateurs" was directed at Eisenhower.[15] A cogent case can be made for reassessing Eisenhower as a veteran bureaucratic politician. But if the portrait of Eisenhower as the humble soldier pushed over his head into a cauldron of high government machinations was a caricature, it should be

12. Richard M. Nixon, *Six Crises* (Pocket Books, 1962), p. 172.

13. Townsend Hoopes, *The Devil and John Foster Dulles* (Little, Brown, 1973), pp. 500–01.

14. Marquis Childs, *Eisenhower: Captive Hero* (Harcourt, Brace, 1958), p. 292.

15. Richard E. Neustadt, *Presidential Power* (Wiley, 1960), p. 180.

noted that it was also a self-caricature, drawn by Eisenhower himself for his own reasons. (Once when asked about a newspaper column at a press conference, the President replied that he could not answer because he never read the columns. The statement was patently false; Eisenhower began each day with a heavy dose of newspaper reading.)

Eisenhower brought with him to the White House very definite notions of staff. They were based on the military model, but as only a professional soldier fully understood, they were adaptable to the fortuities of circumstance. They worked for him; later they would not work for Nixon, who did not understand their subtleties. "The use of staff is a kind of art," David Lilienthal once mused in his diary.[16] Another New Dealer, Rexford G. Tugwell, wrote of Eisenhower that "no President had ever known so well how to use a staff" and that Eisenhower "was more skilled in using staff and more willing to delegate than any of his predecessors."[17] Tugwell profoundly disagreed with the aims of the Eisenhower administration. Still, there was no sense confusing Eisenhower's constricted aspirations for his government with his means of achieving them. Tugwell was simply stating what he knew to be a fact.

The Eisenhower staff was an entirely different sort of entity—with different functions and a different kind of personnel—from the Eisenhower Cabinet. As personal assistants they were better known to the President. Of the original thirty-two professional members of the staff (excluding military aides), twenty-two had worked in the presidential election (often on board the campaign train), five had served under Eisenhower in the army, and two had been with him at Columbia University. Twelve stayed in the administration for the full eight years.[18]

The staff, much more than the Cabinet, was likely to have had previous employment in the federal government. Five had worked in congressional offices, one had served in Congress, and seven had held appointments in the executive branch. As in all administrations, top

16. David E. Lilienthal, *Journals*, vol. 2: *The Atomic Energy Years, 1945–1950* (Harper, 1964), p. 7.

17. Rexford G. Tugwell, *The Enlargement of the Presidency* (Doubleday, 1960), pp. 458, 488.

18. All computations on Eisenhower's staff are based on a remarkable little volume, *White House Staff Book, 1953–1961*, prepared and privately printed as a sort of "college yearbook" by two staff members, Frederick Fox and James Lambie, and presented as a farewell gift to all those who had served in the Eisenhower White House.

White House aides generally were younger than Cabinet officers, although this did not create friction as it has in other presidencies.

Thus while the Eisenhower Cabinet was unique in its pervasive business background and in its lack of Washington experience, the Eisenhower presidential staff was more in the traditional mold. It did have more members from the corporate world than would have been found in a Democratic administration, but the Eisenhower staff businessmen seemed to have a more contemplative cast of mind than the Eisenhower Cabinet businessmen.[19]

Whereas the staffs under Roosevelt and Truman were composed largely of people whose talents were to be found in their finely tuned political antennae, or their overarching loyalty, or in high creativity, the top-echelon Eisenhower staff was noted for its functional professionalism. James Hagerty was a *professional* Press Secretary. That had been his occupation since 1942. (Hagerty had also been a reporter, which may have given him certain insights but was not his chief qualification; Truman chose his Press Secretaries directly from the ranks of working newsmen without notable success.) General Wilton (Jerry) Persons, who headed Eisenhower's congressional relations office, was a *professional* congressional lobbyist. That had been his role for the army during World War II. Special Counsel Bernard Shanley was hired as a lawyer, not as a ghostwriter in mufti. The writing was to be done by Emmet Hughes of *Time* and *Life* magazines—a sharp break with the past, where the distinction between policymaking and word production was left deliberately fuzzy. Besides relying on the statutory Council of Economic Advisers, Eisenhower added a personal economist to the staff, Gabriel Hauge. Robert Montgomery, the actor-producer, was on call to advise the President on the use of television. The Chairman of the U.S. Civil Service Commission was given the additional duty of advising the President on personnel management. And experts were eventually added in the fields of science, foreign economic policy, aviation policy, public works planning, agricultural surplus disposal, disarmament, and cold war psychological planning.

A review of the organization of the White House under Eisenhower

19. Among the men with business backgrounds on the Eisenhower staff who fit this description were Robert Cutler (Old Colony Trust Co., Boston), Clarence Francis (General Foods), Meyer Kestnbaum (Hart Schaffner & Marx), and Clarence Randall (Inland Steel). Cutler, Francis, and Randall were involved in aspects of foreign policy; Kestnbaum advised on intergovernmental relations.

must begin with the Assistant to the President, Sherman Adams. Eisenhower's recollection of his chief aide differs in no respect from the way Adams appeared to those who served under him:

From our first meeting in 1952 Sherman Adams seemed to me best described as laconic, businesslike, and puritanically honest. Never did he attempt to introduce humor into an official meeting. On the many occasions during our White House years when I called him on the telephone to ask a question, he never added a word to his "yes" or "no" if such an answer sufficed. It never occurred to him to say "Hello" when advised by his secretary that I wanted him on the phone or to add a "Good-bye" at the end of the call. For Sherman Adams this was neither bad manners nor pretense; he was busy. Absorbed in his work, he had no time to waste.[20]

Eisenhower saw the function of his Chief of Staff as that of being his personal "son of a bitch," a role ably played for him by Walter Bedell Smith during World War II, and he deliberately sought a person with the same appropriate talents to head his White House operation. After Adams was forced out in late 1958, his place was taken by Jerry Persons, a totally different sort. Persons, a gentle, humorous southerner, whose career had been as a conciliator, was less concerned with running a taut ship. More staff members were given direct access to the President, and Persons was less interested in the careful scrutiny of all matters that were to be put before his boss. This change did not notably affect the operations of the government one way or another, but by this time staff members were proficient in their assignments, comfortable in their relations with each other, and part of a waning administration. It was the Adams style that set the tone of the Eisenhower White House.

All activities except those relating to foreign relations came under Adams. These included appointments and scheduling, patronage and personnel, press, speechwriting, Cabinet liaison, congressional relations, and special projects. A newly created staff secretariat (proposed in the Hoover Commission report, a well-thumbed document during the 1952–53 transition) kept track of the status of all pending presidential business and assured the proper clearances on all papers that reached the Oval Office. A two-man operation within the secretariat prepared daily staff notes for the President, giving him advance notice of actions that were to be taken by the departments and agencies. Adams coordinated White House work through frequent early morning staff meet-

20. Dwight D. Eisenhower, *The White House Years: Waging Peace, 1956–1961* (Doubleday, 1965), p. 311.

ings, generally three times a week. These sessions also were used for briefings by the CIA and to prepare suggested answers to questions that might be asked at presidential press conferences.

Although there had been some formalized responsibility for lobbying Congress in the Truman White House, it was still essentially a closet operation. Doing it without acknowledging that it was being done presumably was least offensive to the legislature's sensibilities as a co-equal branch of government. From Eisenhower's point of view, however, the best reason to end this fiction was that he wanted a staff in position between himself and all those nattering Congressmen. The six key aides who served at some point in the White House congressional relations office had had considerable experience on Capitol Hill; one had been a member of the House of Representatives, and three had more substantial ties to the Democratic party than to the GOP. Given that the Democrats controlled Congress for three-fourths of the time that Eisenhower was in office, these relationships were not without significance. The Republican congressional leadership, on the other hand, was wooed through weekly meetings with the President for which the staff prepared detailed agenda. Eisenhower confessed that "these Legislative meetings were sometimes tiresome."[21] But in general the Eisenhower program fared well—because of his great popularity, because of his personal friendships with Democratic leaders Sam Rayburn and Lyndon Johnson, because of the skill of his staff, and probably in largest part because he did not ask for a great deal. The White House conducted a major assault on Congress for a legislative objective only once or twice a year; the rest of the time the departments were on their own.

In dealing with reporters, Eisenhower saw less of them and had his Press Secretary see more of them than in previous administrations. Roosevelt had held press conferences twice a week, Truman once a week, and Eisenhower once every two weeks on the average. (Illnesses accounted for some of this decline; there was a five-month hiatus in press conferences caused by Eisenhower's heart attack in 1955 and another two-month break in 1956 as a result of the President's ileitus operation.) On the other hand, Hagerty doubled his press briefings, conducting such sessions each morning and afternoon. He also managed to coax greater mileage out of fewer presidential appearances by releasing full transcripts within hours after a press conference and by allowing them to be taped for radio and filmed for later use on television.

21. Eisenhower, *Mandate for Change*, p. 300.

Since Eisenhower did not grant personal interviews and since staff members generally referred reporters' inquiries to Hagerty, the Press Secretary emerged for the first time as the principal spokesman for the government.

Eisenhower generally received favorable coverage despite his bland and sometimes confusing press conference performances. For his part, Eisenhower seemed to regard the White House press corps as a necessary though less pleasant aspect of being President. He could not and would not manipulate them in the manner of Roosevelt, nor did they irritate him to the degree that they had Truman. If he could not point to his meetings with the reporters as a positive accomplishment, he did take some pride in having survived: "I was able to avoid causing the nation a serious setback through anything I said in many hours, over eight years, of intensive questioning. . . . It is far better to stumble or speak guardedly than to move ahead smoothly and risk imperiling the country."[22]

The reputation for efficiency the White House staff had under Adams's direction was well earned, but the reputation for organizational rigidity was somewhat overstated by contemporary observers. There was a box on the chart for "speechwriter," but other staff members, notably Gabriel Hauge and Bryce Harlow, were pressed into service from time to time. Maxwell Rabb, the Cabinet Secretary, also handled relations with Jewish and other minority groups. Frederic Morrow was the administrative officer for special projects as well as being deeply involved in civil rights (he was the first black professional on a White House staff). Paul Carroll and Andrew Goodpaster, both military officers, successively headed the staff secretariat, while also being responsible for the day-to-day liaison on national security affairs. Although such mixed assignments were exceptions, there was some flexibility in the system to take advantage of special talents.

There was more organizational rigidity in the redesign of the White House foreign policy machinery. Eisenhower turned first to retooling the National Security Council; the Cabinet secretariat was not created until October 1954, and then largely followed the NSC model on a much smaller scale. (The Cabinet secretariat was always a two-man operation; the NSC staff in 1956 consisted of twenty-eight members, of whom eleven were considered "think people.")

Eisenhower was the first President to appoint a Special Assistant for

22. Ibid., p. 233.

National Security Affairs with responsibility for long-range planning. Day-to-day liaison, as has been noted, was handled by the Staff Secretary. Neither were operational so that even together their duties did not add up to the White House portfolio later assumed by Henry Kissinger. The first Assistant for National Security Affairs, Robert Cutler, described his domain as "the top of Policy Hill."[23] On the upside of the hill was the Planning Board (basically Truman's NSC senior staff renamed). It was made up of departmental representatives at the Assistant Secretary level with the presidential assistant as its Chairman. The Planning Board developed position papers, which the presidential assistant carried up to the crest, the National Security Council, and assuming that decisions were made by the President at the summit, the decisions then went down the hill to be implemented by the departments. On the downside, Eisenhower placed a new mechanism, the Operations Coordinating Board, consisting of officers at the Under Secretary level, whose job was to give decisions an extra shove as "an expediter and a follower-up."[24]

The NSC Planning Board met twice a week, on Tuesday and Friday afternoons, usually for three hours. It normally took three or four meetings before a paper was ready to be sent forward. Gordon Gray, Special Assistant for National Security Affairs, cited one paper that consumed "all or part of 27 meetings" and on which twenty-three consultants worked.[25] After reviewing a paper, the Planning Board would return it to a subordinate group of assistants, who met for four to eight hours on each redraft. This laborious process was designed to force agreement, but "despite the best efforts of the Chairman of the Planning

23. Robert Cutler, "The Development of the National Security Council," *Foreign Affairs*, vol. 34 (April 1956), p. 448. All three men who held the post of Special Assistant for National Security Affairs under Eisenhower have written about the NSC operations: Robert Cutler (1953–55, 1957–58), as cited above; Dillon Anderson (1955–56), "The President and National Security," *Atlantic*, January 1956, pp. 42–46; and Gordon Gray (1958–61), "Role of the National Security Council in the Formulation of National Policy," Paper delivered at the annual meeting of the American Political Science Association, Washington, D.C., September 10–12, 1959, in Subcommittee on National Policy Machinery of the Senate Committee on Government Operations, *Organizing for National Security: Selected Materials*, 86 Cong. 2 sess. (Government Printing Office, 1960), pp. 62–71. (The Cutler and Anderson articles also appear in this document.) See also Cutler's *No Time For Rest* (Little, Brown, 1966).

24. Cutler, "Development of the National Security Council," p. 449.

25. Gray, "Role of the National Security Council," p. 65.

Board" this was not always possible, and Gray mentioned one policy paper that was finally forwarded to the NSC with nineteen "splits."[26]

The President regularly chaired the weekly NSC meetings. During Eisenhower's two terms there were 366 NSC meetings, and he presided over 329 of them. This mechanism was particularly useful during the first two years of the administration when the work of the council was largely taken up with examining all the policies of the prior administration. (The council met 115 times during the first 115 weeks.) But the machinery kept getting more cumbersome. Meetings were attended by the five statutory members (President, Vice President, Secretary of State, Secretary of Defense, and Director of the Office of Civil and Defense Mobilization); the two statutory advisers (Chairman of the Joint Chiefs of Staff and Director of the CIA); three officers the President added to the NSC (Treasury Secretary, Budget Director, and Chairman of the Atomic Energy Commission); and the following regular invitees: the Assistant to the President; the Director of the U.S. Information Agency; the Under Secretary of State; the Special Assistant to the President for Foreign Economic Policy; the Special Assistant to the President for Science and Technology; the White House Staff Secretary; the Special Assistant to the President for National Security Affairs; the Special Assistant to the President for Security Operations Coordination; and the Executive Secretary and Deputy Executive Secretary of the National Security Council. This added up to twenty persons around the Cabinet table. In addition there were others whose presence was requested because of specific agenda items, such as the Attorney General or the Administrator of the National Aeronautics and Space Administration. Cutler early warned that there is a point at which a group turns into a town meeting and "once this invisible line is passed, people do not discuss and debate; they remain silent or talk for the record."[27]

When Eisenhower met with the President-elect on December 6, 1960, he told Kennedy that "the National Security Council had become the most important weekly meeting of the government."[28] Yet in one of the "afterthoughts" in his memoirs, he expressed flagging enthusiasm for some of the machinery he had created and suggested that part of the committee structure could be usefully replaced "by a highly competent

26. Ibid., p. 69.
27. Cutler, "Development of the National Security Council," p. 453.
28. Eisenhower, *Waging Peace*, p. 712.

and trusted official with a small staff . . . who might have a title such as Secretary for International Coordination"[29]—a sort of Henry Kissinger. Still, as tedious as some of Eisenhower's NSC procedures were, there is no evidence that they caused unreasonable delay when prompt action was necessary, as in the Lebanon crisis of 1958. The decision to dispatch U.S. troops to Lebanon did not emanate from an NSC discussion; it was considered by a smaller gathering in the President's office after an NSC meeting. The more urgent the stakes, the less likely is a decision to be the result of large, formal sessions. By the end of the administration, however, the NSC apparatus was coming under heavy attack from Senator Henry Jackson's Subcommittee on National Policy Machinery, whose reports would influence Senator John Kennedy.

John Foster Dulles had the abiding faith of the President and was the towering figure in the Cabinet. Yet much of the growth in the White House staff came in the area of foreign relations. Besides the elaborate NSC operation, the presidential establishment included new offices for psychological warfare, disarmament, foreign economic policy, overseas food disposal, and the international aspects of science and atomic energy; and Eisenhower also made ad hoc use of his brother Milton for advice on Latin America. Dulles viewed these specialists with suspicion and, when possible, cut their ranks down to what he thought was an appropriate size. Neither Nelson Rockefeller nor Harold Stassen could long survive the Secretary's enmity.

To explain the apparent paradox—the giving and taking of Dulles's power—it is necessary to consider the role of Eisenhower's growing staff. And grow it did. There were thirty-two presidentially appointed professionals in the White House at the beginning of his first term; forty-seven at the beginning of his second term; and fifty when he left office.

The addition of new aides fitted into four categories, each a perceived need of the President. What initially caused the spurt in size was Eisenhower's desire for efficiency. "Organization cannot make a genius out of an incompetent," he wrote. "On the other hand, disorganization can scarcely fail to result in inefficiency."[30] This was the reason for the creation of the Staff Secretary system. Eisenhower's second need was for coordination, which brought about the Cabinet secretariat and the NSC

29. Ibid., p. 634.
30. Eisenhower, *Mandate for Change*, p. 114.

machinery. In certain areas, such as science and economics, Eisenhower felt the need for his own experts. In paying tribute to the Science Adviser, a post he established in 1957 after the Russians launched Sputnik, Eisenhower wrote, "Without such distinguished help, any President in our time would be, to a certain extent, disabled."[31] And what was probably behind the increase in foreign policy advisers was Eisenhower's quest to fill gaps in the regular advice system of the government, to seek ways to make up for what he felt were deficiencies in his Cabinet members. As Adams put it, "Granted that Dulles was a man of great moral force and conviction, he was not endowed with the creative genius that produces bold, new ideas."[32] Therefore Eisenhower turned to such special assistants as C. D. Jackson and Rockefeller to provide what he was not getting from his Secretary of State. Eisenhower's two "bold, new ideas"—the Atoms for Peace (1953) and Open Skies (1955) proposals—did not come from the State Department and were met with skepticism by Dulles. All Presidents have shared Eisenhower's need for coordination and expertise, but the desire for staff efficiency has been a uniquely Republican motivation, which may relate to the differences in philosophy and personnel of the two parties.

Within the Executive Office, Eisenhower had an opportunity to kill off the Council of Economic Advisers in 1953. The Republican Congress, disenchanted with the politics and economics of Leon Keyserling, had drastically cut the CEA budget. But Hauge convinced the President to keep the council and to hire Arthur Burns as its chairman. Under the 1946 enabling act, the three members of the council were to be coequal; Eisenhower quickly won approval of a reorganization plan giving operating responsibility to the Chairman, a variation of a Hoover Commission proposal. Burns chose his staff largely from the academy rather than from government service. While Adams feared that Eisenhower and Burns would not get along, his worry proved groundless. When the 1954 downturn began, Burns introduced regular briefings at the Cabinet meetings—often lasting thirty minutes—and according to Adams, "Eisenhower listened to him with fascination."[33] The CEA survived its first crucial transition in administrations because of the increased stake of the President in the behavior of the economy, because the

31. Eisenhower, *Waging Peace*, p. 224.
32. Adams, *Firsthand Report*, p. 110.
33. Ibid., p. 156.

council members and their staff were congenial to the President, and because they provided the President with information that he considered immediately useful.

The Bureau of the Budget did not fare quite so well. Two of Eisenhower's four Budget Directors were bankers and two were accountants, whereas their predecessors had backgrounds in public administration.[34] For instruction in management reorganization the President was more apt to look to the second Hoover Commission and to his Committee on Government Organization (Nelson Rockefeller, Arthur Flemming, and Milton Eisenhower). Otherwise the Budget Bureau continued to do about what it had always done, but it was just not as central to the making of policy. This was caused less by suspicion of the careerist than by a simple law of physics—everyone could not occupy the same space, and Eisenhower's system of an expanded White House staff and a more powerful Cabinet left less room at the center for the Budget Bureau to occupy.

The testing of Eisenhower's staff-and-Cabinet system came during his extended illnesses. The illnesses happened to coincide with periods of considerable calm in the nation and the world, for which the White House–Cabinet arrangement could hardly take credit. But from Eisenhower's viewpoint, these periods proved that his organizational design would work as intended—efficiently, without friction, confidently. And this was Eisenhower's objective for his government and his country.

DWIGHT EISENHOWER chose a way of organizing the presidency that was very different from that of his predecessors. His highly structured staff system increased the size of the White House, yet the White House was to continue to grow even when it returned to more fluid designs. However, as a result of Eisenhower's having asked for—and received— substantially increased appropriations from Congress for staff purposes, a new "floor" was established.

The emphasis on creating new staff mechanisms did not have an adverse effect on the efficiency of domestic operations but became burdensome on the foreign relations side. Eisenhower's White House

---

34. Eisenhower's Budget Directors were Joseph Dodge (1953–54), Chairman, Detroit Bank; Rowland Hughes (1954–56), Comptroller, National City Bank of New York; Percival Brundage (1956–58), Price Waterhouse and President, American Institute of Accountants; Maurice Stans (1958–61), Executive Partner, Alexander Grant & Co. (certified public accountants).

showed that a large staff need not be operational, at least if it is balanced with tenacious Cabinet officials. Indeed the smaller Truman staff may have been more operations-minded. Still, as future Presidents would prove, the larger the staff, the greater the temptations to try to run the departments from the White House.

The use of the Cabinet for collective advice was particularly suited to the President's preferences for receiving information and was relatively frictionless because of the homogeneity of the Cabinet members. The rudimentary Cabinet secretariat, however, was not a complete success in forcing the most important decisions up through the system.

The combination of an efficient and orderly White House staff and unusual reliance on the Cabinet fit the President's personal needs and limited objectives. The liabilities of the administration—the absence of a steady stream of creative proposals and the failure to recognize the boiling point of certain domestic conditions—have been blamed on Eisenhower's techniques of management. Could the same system that worked for an intrinsically conservative and nonactivist President be adapted to the needs of a liberal, activist President?

The proposition was not tested by Kennedy and Johnson, who simply assumed that it could not. Nixon was an activist, but while he favored a highly structured White House staff, he quickly rejected a collegial use of the Cabinet. Moreover, lacking Eisenhower's skill in the art of using staff, his methods turned out to be more a perversion than an extension of the Eisenhower system.

In the wake of Eisenhower, conservative results and a structured staff system were often equated by social scientists who may have been personally uncomfortable with structured organizations and may have been less familiar with how they operate. It is hardly surprising that they would propose systems that seemed most congenial to them. Yet there is no evidence to prove that they were wrong. Certainly more imaginative people prefer to work within systems of least constraint. On the other hand, it is unlikely that a liberal President with liberal personnel would produce a conservative administration even if the President chose to organize his presidency along more structured lines.

☆ ☆ ☆ ☆ ☆ ☆ ☆ ☆ ☆ ☆ ☆ ☆ ☆

CHAPTER FIVE

John F. Kennedy
☆ 1961-1963 ☆

☆ ☆ ☆ ☆ ☆ ☆ ☆ ☆ ☆ ☆ ☆ ☆ ☆

WHEN John F. Kennedy became President, he promptly dismantled the Operations Coordinating Board of the National Security Council; abolished scores of interdepartmental committees; determined that there would be few Cabinet meetings and that those held would be for primarily symbolic purposes (because "public confidence [is] inspired by order and regularity");[1] and redesigned the White House organizational chart, eliminating the staff secretariat. There would be no Chief of Staff. Top aides would be generalists and would have roughly equivalent titles, usually Special Assistant. The pyramid was to be replaced by the wheel, with the President at the hub.

Kennedy proceeded on the assumption, later articulated by Roger Hilsman, that the way Eisenhower organized the government produced "the basically conservative policies that . . . the Eisenhower administration desired." Eisenhower's operation discouraged "new and innovating policies," forced agreement on "the lowest common denominator," and supported "the status quo."[2] To change policies the new administration had to change mechanisms.

The new President would have been thoroughly uncomfortable with the Eisenhower machinery even if he had wished to make use of it. Harold Seidman was one of many scholars to observe that "President Kennedy evinced little interest in organization structure and administration."[3] Whereas Eisenhower was a product of a rigidly structured

1. Theodore C. Sorensen, *Decision-Making in the White House* (Columbia University Press, paperback ed., 1964), p. 58.
2. Roger Hilsman, *To Move a Nation* (Doubleday, 1967), pp. 19–20.
3. Harold Seidman, *Politics, Position, and Power* (Oxford University Press, 1970),

organization—the military—Kennedy's background had been as a back-bencher in the legislature, operating as a sort of free lance in the competition for public attention. His career, made possible by family wealth, had been decidedly individualistic, an occurrence relatively uncommon in a society where most people's status is determined by position in an organization. Kennedy could be expected to produce a singularly personal presidency.

For this kind of Chief Executive there existed another operating model. As Richard Neustadt wrote Kennedy, "If you follow my advice you will commit yourself not to each detail of Rooseveltian practice—some details are out of date, others were unfortunate—but to the *spirit* of his presidential operation."[4] This was congenial advice. The style of Franklin Roosevelt was attractive to one who was fascinated by the techniques of power, at which Roosevelt was a master. And Roosevelt had created the modern activist presidency, which was partly a product of his techniques. Early in 1960 Kennedy told the National Press Club that the presidency must be "the vital center of action in our whole scheme of government . . . the President [must] place himself in the very thick of the fight."[5] Young, restless, highly intelligent, pragmatic, with a strong sense of history, John Kennedy knew what kind of President he wanted to be even before he knew what he wanted his presidency to do.

William Manchester once accused Kennedy of being "a generational chauvinist." Kennedy agreed, saying he "felt more comfortable with people with a common experience."[6] Kennedy was forty-three years old when he took office. The three original members of his Council of Economic Advisers, for example, were forty-five, forty-four, and forty-two. Among the common experiences of those around Kennedy were military service in World War II, often in intelligence or guerrilla warfare at the line officer level; an excellent education (there were fifteen Rhodes scholars in the administration); and participation in one of the

p. 92. See also Marver H. Bernstein, "The Presidency and Management Improvement," *Law and Contemporary Problems*, vol. 35 (Summer 1970), p. 512; and Rexford G. Tugwell, "The President and His Helpers," *Political Science Quarterly*, vol. 82 (June 1967), p. 262.

4. Richard E. Neustadt, "Memorandum on Staffing the President-Elect," October 30, 1960, Kennedy Library.

5. Quoted in Arthur M. Schlesinger, Jr., *A Thousand Days* (Fawcett, 1967), p. 117.

6. Quoted in Jean M. White, "Catching the Flavor of the Way We Were," *Washington Post*, November 25, 1974.

longest presidential campaigns in history. In a very real sense Kennedy's active quest for the nomination began in 1956 and, with the exception of McGeorge Bundy, his top White House aides had been his top campaign aides. Quoting Shakespeare in *King Henry V*, they would speak approvingly of themselves as "we band of brothers." This was not a phrase that would have quickly come to mind among Roosevelt's helpers (until much later, when sentimentality had set in). Yet it was not an inexact characterization of the Kennedy White House. There was little friction. Kennedy was not one to create conflict among his subordinates, and when he inadvertently gave competing assignments, his assistants were apt to sort them out among themselves.

There were no substantive factions as there had been at the Truman White House. The press expected a power struggle between the so-called Irish Mafia—Kenneth O'Donnell (Appointments Secretary), Lawrence O'Brien (in charge of congressional relations)—and the so-called eggheads, such as Special Counsel Theodore Sorensen and Arthur Schlesinger, Jr. It was a fight that never came off. First, because the intellectuals-in-residence did not place politics lower in the scheme of things than the politicians. George Ball was to complain that the academics drawn to "the yeasty air of the Potomac" had been "so seduced by the challenge of operational problems as to renounce any attempt at conceptual thinking as 'theology.' "[7] Whether there had been seduction or not, the dichotomy of the press was more apparent than real. Second, the centripetal forces were underestimated—not only the personality of the President and the staff's loyalty to him, but the length of time he and his staff had been together. Informal arrangements at the Kennedy White House were more than a result of the informality of the actors; they reflected a division of labor and the trust that had developed in the pre–White House period. Eisenhower's organizational design was a working plan for a group of relative strangers, a substitution of procedures for group instinct and experience. Kennedy could do without procedures as long as other arrangements kept his aides from tripping over each other. If Kennedy had served a second term and there had been a high personnel turnover, it is possible that his White House also would have become more procedurally oriented.

In contrast to the White House staff, dominated as usual by former campaign workers, friends of the President, and persons who had previously served under him, the Kennedy Cabinet reflected the tradi-

7. George W. Ball, *The Discipline of Power* (Little, Brown, 1968), p. 27.

tional, political balances and consisted largely of persons who had been elected to high offices in their own right. Cabinet secretaries are always apt to be older than White House staff members and to have more tenuous personal connections with the President. Even if no institutional gulf existed between White House and Cabinet, the distinctly different personnel profiles of the two groups would create tensions.

In choosing the Cabinet, Kennedy may have felt restrained by the slim margin of his victory. Having been elected with little more than 100,000 votes to spare, he viewed the appointment of department secretaries as an opportunity to impart reassurance to uneasy factions in his party and to important constituent groups whose acquiescence was needed to govern. So a Republican investment banker, C. Douglas Dillon, became Secretary of the Treasury; Luther Hodges, a southern Governor-businessman was named Secretary of Commerce; a New England Governor, Abraham Ribicoff, was picked for the Department of Health, Education, and Welfare; a midwestern Governor, Orville Freeman, for Agriculture; and Stuart Udall, a western Congressman for Interior. The General Counsel for the industrial union department of the AFL-CIO, Arthur Goldberg, was made Secretary of Labor; and incumbent directors, J. Edgar Hoover and Allan Dulles, were retained at the Federal Bureau of Investigation and the Central Intelligence Agency.

There were, however, three surprising choices: Attorney General Robert Kennedy, Defense Secretary Robert McNamara, and Secretary of State Dean Rusk.

For a President to select his younger brother and campaign manager, a person with limited experience as a practicing attorney, to be his chief legal officer was an audacious decision. McNamara and Rusk, on the other hand, were unknown to Kennedy and were the products of an informal network of talent hunters that generally produces the same types of people regardless of party—certain corporate executives, foundation officials, members of major law firms, and university administrators—with interesting subcategories, such as Republicans who turn up consistently in Democratic administrations. McNamara, the president of Ford Motors and a nonpolitical Republican, delighted Kennedy from the start. He was self-confident, articulate, energetic, and comfortable at the helm of large organizations. The President would not have to concern himself with running the Pentagon. This was no small recommendation to a President who had no background or interest in

management. But Rusk was of another nature—a nonassertive southerner, guarded in speech, with an infinite patience for the folkways
of the State Department, where he had served as an Assistant Secretary
during the Truman administration.

"Foreign affairs," Sorensen wrote of Kennedy, "had always interested
him far more than domestic."[8] Kennedy, however, initially expected to
move the focal point of foreign policy formulation from the White
House to the State Department, which was a reason why he cut the staff
and mechanisms of the National Security Council. Yet as if subconsciously, Kennedy created a hierarchy that left him "discouraged with
the State Department almost as soon as he took office. . . . It was never
clear to the President who was in charge."[9] The selection of the Secretary was simply one of those risks that confront all Presidents. "I must
make the appointments now," Kennedy told John Kenneth Galbraith
in December 1960. "A year hence I will know who I really want to
appoint."[10] Although this risk has increased since the Constitution
shortened the transition period between election and inauguration to
ten weeks, it was lack of forethought, not time, that was at the root of
Kennedy's frustration. In constructing a national security triumvirate
of Rusk-McNamara-Bundy, the President put the most diffident in the
post that required the most assertive. This decision was to have profound consequences as the Vietnam issue developed. A McNamara in
the State Department, where he would have represented the institutional interests of diplomacy rather than national security, would not
automatically have advocated a different foreign policy, but he would
have shifted the balance of advocacy.

The problem was compounded when Kennedy personally chose
many of the key secondary personnel at State, even announcing some
of these lesser appointments before Rusk's. Reflecting on government
in 1968, Bundy thought it "nonsense" not to allow a department head
to pick his own subordinates. "The historical record is full of examples
of the trouble and frustration for all concerned that can come from
the oh-so-skillful insertion of a President's man into the second or third
level of a department."[11] Although Kennedy soon lost interest in the

8. Theodore C. Sorensen, *Kennedy* (Bantam Books, 1966), p. 573.

9. Ibid., p. 322.

10. John Kenneth Galbraith, *Ambassador's Journal* (Houghton Mifflin, 1969),
p. 7.

11. McGeorge Bundy, *The Strength of Government* (Harvard University Press,
1968), pp. 39–40.

tedious chore of personnel selection, in the beginning he found it fascinating, and in staffing the State Department he filled at least three secondary positions with men who were more highly qualified than Rusk to be Secretary (Adlai Stevenson, Chester Bowles, Averell Harriman), and a number of others, such as G. Mennen Williams, had strong constituencies of their own. It was a design calculated to diffuse power and promote intrigue.

This hiring pattern contrasted sharply with that at the Defense Department. McNamara took his job with a guarantee that he could select or veto the selection of subordinates. His only personnel problems came from the secretaries of the military services, where White House political considerations weighed most heavily, and even here he eventually inserted his own people.

Length of time in office is not always a fair measurement of how well an appointee performs, but usually there is a relationship. And by this rough standard, Kennedy's appointments were highly satisfactory at Defense and equally unsatisfactory at State. Eleven of the sixteen key State Department people "served an average (mean) of fourteen months in their positions"[12]—a much shorter record of service than that of the Pentagon personnel.

In filling the top echelons of the State Department, Kennedy was influenced by the strong presumptive claims in foreign policy experience of the Stevensonian wing of his party. The appointment of so many liberals at State and in the ambassadorial ranks in turn heightened the pressures on the President to tilt in the other direction—what Schlesinger repeatedly called a "strategy of reassurance."

Kennedy picked each of his conservatives for slightly different reasons, although the overall strategy was to diminish partisan divisions or, if things went wrong, to help redistribute the blame. McNamara's Republicanism was irrelevant, just as Henry Wallace's had been in 1933; they were chosen for their special abilities. Douglas Dillon at Treasury was the person most congenial to the President who would still be acceptable to Wall Street. In choosing John McCloy, William Foster, and Arthur Dean at the Disarmament Agency, Kennedy was "following his customary practice of seeking a conservative to execute a liberal policy."[13] Kennedy sent Henry Cabot Lodge to Saigon as U.S.

12. David T. Stanley, *Changing Administrations: The 1961 and 1964 Transitions in Six Departments* (Brookings Institution, 1965), p. 21.

13. Schlesinger, *A Thousand Days*, p. 437.

ambassador; "the thought of implicating a leading Republican in the Vietnam mess appealed to his instinct for politics," wrote Schlesinger.[14] Generally these appointees served the purposes of the President's choosing, despite the inherent risks, as when Lucius Clay's blue-ribbon commission on foreign aid produced a report that was considerably less supportive than Kennedy expected.

Kennedy had Cabinet meetings as seldom as possible. He dealt with his department heads individually, allotting time according to the degree of his interest in a department's activities. He listened to them as a group "with thinly disguised impatience," in the opinion of his Postmaster General.[15] The President is quoted as saying, "Cabinet meetings are simply useless. Why should the Postmaster General sit there and listen to a discussion of the problems of Laos?"[16] (The example is somewhat moot: the Post Office as a Cabinet position was an anachronism and eventually would be removed from such exalted rank.) On the other hand, many of the departments contained substantive areas of broad concern, such as Interior (environment), Agriculture (food), and Labor (manpower). Moreover, there were men in the Kennedy Cabinet whose perspective was hardly parochial, as evidenced by Labor Secretary Arthur Goldberg's subsequent service on the Supreme Court and at the United Nations. Germaneness was not really the issue; the National Security Council, whose members all shared involvement in common questions, met only sixteen times in the first six months of the administration. Rather, Kennedy was too restless to sit for long periods, too impatient with long-winded speakers, and too mentally agile to accept repetitious, circuitous Cabinet-NSC discussions as a tolerable method of receiving information. It is possible that Kennedy scrapped the concept of collective advice because he hated meetings, just as Eisenhower may have accepted it because of his high tolerance for meetings. If so, both made theories about the proper way to run a government that were ultimately founded on the rates of their respective metabolisms.

In mid-April of Kennedy's first year in office, a brigade of guerrillas, trained and supported by the United States, invaded Cuba and was easily repulsed. "The lessons of the Bay of Pigs," according to Sorensen,

14. Ibid., p. 902.

15. Quoted in Thomas E. Cronin, " 'Everybody Believes in Democracy Until He Gets to the White House . . .': An Examination of White House-Departmental Relations," *Law and Contemporary Problems*, vol. 35 (Summer 1970), p. 608.

16. Schlesinger, *A Thousand Days*, p. 632.

"altered Kennedy's entire approach" to executive management.[17] The plans for a possible invasion had been initiated by the Central Intelligence Agency during the Eisenhower administration. They were reviewed at many sessions with Kennedy. In opposition to the CIA were Arthur Schlesinger, Jr., of the White House staff; William Fulbright, Chairman of the Senate Foreign Relations Committee; and Under Secretary of State Chester Bowles, whose views did not filter through Rusk to the President. Kennedy made a number of modifications and gave his approval. When the operation failed he took full responsibility.

The chief lesson of the Bay of Pigs to Kennedy seems to have been the need for him to turn first to those he trusted most and, conversely, to trust little in those he knew least. The President now treated the advice of the permanent government with suspicion. He inserted his own people into the system whenever possible—Maxwell Taylor for Lyman Lemnitzer as Chairman of the Joint Chiefs, for example. Bundy's NSC staff would become a "little State Department" at the White House, with its own area specialists, such as Michael Forrestal (Far Eastern Affairs), Robert Komer (Near East), and Carl Kaysen (Europe). The Foreign Intelligence Advisory Board was reactivated to keep an eye on the CIA. The President's two closest associates, Robert Kennedy and Theodore Sorensen, previously involved only in domestic matters, were given a broad mandate to concern themselves with foreign policy as well. Ad hoc task forces were created to make foreign policy recommendations, thus superseding the regular channels of the State Department. The first two task forces, on Laos and Cuba, formed in the spring of 1961, were presided over by Defense Department officials, Deputy Secretary Roswell Gilpatric and Assistant Secretary Paul Nitze, respectively. One result of these changes was that when confronted with the second Cuban crisis—the installation of Soviet missiles in the fall of 1962—and the choice was between air strikes or a blockade, the President accepted the advice of those he trusted most (his brother, Sorensen, McNamara) and rejected the advice of those he trusted least (the Joint Chiefs of Staff, CIA, Rusk).[18]

17. Sorensen, *Kennedy*, p. 710.
18. See Graham T. Allison, *Essence of Decision* (Little, Brown, 1971), pp. 203–04. Abram Chayes seems to imply that one reason for restraint in the second Cuban crisis was the number of lawyers offering advice. But since Kennedy rejected the suggestions of lawyers Dean Acheson (a hawk) and Adlai Stevenson (a dove), the proposition is not persuasive. (See Chayes, *The Cuban Missile Crisis* [Oxford University Press, 1974], pp. 13–14.) John Franklin Campbell seemed to blame the

Yet except for the addition of Sorensen and Robert Kennedy, the makeup of the advisory groups during the two Cuban crises were not markedly different. Irving Janis presented a convincing case that the participants approached the crises in entirely different deliberative manners. The sense of U.S. invulnerability, the suppression of personal doubts in favor of a forced unanimity, the stereotyping of the enemy—all present in the meetings leading to the Bay of Pigs decision—were replaced by a vigilant appraisal of the options during the missile crisis.[19] But, one suspects, the underlying reason why Kennedy's advisers were able to engage in such successful decisionmaking in the Cuban missile crisis is that they had earlier produced "a perfect failure" at the Bay of Pigs. Opting for a naval blockade, a low-level response, proved to be the right decision during the missile crisis, but it was also the decision of men who had previously risked greatly and lost. On the other hand, the Bay of Pigs invasion had all the hallmarks of a decision taken in the glow of election victory, just as Roosevelt's attempt to pack the Supreme Court and Johnson's escalation in Vietnam did. Thus the most lasting lesson of the Bay of Pigs may be that the early period of an administration, when arrogance and the illusion of invincibility hangs over the White House, is a time of potential high risk for a President.

The Kennedy administration had a firmer grasp of the importance of sub-Cabinet appointments than did former administrations. Under the direction of the President's brother-in-law, Sargent Shriver, an informal network of talent scouts was positioned around the country. There was nothing systematic about this search, but it did manage to cast the net more widely and to reach out for recruits rather than to merely respond to the entreaties of office-seekers. As a rule of thumb, Shriver sought persons who could be described as "action intellectuals" —businessmen who had written books or professors who had run businesses. Transition task forces also gave the incoming government an opportunity to assess a large number of prospective appointees and at

---

decision in the first Cuban crisis on the absence of advice from career diplomats. But, on the other hand, the successful response to the second crisis cannot be attributed to State Department presence. (See Campbell, *The Foreign Affairs Fudge Factory* [Basic Books, 1971], p. 51.)

19. See Irving L. Janis, *Victims of Groupthink* (Houghton Mifflin, 1972), pp. 14–49 and 138–66.

least twenty-four task force participants were given positions during the initial hiring period.[20]

Every President who succeeds a President of the other party, especially when the other party has been in office for some time, looks upon the bureaucracy as a hotbed of covert oppositionists. The assumption, to some degree correct, is that the outgoing administration has insinuated its politicians into the civil service. The Kennedy people came to office with a low quotient of paranoia. Yet before long they thought of the rest of government as a resistance movement, not a political resistance movement, but an *institutional* resistance movement, "a bulwark against change . . . a force against innovation with an inexhaustible capacity to dilute, delay and obstruct presidential purpose."[21] This frustration was deepened by generational differences. The careerist works his way up a hierarchical ladder; the political appointee short-circuits the system—his rise to the top is quick, if brief. When the two intersect they are at different ages, have different metabolisms, different reward systems, a different sense of time. While the age difference between the staffs of the permanent government and the Kennedy White House was substantial, friction was also a product of contrasting styles. The Schlesingers and the Salingers were the antithesis of the Brownlow Committee's stereotypical presidential assistant with "a passion for anonymity."[22] Not only did they have a personal flair that attracted attention, but for them to have waited for problems to work themselves up through the bureaucracy would have been an act of unattainable self-control and a violation of their instructions. Their President expected them to seek out incipient crises. At times the White House staff may have confused the pace of the permanent government with its intent; the bureaucracy moved slowly, but it did not necessarily move in the opposite direction, nor was it totally immune to political leadership. Suspicions of the civil service, first evidenced in the Kennedy White House, were to increase under Johnson and to become pathological under Nixon.

While the underlying reason for the growth of the White House un-

20. See "Pre-Inaugural Task Forces Unprecedented in History," *Congressional Quarterly Weekly Report*, vol. 19, April 7, 1961, pp. 620–23.

21. Schlesinger, *A Thousand Days*, pp. 625–26.

22. Brownlow Report, p. 5. See also Louis W. Koenig, *The Chief Executive* (Harcourt, Brace and World, 1968 ed.), p. 174.

der Eisenhower had been his belief in management (a staff secretariat, a Cabinet secretariat, and so forth), the growth of the Kennedy White House was based on the President's belief that if a task was important enough it was necessary to have someone at the White House with responsibility for prodding the bureaucracy. Whereas Roosevelt's favored technique was to spawn new agencies, Kennedy more often chose White House expediters.

There was a variety of specific causes for Kennedy's expansion of the White House—Executive Office complex: congressional enactment (Office of Special Representative for Trade Negotiations); to save face for an official who was discharged from another position (Chester Bowles); to provide a good address from which to run for office (placing Food for Peace Director George McGovern in the White House); to find a useful activity for the Vice President (chairing the National Aeronautics and Space Council); in order to lobby a bill through Congress (Howard Petersen's operation in support of the Reciprocal Trade Act); because of the personal interest of the President's wife (the arts); and because no one else in government cared (the District of Columbia).

The White House was allowed to keep growing because there was no resistance to growth. Indeed creating another White House office was often the easiest way to solve a personnel or constituent problem, a conferring of high status with little effort. The White House was the one place in government where the President could totally control expenditures and was free to move personnel and establish units at will. It was not until Gerald Ford became President that even a modest attempt was made to cut back on staff. Ford, however, was primarily interested in trimming numbers, not functions; he had evidently recognized that the White House had become costly and that perhaps some of its workers were underemployed, but he was not necessarily aware that his staff had acquired inappropriate duties that might be performed better elsewhere.

Much of the emphasis at the Kennedy White House was on crisis management and the public (nonmanagement) aspects of the presidency. Kennedy's habits, which predisposed him to informal arrangements anyway, were further pushed in this direction by the large number of international crises that occurred during his thousand days in office. Crisis management, almost by definition, is jerry-built—the intensive, high-level consultations during the Cuban missile crisis, for instance, fit the needs of a short-term crisis, but would have been quite difficult to sustain over a very long period of time. The public aspects of the presidency—speeches, press conferences, symbolic activities—were in keeping with Kennedy's conception of the office, what Roosevelt called "moral leadership." Under the direction of Pierre Salinger, more elaborate preparations than ever before were made for briefing the President before press conferences, which now were carried on live television. Kennedy held these meetings slightly less often than Eisenhower had, but they were infinitely more effective. The production of speeches again became a major White House activity. Instead of isolating this function on the organizational chart, as had been the case in the Eisenhower White House, Kennedy returned to the Rooseveltian practice and to the title that had been invented for Rosenman and that had been continued through the Truman period. As chief draftsman, Sorensen was Special Counsel and primary White House adviser on domestic policy.

The only White House unit that attempted to build more systematic links with the rest of government was the Congressional Relations Office, headed by O'Brien, whose staff remained about the same size as that of the Persons-Harlow operation under Eisenhower. But O'Brien greatly expanded his outreach through the placement and coordination of legislative liaison officers in the departments and agencies. These operatives sent O'Brien weekly reports and future projections, which were analyzed for the President and formed the basis of his meetings with congressional leaders. Periodically O'Brien would also call together his network, which numbered approximately forty.[23]

If the golden age of the Bureau of the Budget coincided with the Truman administration, the Council of Economic Advisers took on its special primacy under Kennedy. The President discontinued Eisenhower's practice of employing a White House economist in addition to the CEA. While the CEA still had competition from other sources, the creation of an economic troika that met regularly had the effect of elevating the CEA Chairman to the level of the Budget Director and the Treasury Secretary, despite the major operational roles and extensive staffs of the Director and the Secretary.

The three members of Kennedy's CEA—Walter Heller (Chairman),

23. See Edward de Grazia, *Congressional Liaison* (American Enterprise Institute for Public Policy Research, 1965); and G. Russell Pipe, "Congressional Liaison: The

James Tobin, and Kermit Gordon—fit the personality profile that the President found most arresting. As Herbert Stein wrote, "They were, for one thing, extremely self-confident."[24] Truman's CEA was drawn from government service, Eisenhower's from the academy, and Kennedy's from both—all three members were professors with a track record in Washington. They were, in short, "action intellectuals." They knew the proper way to lecture the President, and a CEA memorandum reached Kennedy's desk on the average of once every third day. Before long CEA members were taking on the sort of programmatic assignments that had been unknown to prior councils, such as developing legislative proposals regarding poverty and transportation. Heller concluded that "the forces of both law and practice make it increasingly natural that the major focus of presidential economic advice should be in the Council."[25] The question is not as settled as Heller suggests, since both law and practice have a way of being disregarded when it suits a President's purposes; what is most convincing is that the two areas that have become of overriding presidential concern are foreign policy and the economy. In this context, the temptations are great for a President to have his chief advisers close at hand.

The CEA, with its small staff of nineteen full-time professionals, was able to relate quickly and comfortably to the President—indeed, to effectively move across the invisible line that separates the Executive Office of the President from the White House staff. The same could not be said of the 500-person Bureau of the Budget. Kennedy preferred to deal with individuals, not institutions. Moreover, two other forces worked to downplay the traditional role of the bureau as an extension of the presidency. The first was Kennedy's disinterest in questions of management, which was an important element in the bureau's portfolio; the second was the tendency for the legislation that was most important to the President to be designed by Sorensen's office after direct negotiations with the departments and renegotiations on Capitol Hill by O'Brien's men. This still left a great deal of work for the Budget Bureau's legislative reference unit, but it was mostly the

Executive Branch Consolidates Its Relations with Congress," *Public Administration Review*, vol. 26 (March 1966), pp. 14–24.

24. Herbert Stein, *The Fiscal Revolution in America* (University of Chicago Press, 1969), p. 379.

25. Walter W. Heller, *New Dimensions of Political Economy* (Harvard University Press, 1966), p. 15.

clearance of the more minor bills.[26] The irony is that as the bureau became less influential, Budget Directors David Bell and Kermit Gordon gained influence, in effect becoming personal and powerful special assistants to the President. As such, the President sought persons with the expertise that he found most helpful. Roosevelt and Truman had picked Budget Directors from the field of public administration; Eisenhower's directors were bankers and accountants; Kennedy's men had backgrounds in program analysis and economic policy.

BY THE SUDDEN end of John Kennedy's life, virtually every aspect of White House staffing arrangements had been altered to conform with the habits and priorities of the President. Only the personal services functions, such as scheduling and appointments, continued to be handled in the traditional way that a Herbert Hoover would have recognized as familiar. Even where boxes remained on the organizational chart, the apparent continuity was deceptive. The roles of the Budget Director and the CEA Chairman, just two examples, were measurably different under Kennedy and Eisenhower.

In practice, as Kennedy found, a new President has full power to appoint his own staff, to make assignments, to create or abolish White House offices, to give or withhold his time and attention, and to seek advice from any source and to measure the consequences of rejecting it. This realization should not be startling, yet the tendency has been to view each President's flexibility as circumscribed by the precedents of his predecessors, which layer like barnacles around the office. The very notion of an institutional presidency implies that a President accepts and uses that which is in place when he arrives at the White House. But within the limits of organizing a presidential advice and service system, the experience of Kennedy, like that of Eisenhower before him, was that each President is remarkably free to make his own mistakes.

Kennedy had little interest in the place of organization in the operations of the executive branch and developed a disdain for its routines. This was partly the result of the early failure at the Bay of Pigs, but also because of impatience, "generational chauvinism," and an emphasis on crisis management.

Personal trust was often substituted for institutional responsibilities in choosing advisers. Cabinet officers, especially in the "lesser" depart-

26. See Robert S. Gilmour, "Central Legislative Clearance: A Revised Perspective," *Public Administration Review*, vol. 31 (March-April 1971), pp. 150–58.

ments, had a difficult time in engaging Kennedy's attention. Chains of command were sometimes scrambled. The boundless energy of presidential assistants worked like a magnet, drawing departmental issues into the White House.

The President's style attracted persons of intelligence and creativity to government service; fostered the redefinition of some issues, particularly in economics; and promoted new initiatives. But he was unable to win approval for his legislative package or to change the habits of the permanent government.

His organization of the administration conformed to his sense of the presidency as the focal point of the national government. His ability to personalize the office was aided by a stunning capacity to draw attention to himself and his family and by the skill of those assistants who helped him in his symbolic duties, such as speechwriter Sorensen and Press Secretary Salinger.

Kennedy had not been unfaithful to the spirit of the Rooseveltian model. A President with public relations skills and a message to impart could continue to marshal public opinion—perhaps regardless of his choice of organizational arrangements. What had changed since Roosevelt's time was the size and complexity of the federal establishment. It could no longer be assumed that a personalized presidency was sufficient to discharge the responsibilities that were expected of central government.

☆ ☆ ☆ ☆ ☆ ☆ ☆ ☆ ☆ ☆ ☆ ☆ ☆ ☆

CHAPTER SIX

Lyndon B. Johnson
☆ 1963-1969 ☆

☆ ☆ ☆ ☆ ☆ ☆ ☆ ☆ ☆ ☆ ☆ ☆ ☆

ON NOVEMBER 27, 1963, Lyndon Baines Johnson, President for five days, declared before a joint session of Congress that the theme of his administration was to be continuity. John F. Kennedy had been assassinated. The nation was in mourning. All appointees of the slain leader were being asked to continue to serve the new President. Unlike Truman, who moved quickly to put his own people in the White House and then in the Cabinet, Johnson made no changes in the Cabinet for thirteen months. At the White House he combined his staff with Kennedy's staff, producing what a Johnson assistant called Noah's Ark. "There's two of everybody."[1]

Much later Johnson gave a variety of reasons for the mass retention of the Kennedy appointees—a decision he regretted. But at the time he felt quite correctly that he had no choice.[2] The nation's paramount need was for stability and reassurance.

Friction was inevitable between some of the Johnson people and some of the Kennedy people. Presidential nominees always have sought running mates who, if necessary, could assure them electoral success.

1. Eric F. Goldman, *The Tragedy of Lyndon Johnson* (Knopf, 1969), p. 22.

2. On November 11, 1968, President-elect Nixon visited the White House, where, according to Mrs. Johnson, he asked Johnson why he had kept so many of the appointees of his predecessor: "Lyndon answered in a measured, thoughtful tone. 'Well, there are several reasons. One, respect for President Kennedy. He had trusted me, and I tried to put myself in his shoes. How would I have felt if, as soon as I was gone, he had disposed of all my people? I wanted to be loyal to him. Two, I didn't know for a good while whether I had an excellent man or an incompetent. And three, I didn't always have all the troops I needed.'" (Lady Bird Johnson, *A White House Diary* [Dell, 1971], p. 808.)

Kennedy was the first to have chosen so wisely as to have actually made the difference. Johnson helped carry enough southern states to win the election. Then, having relinquished the substantial powers of Senate Majority Leader, Johnson endured the vice presidency in conventional isolation, performing the marginal duties of a constitutional appendix. It is easy to forget a Vice President; one must, in fact, make an effort to do otherwise. While President Kennedy made the effort and acted toward his Vice President with civility and respect, many in the Kennedy White House looked upon Johnson, when they thought of him at all, as akin to a blood relation whose table manners leave room for improvement. He was a southerner in a North-Northeastern regime; nouveau riche, uncultured, and middle-aged in a patriciate that celebrated youth; a Protestant fundamentalist in the government of the first Catholic President. Although the Kennedyites could not disclaim him, they could limit supping with him to official occasions.

When Johnson became President some of his inherited staff, as Eric Goldman reported, viewed him as "a usurper, and an ignoble one at that. They snickered and sniped, half performed their tasks, and engaged in petty sabotage."[3] Others, notably McGeorge Bundy and Lawrence O'Brien, Kermit Gordon and Walter Heller, continued their duties without loss of energy. Those willing to transfer loyalty to the new President were to have their effectiveness enhanced. O'Brien eventually was elevated to the Cabinet; Gordon was offered and declined a Cabinet post.

It took about six months for the Kennedy incorrigibles to drift back to private life and be replaced by people who sounded more like the President. The most obvious characteristic of the Johnson White House was that it contained so many Texans. Over the years the staff manifest included Walter Jenkins, Bill Moyers, Jack Valenti, Horace Busby, Marvin Watson, Harry McPherson, George Christian, Liz Carpenter, H. Barefoot Sanders, Price Daniel, Jake Jacobsen, and Larry Temple.[4] This was not a distinction that defined ideology. Watson was considered a conservative; Moyers and McPherson were known as liberals. Many of the others, as on all White House staffs, were technicians of no known convictions.

3. Goldman, *The Tragedy of Lyndon Johnson*, p. 18.
4. See David S. Broder, "Texas, D.C.," *Atlantic*, March 1975, p. 113. Three Texans served in Johnson's Cabinet: W. Marvin Watson, Postmaster General; C. R. Smith, Secretary of Commerce; and Ramsey Clark, Attorney General.

By and large, the Johnson staff was very young, younger even than Kennedy's aides, most of whom were near-contemporaries of their President; and since Johnson was a decade older than Kennedy, the age gap between President and staff was considerable. It was unusual even for the Johnson White House that Moyers attained the highest rung of staff assistant before reaching the age of thirty.

The average age of presidential aides steadily and markedly declined from the time of Eisenhower through the Nixon administration. The latter's staff was the youngest yet, one of those "historic firsts" of which he was inordinately proud. The relationship between President and staff is not meant to be one of equals; still, it follows that the greater the age difference, the more inherently unequal it is apt to be. Johnson's and Nixon's young men (there were hardly any women on the professional staff) were less able to dispute the decisions of their Presidents than the older (and wealthier) staff of Eisenhower. This is not meant to imply that Eisenhower's staff often disputed him, only that they were in a better position to do so. Some young people challenge authority more than their elders, but these are not the ones who are attracted to the White House. While some of Johnson's aides—notably Moyers and McPherson—persisted in presenting an opposing view of the war in Vietnam, if they were not the exceptions that proved the rule, certainly they were uncommon young men.

The average age of the White House staffs did not drop because succeeding Presidents desired less and less back talk from their assistants, but rather as a result of Presidents wanting more and more activities to originate in the White House and to be accomplished faster and faster. The youthfulness of the Kennedy, Johnson, and Nixon staffs reflected the biological probability that older persons could not long have sustained the pace and that more routine functions had been assumed by White House personnel.

"I'll get my action from the younger men and my advice from the older men," Johnson used to say.[5] The President's older men were contemporaries who had been drawn to the heady atmosphere of the New Deal and had stayed on to get rich in Washington in the practice of law. The "Kitchen Cabinet"—that Jacksonian phrase for a group of outsiders to whom a President regularly turns for advice—is a notion that has difficulty surviving in this age of the modern presidency. (One

5. See "The White House Staff vs. the Cabinet: Hugh Sidey Interviews Bill Moyers," *Washington Monthly*, February 1969, p. 78.

suspects it always was an exaggeration and that presidential friends were more often close listeners than close advisers.) A new President, particularly a President by accident, turns at first to old friends from outside the government. Some of them eventually enter his administration and the influence of the others begins to fade as the President takes the measure of officials within his chain of command. Moreover, the usefulness of the outsider declines in direct proportion to the increase in information needed to make a decision, the speed with which the decision must be made, and the degree of agreement among insiders that is necessary in order to make a decision stick. Johnson, however, continued throughout his presidency to have extensive outside advice. Those most often in attendance at the White House were Abe Fortas and Clark Clifford. Fortas continued to counsel the President even after he became a Supreme Court Justice; Clifford became Secretary of Defense for the last eleven months of the administration. In foreign policy, Johnson regularly met with eleven nongovernmental advisers, who became known as the Wise Men.[6]

There were a number of other groups of outsiders on tap. At a level once removed from the President were his task forces, which will be discussed later. There was a steady procession of meetings with special interest representatives, such as George Meany of the AFL-CIO, for Johnson loved meetings as much as Kennedy hated them. There were the constant sessions with congressional leaders, although Johnson frequently sought the Congressmen's opinions after the critical point had been reached in decisionmaking.[7] And there was advice given by ex-Presidents. Johnson called on the elderly Truman out of courtesy. He was anxious to solicit Eisenhower's opinions, especially when they proved supportive. The war in Vietnam led to the repeated accusation that Johnson walled himself off from outsiders, but in fact he was the most accessible President since Roosevelt. Yet Johnson's outside ad-

6. Johnson listed the members of his advisory group, known as the Wise Men, as "former Secretary of State Dean Acheson, former Under Secretary of State George Ball, General Omar Bradley, McGeorge Bundy [former Assistant to the President for National Security Affairs], Arthur Dean (who had negotiated the Korean War Settlement), former Treasury Secretary Douglas Dillon, Ambassador Henry Cabot Lodge, retired diplomat Robert Murphy, General Matthew Ridgway, General Maxwell Taylor, and former Deputy Secretary of Defense Cyrus Vance." (Lyndon Baines Johnson, *The Vantage Point* [Holt, Rinehart, and Winston, 1971], p. 416.)

7. "Bill Moyers talks about LBJ, Power, Poverty, War and the Young," *Atlantic*, July 1968, p. 31.

visers, it should be noted, were not unlike his inside advisers. Johnson's Wise Men had been officials in the White House or in the State and Defense Departments. Their former association with decisionmaking at the highest level ensured that they would provide advice that took account of Washington constraints and realities. At the same time, they might be expected to provide a greater degree of skepticism and detachment than those with daily responsibilities. But by choosing outsiders who had been insiders, Johnson was not calling for advice that could be expected to be different in kind.

The pace under Johnson became so fierce that even many young men could not keep up. The President worked a two-shift day, 7 A.M. to 2 P.M., 4 P.M. to 9 P.M. Between two and four he took a walk or a swim, ate lunch, had a nap, showered, and changed clothes. Then, returning to his office, Johnson was known to say, "It's like starting a new day." His top assistants were expected to be available at all times, for both shifts.[8]

Johnson seemed at war with time, relentlessly pursuing a battle against the clock to do more of everything for as long as he would be in office. Speechmaking is one example. In 1964, an election year, he made 424 speeches. Liz Carpenter was in charge of one group of aides who met every Monday at 5 P.M. for the sole purpose of providing the President with jokes for his public appearances. Almost everyone on the staff was pressed into service as a presidential draftsman at some time. The demand for Johnsonian words meant that replacements were constantly needed to replenish what Liz Carpenter called "our stable of speechwriters." She noted that "everyone joined in the talent search for speechwriters, turning them up in unlikely places and confiscating them for White House use."[9]

It was not just the length of the day or the intensity of the work that made Johnson a tough employer. Herblock's much-noted cartoon of the President with a cat-o'-nine-tails, which Johnson had obviously just applied to the backs of his aides, was a pictorial representation of his reputation for verbally abusing those close to him. The ceaseless turnover of presidential assistants, according to Eric Goldman, gave the White House "the appearance of a well-slept rooming house."[10]

8. Charles Roberts, *LBJ's Inner Circle* (Delacorte, 1965), pp. 42–43.
9. Liz Carpenter, *Ruffles and Flourishes* (Doubleday, 1970), p. 253.
10. Goldman, *The Tragedy of Lyndon Johnson*, p. 272.

Another consequence of the Johnson style was the difficulty of attracting people to Cabinet and sub-Cabinet positions.[11] Some, of course, may have declined because they did not agree with the President's policies; others—especially after Johnson announced that he would not run for reelection—may have viewed the administration as a poor job risk. Johnson turned for help to John Macy, the Chairman of the Civil Service Commission. As the new White House talent hunter, Macy attempted to bring some scientific management to the task of political recruitment, previously known as BOGSAT ("a bunch of guys sitting around a table"). One of his innovations was to design a computer system, the White House Executive Biographic Index, which eventually provided the President with prompt information about 16,000 people.[12] The operation was particularly useful in putting together presidential commissions where demographic considerations played a key role. The Macy office was also successful in forcing vacancies to be filled as they occurred.

The administration came to rely heavily on promotions from the career service to fill important second-echelon slots. While this was undoubtedly a tribute to the work of some civil servants, it also was an indication that the President was less able to attract outsiders to government. According to Theodore Sorensen, "Lyndon Johnson complained privately that too many of his policy positions went by default to career civil servants who were willing, available, and technically competent but had no 'fire in their bellies.' "[13] Careerists received nearly half of Johnson's 265 major appointments in his first eighteen months as President.[14]

At first the President's staff had a semblance of hierarchy because of the presence of Walter Jenkins, who had served Johnson since 1939 and who functioned loosely, if not in title, as the White House Chief of Staff. Jenkins's age was closer to the President's, which also fortified

11. Among those who are known to have declined Cabinet appointments were Donald C. Cook of American Electric Power Co.; Thomas J. Watson, Jr., International Business Machines; Frank Stanton, Columbia Broadcasting System; Abe Fortas; Ben Heineman, Chicago Northwestern Railroad; and Kermit Gordon, who went to the Brookings Institution in preference to becoming Secretary of the Treasury. (See Lady Bird Johnson, *A White House Diary*, pp. 220–21; Lyndon Johnson, *The Vantage Point*, p. 545; and Rowland Evans and Robert Novak, *Lyndon B. Johnson: The Excercise of Power* [New American Library, 1966], p. 506.)

12. John W. Macy, Jr., *Public Service* (Harper and Row, 1971), pp. 227–28.

13. Theodore C. Sorensen, *Watchmen in the Night* (MIT Press, 1973), p. 36.

14. Roberts, *LBJ's Inner Circle*, p. 160.

his claim to authority over the younger assistants. The other figure of some presumptive claim to rank was George Reedy, whose service to Johnson went back to 1951. Reedy, a former UPI reporter, replaced Pierre Salinger as Press Secretary when the latter resigned in March 1964 to run for the Senate from California.

Reedy, however, eventually became a victim of poor health and of Johnson's war with the press. After an initial period in which the President wooed the reporters, his penchant for news management created a new phrase in the political vernacular, "credibility gap." The 1968 Freedom of Information report of Sigma Delta Chi, the journalism society, declared, "Secrecy, lies, half-truths, deception—this was the daily fare. . . . President Johnson is leaving office with perhaps the worst record for credibility of any President in our history."[15]

Reedy was replaced by Moyers in July 1965 for roughly the same reasons that a losing coach is fired. For the first time, a Press Secretary's downfall was based not on his performance, but on the performance of a President.

The sudden resignation of Jenkins during the 1964 campaign began the process of turning the staff into what Goldman has called "a shifting band of individuals and groups moving in mutual suspicion around the commanding, demanding figure of Lyndon Johnson."[16] At the same time, perhaps paradoxically, a countervailing force welded the President's men closer together. The force was adversity. As the administration's Vietnam policy left those on the inside feeling increasingly beleaguered, they turned more and more to each other for reassurance and support.

The Johnson White House moved closer to approximating the FDR model than at any time since the death of the founder of the modern presidency. The parallel with Roosevelt's White House is apparent in the following comment by a young Johnson assistant: "President Johnson tended to build his staff around people in a very unstructured way. . . . There was no domestic policy council, very little in the way of formalized staff interaction, meetings, and the like."[17]

Despite a gradual trend of nearly twenty years toward sharper definition of White House assignments, Johnson (in the Roosevelt man-

15. Quoted in William J. Small, *Political Power and the Press* (Norton, 1972), p. 119.

16. Goldman, *The Tragedy of Lyndon Johnson*, p. 275.

17. James Gaither, "Advising the President: A Panel," *The Bureaucrat*, vol. 3 (April 1974), p. 25.

ner) expected his top people to be general handymen. Reedy was Press Secretary and also liaison with labor; Watson was Appointments Secretary as well as liaison with business. In addition to their other duties, Valenti, a Catholic, and Lee White, a Jew, maintained contact with their organized coreligionists. At lunch in the White House mess, the staff joked among themselves that the President had dealt each of them a "resident" assignment: resident Italian, resident youth, resident hawk, resident dove.[18] Moyers came closest to being generalist in chief, meaning, as in the earlier case of Harry Hopkins, that he was more directly concerned with more matters that the President cared about than any other assistant. His amazing string of responsibilities included Press Secretary, speechwriter, domestic policy adviser, designer of the media campaign during the 1964 election, conduit to the bureaucracy, and foreign policy gadfly.

Johnson also followed the Rooseveltian practice of expecting his assistants to remain anonymous. Indeed Moyers's fall from grace was partly a result of his ability to attract favorable publicity to himself, especially at a time when the President's publicity was not favorable. The facelessness imposed on the staff kept the public from a true recognition of its worth. Undoubtedly Johnson's reputation as a wheeler-dealer rubbed off on those around him, although his administration produced none of the petty scandals that had plagued Truman. The Washington press corps, moreover, may have viewed his band of Texans (and others) with a certain disdain for their style. One indication that the intellectuality of the Johnson staff was underrated at the time is the high quality of the books written by them after they left government.[19]

18. George Christian, *The President Steps Down* (Macmillan, 1970), pp. 16–17.

19. Among the books written by Johnson aides after they left the White House (in addition to those cited that were written by Carpenter, Christian, Goldman, Macy, and Reedy): Peter Benchley, *Jaws* (Doubleday, 1974) and *The Deep* (Doubleday, 1976); Joseph A. Califano, *The Student Revolution* (Norton, 1969) and *A Presidential Nation* (Norton, 1975); Douglas Cater, *Dana* (McGraw-Hill, 1970); Harry McPherson, *A Political Education* (Atlantic-Little, Brown, 1972); Bill Moyers, *Listening to America* (Harper Magazine Press, 1971); John P. Roche, *Sentenced to Life* (Macmillan, 1974); Will Sparks, *Who Talked to the President Last?* (Norton, 1971); Jack Valenti, *Bitter Taste of Glory* (World, 1971) and *A Very Human President* (Norton, 1976); and Ben J. Wattenberg (co-author, Richard M. Scammon), *The Real Majority* (Coward-McCann, 1970) and *The Real America* (Doubleday, 1974). This list does not include books by those members of the Johnson staff who also had served under Kennedy, by careerists, or by those who served on the Johnson staff as White House Fellows, such as Doris Kearns, Thomas E. Cronin, and Sanford D. Greenberg.

How deliberately did Johnson try to emulate Roosevelt's system? Having been elected to the House of Representatives in 1937 as a staunch New Dealer, Johnson often said, "FDR was a second daddy to me." He thought of Roosevelt as "a book to be studied, restudied, and reread."[20] Yet such statements should not be taken too literally. Johnson was not a student; rather, like Roosevelt, he was a politician of great energy and ego who instinctively chose systems that kept all components dependent on him, that depended largely on personal loyalty (of which, of course, he was the sole judge), and that were adjustable to his idiosyncratic work habits.

The two Presidents, Johnson and Roosevelt, arrived at superficially similar staff arrangements out of conceptions of the presidential role that were profoundly different. Roosevelt was a public President. Johnson was a congressional President. Roosevelt moved in a mysterious symbiotic relationship with public opinion, nudging it forward, retreating when he was too far ahead. It was the reference point around which his actions were planned. He measured his success in terms of "moral leadership," which placed heavy emphasis on mass communication. Johnson, on the other hand, saw his reference point as the Congress, with whom he shared an equally mysterious and symbiotic relationship on domestic matters. He measured his production in terms of legislative proposals; his success, in enactments. Of all the modern Presidents, Eisenhower was the only one whose "special relationship" was with the so-called permanent government. To maintain this relationship, he needed a staff system that emphasized order and routine and that was geared to responding to the departments. Roosevelt and Johnson had greater need for creativity and flexibility and for aides capable of quickly producing words or proposals and of maneuvering legislators rather than reassuring civil servants.

Thus Johnson, the lifetime legislator, who viewed legislation as the end result of governance, sought a staff system capable of mass-producing legislative initiatives. But he demanded proposals of a certain kind—bold and innovative, in the Rooseveltian manner, yet uniquely his own in a manner that distinguished him from his predecessor. A driving force of this President—not always a constructive one—was the compulsion to prove himself "better" than the Kennedy brothers. Traditionally, the path traveled by proposed legislation in

20. Bill Moyers, quoted in Henry F. Graff, *The Tuesday Cabinet* (Prentice-Hall, 1970), p. 52.

the executive branch was from departments and agencies through the Bureau of the Budget to the President. From Johnson's vantage point, this was ponderous, when what he wanted was speed; it excluded him until the final decision, when what he wanted was a system that continuously responded to his wishes; and it often produced the same ideas year after year, when what he wanted were fresh ideas that could carry his brand.

Johnson supplemented the existing department-centered system with one that was White House–centered and that in the President's opinion operated "almost as a separate arm of the government."[21] Under the direction of Joseph Califano, who took over Moyers's job as chief of the White House domestic office, a series of task forces had been established by 1965 that functioned on an annual cycle, roughly along these lines:[22]

March-April: Compile "idea book." (In 1968, for example, this contained more than 100 possible topics for task force investigation.)

May-June: Select task force subjects (fifty in 1967); gather names of potential members.

July-August: Select task force members; assign staffs from Bureau of Budget and Califano's office.

September-October: Task forces in session. All meetings and reports to be secret.

November-December: Agencies comment on task force reports; Budget Bureau review of budget implications; LBJ decisions on which recommendations to accept.

January-February: Preparation of messages to Congress; introduction of bills. And the cycle begins again.

The President was proud of this innovation. The task forces harnessed the energy of about 300 business people, labor leaders, and educators. Much of his Great Society originated in this way, including Titles III and IV of the Elementary and Secondary Education Act of 1965, the rent supplement and model cities programs of 1966, and the Head Start program. Through the inclusion of key agency people on the task forces, the staff help of the Budget Bureau, and total secrecy,

21. Lyndon Baines Johnson, *The Vantage Point*, pp. 326–29.
22. See Norman C. Thomas and Harold L. Wolman, "The Presidency and Policy Formulation: The Task Force Device," *Public Administration Review*, vol. 29 (September-October 1969), pp. 459–71.

Johnson felt he had avoided the problems that he associated with Kennedy's pre-inauguration task forces—unrealistic recommendations, opposition by those inside government, and the embarrassment of publicizing proposals that the President would not accept. Looking back on the Johnson process, Califano said in 1973: "Programs might originate at the department level in routine areas. In new areas . . . a lot of stuff we just did and handed it to the department concerned."[23]

Nor did White House involvement end with the formulation of policy. Truman had brought labor-management relations into the White House when he wanted to settle a rail strike, but he had left the negotiating to an assistant; when Johnson tried to avert a rail strike he did the negotiating himself. And a White House staff conducts itself in the image and likeness of its President. Then, too, the coordination of policy was becoming more crucial and complicated as Great Society programs proliferated. Califano noted: "The President can't pick up the phone any longer and call the Secretary of Labor and assume that the Secretary of Labor can tell him what is happening in manpower training."[24] Now there were manpower training programs in the Departments of Defense, Labor, Commerce, Health, Education, and Welfare (HEW); the Veterans Administration; and the new Office of Economic Opportunity. When the President wanted action—with one phone call—he called Califano, not Labor Secretary Willard Wirtz.

Observing this scene from across the street in the Bureau of the Budget, Assistant Director William Carey saw "Califano's office [become] a command post, an operational center within the White House itself, the locus for marathon coffee-consuming sessions dedicated to knocking heads together and untangling jurisdictional and philosophical squabbles."[25] One person who did not like what was happening was Robert Wood, Under Secretary of the Department of Housing and Urban Development:

Confusion is created when men try to do too much at the top. In order to know what decisions are being made elsewhere in government, the White House tends either to spend time reviewing programs or to take more and more decisions on itself. The separate responsibilities of the White House, the Executive Office, and the agencies are fudged, and the demarcations of who

23. Charles Roberts, ed., *Has the President Too Much Power?* (Harper's Magazine Press, 1974), pp. 152–53.

24. Ibid., p. 141.

25. William D. Carey, "Presidential Staffing in the Sixties and Seventies," *Public Administration Review*, vol. 29 (September-October 1969), p. 454.

does what become uncertain. The result is a blurring of the distinction between staff and line, between program and policy. . . .[26]

The strange inversion of White House staff and domestic Cabinet was symbolically illustrated when Johnson secretly moved Labor Secretary Wirtz into the Executive Office Building as his chief speechwriter during the 1964 campaign.[27]

Nothing, however, was simple to chart in the Johnson White House. While Califano and his staff (never exceeding seven professionals) were the primary domestic policy assistants, they were not the only ones. The Council of Economic Advisers under Heller, Gardner Ackley, and Arthur Okun gained influence as the Vietnam involvement affected the economy. Budget Directors Kermit Gordon, Charles Schultze, and Charles Zwick gained influence as federal spending increased, as deficits mounted, and as new programs cut across agency lines. Consumer Affairs was placed in the Executive Office, directed first by Esther Peterson and then by Betty Furness, reflecting the growing power and cohesiveness of the consumer movement. The Office of Economic Opportunity, the Johnson-created operating arm of the "war on poverty," also was given preferred position in the Executive Office, a presidential cue to the importance he placed on this effort. Within the White House, various aides were assigned discrete portions of the action. Douglass Cater had a major voice in health and education; Roger Stevens was concerned with the arts; Clifford Alexander with civil rights.

For a while the President retained Eric Goldman as an intellectual-in-residence. Johnson seems to have hired the Princeton historian for a number of reasons: in an effort to treat intellectuals as an interest group (with its own "resident"); under the misconception that intellectuals produce instant ideas on demand; and because someone in the White House should know "the kind of thing a President should do"[28] —such as invite Lincoln scholars to lunch on Lincoln's birthday. Kennedy had also employed a resident intellectual, Arthur Schlesinger, Jr. But Schlesinger had a more political role because of his considerable experience in the liberal wing of the Democratic party, where the President was initially viewed with suspicion. In addition, it is probable that

26. Robert Wood, "When Government Works," *The Public Interest*, no. 18 (Winter 1970), p. 42.

27. See Evans and Novak, *Lyndon B. Johnson*, p. 466; and Roberts, *LBJ's Inner Circle*, p. 146.

28. Quoted in Goldman, *The Tragedy of Lyndon Johnson*, p. 278.

Kennedy retained Schlesinger for the same reason Johnson confided in Doris Kearns, a White House Fellow on leave from Harvard—as a hedge against history (or historians). In general, intellectuals have fared poorly on the White House staff unless they have had some reason to be there other than their identification with university life. Goldman finally went back to the campus because Johnson felt uncomfortable in his presence (and thus saw as little of him as possible) and blamed Goldman for the hostility of intellectuals, just as he seems to have blamed Reedy for the hostility of reporters.

By the mid–1960s a variety of forces were coming together to promote a more "operational" White House. These included the personality of the President, who was impatient with the pace of government and distrustful of those beyond his immediate reach; the collectivity of new presidential programs that Johnson had pushed through Congress, grander in scale and more complex in execution than the machinery of government was capable of coping with; and the new prevailing view of public administration—nurtured by scholars who had come of age during the New Deal period—that was supportive of centralizing the management of the executive branch in the Office of the President. An expanded presidential role was reflected in the report (never made public) of the President's Task Force on Government Organization, whose Chairman was industrialist Ben Heineman.[29] On June 15, 1967, the task force proposed to Johnson that he create an Office of Program Coordination (within his Executive Office, but outside the Budget Bureau), which would be different from what existed in two ways. First, the Director would be more powerful than Cabinet officers in the key areas where departments were in conflict. ("The President must inform Cabinet subordinates that he expects them to meet upon the call of the Director; that he expects major matters of interdepartmental program coordination to be settled in the forum provided by the Director; and that, when agency heads remain unable to compose agreement, he expects agreements to emerge and 'to stick' along lines prescribed by the Director.") And second, senior presidential assistants would be located throughout the country, serving "as the President's eyes and ears in the field." ("Only a formidable field force of Presidential representatives

29. The other members of the task force were McGeorge Bundy, William Capron, Hale Champion, Kermit Gordon, Herbert Kaufman, Richard C. Lee. Bayless Manning, Robert S. McNamara, Harry Ransom, and Charles L. Schultze. The report is available at the Johnson Library, Austin, Texas.

tied into, and reflective of, the Presidential perspective will overcome
the serious gap that has opened between planning in Washington and
making the programs work back home.") Johnson did not implement
this recommendation, though his failure to act probably was caused
less by disagreement than by Vietnam, which was then consuming his
attention and limiting his ability to engage in other controversial
activities.

Johnson did not set out to downgrade the Cabinet as Kennedy had
done. Reedy recalled: "Cabinet meetings were held with considerable
regularity, with fully predetermined agendas and fully prewritten
statements. In general, they consisted of briefings by cabinet members
followed by a later release of the statements to the press. It was regarded
by all participants except the President as a painful experience."[30] The
influence of the domestic cabinet members was an individual rather
than a collective matter. Some, such as John Gardner, were held in
high regard by the President; others, such as Wirtz and Stewart Udall,
were in nearly open rebellion by the end of the administration.[31]

The Cabinet departments increased by two under Johnson with the
creation of Housing and Urban Development (1965) and Transportation (1966). He made an unsuccessful attempt to merge the Departments
of Commerce and Labor, and he rejected until he was about to leave
office a commission recommendation to remove the Post Office from
Cabinet status. Twenty-five men served in Johnson's Cabinet. Ten he
inherited from Kennedy.[32] Of the other fifteen appointees, only four
were recruited from outside government—Washington lawyer Clark
Clifford at Defense; foundation executive John Gardner at HEW; and
two businessmen who became Secretaries of Commerce, John Connor
and C. R. Smith. The other eleven were internal promotions, such as
Wilbur Cohen, Jackson's last Secretary of HEW, who had spent most
of his career in the Social Security Administration. The people that

30. George E. Reedy, *The Twilight of the Presidency* (New American Library,
1970), p. 74.

31. See Christian, *The President Steps Down*, pp. 235–43.

32. Four of the Kennedy Cabinet—Dean Rusk, Udall, Wirtz, and Orville Freeman—stayed until the end of the Johnson administration. In getting rid of holdover appointees, the practice is to offer them some face-saving position. Judgeships
and ambassadorships are considered appropriate. HEW Secretary Anthony Celebrezze
was made a federal judge and Postmaster General John Gronouski became Ambassador to Poland.

Johnson picked (rather than retained) were competent and well regarded by the "clients" of their agencies but were usually not household names of independent, political reputation.

On national security matters, the President relied increasingly on a subcommittee of a subcommittee of the Cabinet. Several iron laws of presidential behavior were at work: as a group grows in size, its value to a President becomes more symbolic, less advisory; the chance of leaks increases; and members speak for the record or not at all. Thus the more important the issue, the smaller the group that a President turns to for advice, and in issues of utmost importance, a President may confer only with himself. Truman had shunned the National Security Council until the outbreak of the Korean war. Then the council replaced the larger and less differentiated Cabinet as his chief forum for policy discussion. As the Vietnam war became the major issue of the Johnson administration, the President turned from the National Security Council to what Henry Graff has called the Tuesday Cabinet. Weekly on that day, Johnson had lunch with the Secretary of State (Dean Rusk), the Secretary of Defense (Robert McNamara, Clark Clifford), his Special Assistant for National Security Affairs (McGeorge Bundy, Walter Rostow), the Director of the Central Intelligence Agency (Richard Helms), the Chairman of the Joint Chiefs of Staff (General Earle Wheeler), and his Press Secretary (Bill Moyers, George Christian). In effect, six officials became the War Cabinet. The National Security Council continued to meet regularly, but it dealt with matters other than Vietnam, and its deliberations took on a symbolic quality. "It was impossible to escape the feeling that everything was scripted," said an attendee.[33]

Even more than in domestic affairs, Johnson relied on the people he had inherited from Kennedy in formulating foreign policy. Rusk, Bundy, and McNamara assumed greater importance under a President who was less experienced in international relations and whose close associates generally had backgrounds in politics rather than in diplomacy. There was a special irony in the case of Secretary Rusk. Whereas Rusk and Kennedy dealt with each other formally and warily across cultural and generational chasms, Rusk and Johnson shared a common background of the rural South and were only six months apart in age. As McNamara became disillusioned with the situation in Vietnam and

33. George E. Reedy, *The Presidency in Flux* (Columbia University Press, 1973), p. 24.

when Bundy was replaced by Rostow, the President was able to report that "Rusk had the best understanding of the way I wished to move."[34] The Secretary of State, a peripheral figure under Kennedy, again emerged in actuality, as he was in protocol, the first member of the Cabinet.

Johnson's Vietnam decisions are often viewed as a product of a malfunctioning advisory system. Alexander George has argued cogently for "multiple advocacy" in the making of foreign policy, with a President listening "in a structured setting to different, well-prepared advocates making the best cases for alternative options."[35] Yet, in practice, how closed off from alternative opinion was Johnson?

Certainly there was no shortage of key advisers who favored increased involvement, notably the Joint Chiefs of Staff, White House assistant Rostow, and the U.S. ambassadors in Saigon. On the other hand, Johnson argued that "there was no shortage of information at any time"—presumably meaning information both supporting and opposing various options.[36] For a man with three TV sets in his office, he was hardly unaware of opposition to his actions. Moreover, the President claimed that he "institutionalized" opposition within the government, and in a sense he did. "Under Secretary of State George Ball had been less than enthusiastic about some aspects of our involvement in Southeast Asia," Johnson said. "Often in our meetings he spoke in opposition to one proposal or another. Especially from 1965 onward he played the role of devil's advocate frequently."[37] Nor was Ball the only internal critic. Moyers and later McPherson had the same function at the White House. The President frequently consulted Llewellyn Thompson, the State Department's Soviet specialist, who was known to caution restraint. Johnson's friend and successor as Senate Majority Leader, Mike Mansfield, also carried the case against the President's policies to the President. Strangely, as the Pentagon Papers disclosed, the CIA was consistently reporting that the war was not going well.

"Simply stated," wrote James Thomson, who served in the White House and the State Department, "dissent, when recognized, was made to feel at home." The President and his allies "felt good (they had given

34. Lyndon Johnson, *The Vantage Point*, p. 410.

35. Alexander L. George, "The Case for Multiple Advocacy in Making Foreign Policy," *American Political Science Review*, vol. 66 (September 1972), p. 751.

36. Quoted in Johnson, *The Vantage Point*, p. 64.

37. Ibid., p. 147.

a full hearing to the dovish option)."[38] The internal opponents were neither unimportant nor inarticulate. Indeed they were among the best people in government. But they were ultimately ineffective for a basic reason: the President disagreed with them. "I am not going to lose Vietnam," Johnson said. "I am not going to be the President who saw Southeast Asia go the way China went."[39]

It would have taken a President with an unconventional cast of mind to have reversed the direction of U.S. policy, or a President schooled in military tactics, such as Eisenhower, who understood the hazards of becoming involved in a massive land war on the Asian continent. The Vietnam experience was in keeping with the cold war legacy that Johnson inherited. And once committed to fighting in Vietnam, a reversal of policy became increasingly difficult. The U.S. system is not one that makes it easy for a President to admit he is wrong, nor was Johnson a man whose psychological stakes in his actions were insignificant.

So the root causes for the Vietnam escalation are not to be found in "captive" theories that stress the preponderance of hawkish advice. Johnson was not a captive of his advisers. He was a captive of what he was and what he believed.

LYNDON JOHNSON's methods of organizing the presidency suggest that Presidents can be too idiosyncratic. The continuing needs of large organizations demand a certain degree of predictability in leaders. Johnson's habits may have made good news copy—when they were printable—but they created a high personnel turnover on the White House staff, an unhealthy sense of insecurity and dependence on the part of those around him, and constant strain in his relations with some members of his Cabinet. A President's right to do things his way, so long a tenet of liberal advocacy of a strong presidency, suddenly appeared to be a double-edged sword.

Johnson's skills as a legislative leader and his attention to congressional lobbying resulted in an extraordinary record of major enactments. His technique of developing legislative packages was innovative.

38. James C. Thomson, Jr., "How Could Vietnam Happen?" *Atlantic*, April 1968, p. 49.

39. Quoted in Tom Wicker, "The Wrong Rubicon: LBJ and the War," *Atlantic*, May 1968, p. 68.

Many of his assistants were talented and all were hardworking. But his legislator's mind-set, when applied to grave questions of world security, produced disaster. He had grown successful by manipulating men in small numbers, a practice based on broad knowledge and careful assessment of colleague politicians whose motor forces he understood. He incorrectly analogized this experience to relations between nations, overpersonalizing whatever entered his field of vision.

The need to become directly involved in all aspects of the presidency that he cared about brought a more than normal quotient of minutiae into the White House and engaged his staff in more operational and policy-formulating matters than ever before. New agencies were added to the Executive Office of the President. Responsibility gravitated to those closest at hand. Personal loyalty to him became an overriding concern and some Cabinet members were increasingly treated with suspicion.

His personal style limited his ability to use public opinion to bolster his position within government. Adversity fed on itself, producing an "us against them" mentality and further isolating the President from the rest of the country—eventually even restricting his freedom of travel.

In the end, Lyndon Johnson turned the presidency into a bunker and then handed it over to Richard Nixon.

☆ ☆ ☆ ☆ ☆ ☆ ☆ ☆ ☆ ☆ ☆ ☆ ☆

CHAPTER SEVEN

Richard M. Nixon
☆ 1969-1974 ☆

☆ ☆ ☆ ☆ ☆ ☆ ☆ ☆ ☆ ☆ ☆ ☆ ☆

IF THE U.S. Civil Service Commission were to choose Presidents by unassembled examination—the way high-level federal executives are picked on the basis of past record rather than written test—Richard M. Nixon in 1968 might have appeared as qualified as any President since the end of the Virginia dynasty. True, he did not have the congressional experience of Lyndon Johnson, although he had been in both the House of Representatives and the Senate for short periods. More important, he was the first President since John Adams to have served as Vice President for eight years. And no other Vice President had been given so many chores. Having been out of office since his defeat by John Kennedy in 1960, presumably Nixon had also had eight years to contemplate the nature of the office that had first eluded him.

That Richard Nixon became the first President to have been forced to resign may say much about the qualities that are most necessary in an American President and that are beyond the scope of this study. It may say something about how little can be known about being President before taking office—a point made by Nixon in a television interview on January 4, 1971, and made earlier, under similar circumstances, by John Kennedy.[1] It may also say something about the way Nixon organized his presidency and the people he picked to assist him, at least that is an assumption made by some in the wake of Watergate.

Nixon was clearly a management-conscious President; the way the White House would be organized was of serious concern to him. Theo-

1. See *Public Papers of the Presidents, Richard Nixon, 1971* (Government Printing Office, 1972), p. 6. See also *Public Papers of the Presidents, John F. Kennedy, 1962* (GPO, 1963), p. 889. (Hereinafter referred to as *Public Papers*.)

dore White felt that an important generalization, basic to an understanding of Nixon, is that he had "a fascination with How Things
Work."[2] John Osborne of the *New Republic*, that most skilled observer of the Nixon White House, stressed the President's "continuing
struggle for neatness," a constant quest for "disciplined order and
precision."[3]

While the organizational arrangements of all administrations change
over time, usually gradually, Nixon's were in a continual state of flux
so that his presidency seems to have evolved through six phases. Phase
I encompassed the pre-inauguration period in 1968 when Nixon laid
out his plans for a Cabinet-centered government in domestic affairs
and a White House–centered government in foreign affairs. Phase II,
from January through September 1969, was a period of policy formulation with relations between Cabinet and White House staff in a volatile
balance. October 1969 through June 1970 was a transitional period,
Phase III, during which the emphasis shifted to program development
and implementation, and internal power started to move decidedly in
the direction of the White House staff. In Phase IV, July 1970–November 1972, control of government became firmly centralized in the White
House; the Domestic Council was created, the Bureau of the Budget
was converted into the Office of Management and Budget, there was
a proliferation of functional and constituent offices in the White House,
and the President proposed fewer and larger domestic departments.
After Nixon's reelection in 1972, Phase V was a movement toward
decentralization, primarily to be accomplished by transferring White
House loyalists to the departments; and in the final phase, starting
with the firing of H. R. Haldeman and John Ehrlichman in April
1973, there was the Watergate-created disintegration of the administration, culminating in the President's resignation on August 9, 1974.

When asked in May 1968 how he would operate if elected President,
Nixon replied:

> For one thing, I would disperse power, spread it among able people. Men
> operate best only if they are given the chance to operate at full capacity.
>   I would operate differently from President Johnson. Instead of taking all
> power to myself, I'd select cabinet members who could do their jobs, and each

2. Theodore H. White, *Breach of Faith: The Fall of Richard Nixon* (Atheneum
and Reader's Digest Press, 1975), p. 62.

3. John Osborne, *The First Two Years of the Nixon Watch* (Liveright, 1971),
"First Year," pp. 28, 96.

of them would have the stature and the power to function effectively. Publicity would not center at the White House alone. Every key official would have the opportunity to be a big man in his field. On the other hand, when a President takes all the real power to himself, those around him become puppets. They shrivel up and become less and less creative.

Actually, my belief in dispersal of power relates to the fundamental proposition of how to make a country move forward. Progress demands that you develop your most creative people to the fullest. And your most creative people can't develop in a monolithic, centralized power set-up.[4]

Nixon, however, made a distinction in foreign policy operations. He looked back with enthusiasm on Eisenhower's use of the National Security Council. "The process was, of course, not flawless, but it was the controlling element in our success in keeping the peace throughout our eight White House years." Nixon saw subsequent foreign policy decisions—presumably those relating to Cuba and Vietnam—as a direct result of the demise of the NSC.

Since 1960, this Council has virtually disappeared as an operating function. In its place there have been catch-as-can talk-fests between the President, his staff assistants, and various others. I attribute most of our serious reverses abroad since 1960 to the inability or disinclination of President Eisenhower's successors to make effective use of this important Council.... I intend to restore the National Security Council to its pre-eminent role in national security planning.[5]

Nixon's White House aides, he said, were to be "generalists in the very best sense of the word." His objective was to avoid surrounding himself with advocates for the various federal departments and other constituencies.[6] Bob Haldeman, who was to be the President's Chief of Staff, told the first post-election meeting of his assistants, "Our job is not to do the work of government, but to get the work out to where it belongs—out to the Departments." One of those in attendance, speechwriter William Safire, later commented that this "was not a matter of being two-faced—Nixon and Haldeman honestly thought in the beginning that was the way it could and should be done."[7]

Still, if the impression given was that Nixon wished to be a latter-day

4. Earl Mazo and Stephen Hess, *Nixon: A Political Portrait* (Harper and Row, 1968), pp. 314–15. See also Harold Seidman, *Politics, Position, and Power* (Oxford University Press, 1970), pp. 74–75.

5. *Nixon Speaks Out* (Nixon-Agnew Campaign Committee, 1968), pp. 242–43.

6. *National Journal*, February 28, 1970, p. 422.

7. William Safire, *Before the Fall* (Doubleday, 1975), p. 116.

Eisenhower, there was another clue in his campaign speeches to suggest otherwise: "The next President must take an activist view of his office."[8] Could an Eisenhower-style system be adaptable to an activist President? Eisenhower's presidential establishment was an extension of staff-and-command routines that he had mastered in a lifetime of military service. Could they be fitted to the style of a politician whose managerial experiences in large organizations were limited? Moreover, despite the political usefulness of identifying himself with Eisenhower, Nixon never viewed his former chief as a presidential model in the sense that Johnson looked to FDR. In *his* administration, Nixon is reported to have told close associates, he wanted no Sherman Adams, no James Hagerty, no John Foster Dulles.[9]

It was in the context of an independent-yet-collegial domestic Cabinet, a retooled NSC machinery that kept foreign policy control in the hands of the President, and a White House staff of generalists that Nixon set out to choose his department heads and personal assistants. The results of his Cabinet-making were announced on December 11, 1968: William P. Rogers, Secretary of State; David M. Kennedy, Treasury; Melvin P. Laird, Defense; John N. Mitchell, Attorney General; Winton M. Blount, Postmaster General; Walter J. Hickel, Interior; Clifford M. Hardin, Agriculture; Maurice H. Stans, Commerce; George P. Shultz, Labor; Robert H. Finch, Health, Education, and Welfare; George W. Romney, Housing and Urban Development (HUD); and John A. Volpe, Transportation.

The President-elect presented the incoming Cabinet to the American people as men of "extra dimension." Others, such as Arthur Schlesinger, Jr., would criticize Nixon's appointees for their lack of national standing. "Historically, the Cabinet . . . has generally contained men with their own views and their own constituencies. . . . But who in President Nixon's Cabinet will talk back to him? . . ."[10]

A more balanced assessment is to be found somewhere between Nixon and Schlesinger. The new Cabinet displayed considerably more diversity and political experience than had Eisenhower's. Nixon, too, had his share of millionaires, but they were neither the patricians of the Roose-

8. *Nixon on the Issues* (Nixon-Agnew Campaign Committee, 1968), p. 76.

9. See Rowland Evans, Jr., and Robert D. Novak, *Nixon in the White House* (Random House, 1971), p. 10.

10. Arthur Schlesinger, Jr., "Presidential War," *New York Times Magazine*, January 7, 1974, p. 28.

velt-Truman administrations nor the major corporation executives of the Eisenhower Cabinet. Rather, Nixon's millionaires were generally self-made owner-operators in the mold of Hickel, Volpe, and Blount. Even Romney, a former president of American Motors, had started life poor and had laterally entered Big Business.

Nixon turned less to Congress for his department secretaries than had Truman. Yet Truman was the exception, not Nixon. The trend was clear—half the Cabinet had come from Congress in the period 1828–60; 40 percent from 1860 until 1896; 20 percent from 1896 to 1932; and only 15 percent since 1932.[11]

The most similarities were between the initial Kennedy and Nixon Cabinets. Each President chose three Governors, appointed his campaign manager to head the Justice Department, turned to one member of the House of Representatives, gave Treasury to a banker, the Post Office to a businessman, Interior to a westerner, and Agriculture to a midwesterner. Kennedy selected one person from the opposition party, which Nixon did not do until John Connally became Treasury Secretary in 1970, although Nixon did try to recruit Senator Henry Jackson as his first Defense Secretary. Both Kennedy and Nixon picked several Cabinet officers who were personally unknown to them and in the cases of McNamara and Shultz (whose surname Nixon did not know how to spell) the unknowns were to emerge as Cabinet strongmen. Nixon turned to two academics; there were none in the Kennedy Cabinet.[12]

In sum, Nixon selected a traditionally balanced Cabinet. If it was a mite short on Washington executive experience, the reason was not difficult to locate. Republicans had had little opportunity for such experience in recent years. And many members of the last Republican

11. See Kevin P. Phillips, *Mediacracy* (Doubleday, 1975), pp. 179–80. Nixon subsequently chose three more members of Congress: Rogers Morton of Maryland, Secretary of the Interior; George Bush of Texas, U.S. Representative to the United Nations; and Senator William Saxbe of Ohio, Attorney General.

12. Secretary of Agriculture Hardin had been Chancellor of the University of Nebraska; Secretary of Labor Shultz had been Dean of the Graduate School of Business, University of Chicago. Two other academics were later appointed to head departments: Henry Kissinger of Harvard (State); and James R. Schlesinger, formerly of the University of Virginia (Defense). White pointed out that in Nixon's second term his "Cabinet and staff . . . were more heavily dominated by Harvard men than those of any of the six Harvard men who had been Presidents of the United States." (*Breach of Faith*, p. 252.)

administration, eight years previously, had been advanced in years. Yet three of Nixon's eleven Cabinet officers had held high positions under Eisenhower.[13]

Department Under Secretaries in some cases were selected by the Cabinet officers. In other cases, they were suggested by the White House. Finch and Romney, for example, gave the number two jobs to old colleagues from their states. The Hickel appointment, which had been subjected to heavy fire from environmentalists, was balanced with the appointment of Russell Train, a dedicated conservationist. The two top officials of the Interior Department were barely on speaking terms. As a general rule—with a notable exception at Defense—the administration was better served when the Secretary made the choice. An absurd attempt was made to expand the recruitment process by sending form letters to all listees in *Who's Who* (including Richard M. Nixon). The major product of this effort was a lot of unanswered letters in the transition office. Prospective Assistant Secretaries and other key aides were located in the usual manner—through participation in the campaign and other Old Boy Networks.

White made an interesting point when relating the Cabinet to the eventual downfall of the Nixon presidency. The large number of people who declined to serve in the Cabinet, White contended, created a situation in which Nixon "would be dependent, thus, for control of his government on the political loyalists of his inner circle." Besides Senator Jackson, it is believed that Nixon was rejected by Senators Hubert Humphrey and Edward Brooke for the UN ambassadorship—a Cabinet appointment only in the most symbolic sense—and William Scranton for Secretary of State.[14] Nixon's rejection rate, in fact, was no higher than that of past administrations (other than Eisenhower's) and possibly even a bit lower than Franklin Roosevelt's and Lyndon Johnson's. Only three members of the Nixon Cabinet can be considered to have been close political allies (Mitchell, the 1968 campaign manager;

13. Secretary of State Rogers had been Attorney General in the Eisenhower administration; Commerce Secretary Stans had been Eisenhower's last Budget Director; and Transportation Secretary Volpe had served under Eisenhower as Federal Highway Administrator. Elliot Richardson, who later held three Cabinet appointments in the Nixon administration, had been an Assistant Secretary of HEW under Eisenhower.

14. White, *Breach of Faith*, pp. 103–04. I believe White is mistaken in assuming that Nixon made serious Cabinet offers to Nelson and David Rockefeller. For a comment on Nixon's offer to Humphrey, see Lady Bird Johnson, *A White House Diary* (Dell, 1971), p. 823.

Stans, the fund raiser; and Finch, the 1960 campaign manager). Rogers qualified as an old friend, not as a political activist. Finch and Rogers did not prove to be outstanding Cabinet officers, but they did not contribute to, and could not have prevented, Watergate. Finch was the first department secretary that Nixon removed; Rogers was picked to be a compliant Secretary of State so that Nixon could run foreign policy from the White House. Mitchell and Stans were deeply involved in the events of Watergate in their subsequent 1972 campaign roles, but not as Cabinet officers. If Nixon was often better served by total strangers than by old friends in the Cabinet—an experience of a number of other Presidents as well—any generalization would have to be followed by a long string of exceptions.

In choosing his personal staff, Tom Wicker reported, "Mr. Nixon at the White House is surrounded by West Coast advertising executives and young merchandising types."[15] This characterization, which gained credence over time, fails to account for the degree to which White House staffs have become differentiated. The Nixon White House operations, before they began to mushroom, were organized around eight discrete functions: a personal services staff, headed by Haldeman; two press relations staffs, under Ronald Ziegler and Herbert Klein; two domestic policy staffs, reporting to Arthur Burns and Daniel P. Moynihan; Henry Kissinger's national security staff; a congressional relations staff, directed by Bryce N. Harlow; a small political operations staff consisting of Harry Dent and John Sears; a personnel staff with Peter Flanigan in charge of high-level recruiting and Harry Flemming in charge of the larger number of more routine appointments; and a speechwriting staff with its own executive editor, James Keogh. There were also the traditional Executive Office staffs, many of which had become closely drawn into the White House operations by the beginning of the Nixon administration. The Council of Economic Advisers and the Office of Science and Technology were on call depending on the importance that the President chose to attach to such specialized advice.

The advertising-merchandising types were clustered on the personal services and public relations staffs. Haldeman had been Vice President in charge of the Los Angeles office of J. Walter Thompson, and he brought with him to the White House four young men who had been employed in that agency, including Ron Ziegler. The other staffs usually

15. See introduction by Tom Wicker in Osborne, *The First Two Years of the Nixon Watch*, "First Year," p. vii.

attracted people with backgrounds and skills appropriate to their functions. Harlow, who had been Eisenhower's congressional lobbyist, picked assistants with extensive staff experience on Capitol Hill. Three of the four chief members of the speechwriting team had been journalists. Kissinger largely borrowed from the Foreign Service and the Defense Department, and Burns and Moynihan had a tendency to make use of people with academic backgrounds. As has been true in the past, the largest professional supplier of White House aides was the law. All of the President's political operatives were lawyers.

There were a number of innovations at the early Nixon White House, although some were veiled from view at the time, and the significance of others would not be perceived until later.

Public relations. Under Kennedy there had been an attempt to co-ordinate the "activities of the various executive agencies in the interest of an integrated administration-wide public relations policy."[16] There was a limit, however, to how much attention Press Secretary Salinger could devote to these expanded duties. Under Nixon these functions were divided. Ziegler handled the traditional chores of Press Secretary, and Klein acted as Director of Communications for the Executive Branch, vaguely empowered with coordinating the flow of information from the departments. Given Klein's reputation as a casual administrator, it may be that this arrangement was primarily motivated by Nixon's desire to keep his old friend away from the daily routine of presidential press operations. By late 1969, however, the actual direction of the operation passed into the hands of Jeb Magruder. The office became obsessed with "selling" the President, and there followed a quantum jump in the scope and scale of White House public relations.

Speechwriting. This function was again isolated from substantive assignments, as it had been under Eisenhower, although now the writers were more active participants in policy negotiations. The writers were organized along the lines of a press newsroom; each had a beat, an executive editor made assignments, and researchers checked facts. Nixon's three favorite writers were Raymond Price, Patrick J. Buchanan, and William Safire. Each held an ideologically distinct position loosely corresponding to left, right, and center within the Republican party. Each had a special style. According to Safire, "When Nixon wanted to take a shot at somebody, he turned to Buchanan. . . . When

16. Elmer E. Cornwell, Jr., *Presidential Leadership of Public Opinion* (Indiana University Press, 1965), p. 222.

Nixon wanted a vision of the Nation's future . . . he turned to Price.
. . . and when he wanted the complicated made simple, or a line to be
quoted" he turned to Safire.[17] Nixon never merged their talents. Rather,
he compartmentalized his staff to serve his separate needs. It was as if
each chamber inside the President was to have its own reflection at the
White House.

News-summary. Buchanan was also in charge of presenting the
President with a daily summary of the news, often fifty pages, which
Nixon used as a supplemental source of information on what was
going on within the federal government. Presidents have always looked
to the press, in varying degrees, as a conveyor belt between themselves
and their administrations. Kenneth O'Donnell related how Kennedy
phoned him early one morning about the closing of a government installation that he had noted in a Detroit newspaper article. "Call Bernie
Boutin [administrator of the General Services Administration] right
now and tell him that I want a written report . . . on my desk no
later than nine o'clock this morning."[18] Nixon turned this process into
a routine. His comments in the margins of the daily news summary,
promptly transcribed, became a formal channel of command between
the President and his staff. And each morning, first thing, the press in
all its inexactitude—as it must look to any President—was served up to
Nixon.

Youth. Below the top echelon in the White House, there was a pre-
cipitous drop in the age of the staff. Many of these younger aides, often
in their late twenties or early thirties, served with distinction, but a
substantial number were to be sucked into the vortex of Watergate.
Jeb Magruder wrote of one assistant, Gordon Strachan: "He was one
of those people, like John Dean, who was capable and could be engaging, but who was obviously always studying all the angles and trying to
manipulate events to his own advantage."[19] Yet not all these young
men were mere seekers of the main chance. Herbert L. (Bart) Porter,
another aide to Magruder, was to attribute his Watergate involvement
to "fear of group pressure," desire to be considered "a team player,"
and unquestioning loyalty to the President.[20] The crimes of Watergate

17. Safire, *Before the Fall*, p. 100.
18. Kenneth P. O'Donnell and David F. Powers, *Johnny, We Hardly Knew Ye*
(Little, Brown, 1972), p. 255.
19. Jeb Stuart Magruder, *An American Life: One Man's Road to Watergate*
(Atheneum, 1974), p. 93.
20. *Presidential Campaign Activities of 1972, Senate Resolution 60*, Hearings be-

were not limited to the inexperienced; beneath the surface of the Nixon administration was a stratum of staff, often young but not always so, that was particularly susceptible to the commands of others.

Investigations. An obscure member of the original Ehrlichman staff was one Jack Caulfield, a former New York City policeman, who was to tell the Ervin Committee that his job was "to attempt to develop and supply" political intelligence. He took special interest in Senator Edward Kennedy's accident at Chappaquiddick. He arranged to place a wire tap on the phone of columnist Joseph Kraft through private arrangements, because, as Ehrlichman told him, "the FBI is a sieve."[21] Reporter Clark Mollenhoff was also hired "to investigate any indications of wrongdoing or questionable ethical conduct" within the government.[22] Caulfield and Mollenhoff were on the White House staff because the President felt he needed information that he did not trust the usual mechanisms of the permanent government or his political party to supply.

If in the beginning there were seeds of Watergate, they were nearly invisible, overwhelmed by the almost Rooseveltian struggle that was taking place over the forging of domestic policy.

Why Nixon chose Daniel Patrick Moynihan to be the Assistant to the President for Urban Affairs is a question that has not been satisfactorily answered. They were strangers. Moynihan was a Democrat, closely associated with the Kennedys, and with a reputation as a colorful controversialist. The absence of a high-level Democrat in an administration that had not received a clear electoral mandate may have been a factor, but if so the placement of Moynihan in an advocacy role at the President's elbow was overcompensation. As with Kissinger, Moynihan's colleague at Harvard, Nixon could have been seeking a bridge to the intellectual community that had not been part of his electoral constituency. The appointments of Moynihan and Kissinger were examples of Nixon initially seeking to act "presidential." For Presidents, although chosen by only a part of the electorate, take office with the mandate to represent "all the people," which often accounts for what may appear to be unlikely behavior—Eisenhower, the army

---

fore the Senate Select Committee on Presidential Campaign Activities, 93 Cong. 1 sess. (Government Printing Office, 1973), bk. 2, pp. 648–49. (Hereinafter referred to as Ervin Committee.)

21. Ibid., bk. 21, pp. 9687, 9713.
22. *Public Papers, 1970*, pp. 470–71.

officer, who warned of the "military-industrial complex"; Kennedy, the Catholic, who was accused of being the most anti-Catholic President since Millard Fillmore; and Johnson, the southerner, who became a champion of civil rights legislation. In the case of Kissinger, the risks for the President were modest. Nixon had read Kissinger's books, agreed with him, and was moving in an area in which he had considerable experience. But the appointment of Moynihan was to carry the President down unfamiliar paths, often against the grain of his stated convictions.

It is possible that Nixon had this in mind when three days after assuming office he suddenly announced the appointment of Arthur Burns, "a longtime friend and trusted adviser.... whose prime responsibility will be the coordination of the development of my domestic policies and programs."[23] Burns was a Columbia professor, an elder among Republican economists, and a Chairman of the Council of Economic Advisers under Eisenhower. Nixon invented a new title for Burns—Counsellor—and bestowed upon him Cabinet status.

The President seemed to be mandating contrasting academics—each with a small staff—to compete for his approval. This was a proven technique of presidential leadership. But it had never been Nixon's style, nor was he employing internal adversaries in other parts of government. More likely Nixon slipped into this mode by inadvertence. Burns had been promised the chairmanship of the Federal Reserve Board when it became available in 1970. In the meantime, Nixon wanted Burns's services and there were not many positions in which to place a person of his background and prestige. That Burns and Moynihan were given vague and overlapping jurisdictions may have most reflected the President's limited attention to domestic policy.

In the competition between the two scholars, Burns should have been the winner. He had rank, the President's trust, and presumably a point of view that was ideologically attuned to Nixon. That it did not always work out this way is a commentary on the importance of chemistry in doing business with a President. Burns was ponderous. His long monologues had fascinated Eisenhower; they bored Nixon. In juxtaposition, the glittering style and wit of Moynihan engaged the President and became a weapon of considerable utility. Moreover, Moynihan's proposals were dramatic; they appealed to the presidential instinct to "do something."

23. *Public Papers, 1969*, p. 12.

Moynihan also had a vehicle, the Council for Urban Affairs, that provided him with regular access to the Oval Office. This Cabinet-level council was chaired by the President, with Moynihan as its Executive Secretary. As long as Moynihan could keep the weekly meetings interesting and important, the President would keep them on his schedule. If the President kept coming, the Cabinet members would keep coming, and policy would be debated through a mechanism that was run by Moynihan. Burns had no comparable process for initiating policy. He was in charge of seeing that pre-inaugural task force recommendations worked their way through the departments—and later would create a series of outside task forces—but these quick reports could not compete with the recommendations of the Urban Affairs Council's subcommittees, which harnessed the desires of the domestic cabinet officers. When the Secretary of Commerce wanted to create a minority enterprise program or the Secretary of Agriculture wanted to increase the food stamp program, the recommendation came to the President through the council. Burns was placed in the position of having to react to the proposals of others, a task he performed with thoroughness, often to the betterment of the proposals under discussion. The principal Burns initiative was revenue sharing, a proposal that had come from a task force.[24]

The Nixon domestic policy reached a climax on August 8, 1969, when the President announced his support for Burns's revenue sharing and Moynihan's Family Assistance Plan (FAP), a form of guaranteed income. Toward the end, Burns and Moynihan shed the veneer of neutral competence and became forceful advocates for their beliefs. The President was particularly proud that in deciding in favor of FAP he had been politely opposed by a majority of the Cabinet.

Within a month the President was turning away from the system that had produced the August 8 message. On October 17 the White House prematurely announced that Burns was to be the next Chairman of the Federal Reserve Board. On November 4, Moynihan was "promoted" to Counsellor, a member of the Cabinet without specific duties, as was congressional specialist Harlow. At the same time, John Ehrlichman, who had entered the White House as Counsel to the President, handling routine legal matters, was named Chief Domestic As-

24. For Moynihan's description of the Council for Urban Affairs, see his *The Politics of A Guaranteed Income* (Random House, 1973), pp. 73-75.

sistant. By late fall the Burns and Moynihan staffs had been disbanded. Some went to work for Ehrlichman, others left the White House.

Why had Nixon chosen to dismantle the system that had produced a series of proposals that he felt would "bring reason, order, and purpose into a tangle of overlapping programs, and show that Government can be made to work"?[25]

The Urban Affairs Council was a flawed instrument in that its jurisdiction did not encompass all domestic policy. It consumed a tremendous amount of the Cabinet's time, which was justifiable in the beginning when all policy was under review but difficult to sustain as the demands of department management built up. Another vehicle was needed at a lower echelon to turn proposals into draft legislation, executive orders, and presidential messages. As the administration's thrust moved from policy formulation to implementation, the President shed his scholars in favor of a manager.

There was another reason why the President scrapped his pre-August 8 system. *It made him uncomfortable.* For a President to opt for a system of staff conflict, he must be prepared to assume a major role in mediation, assignments, and even hand-holding. This Nixon was unwilling to do.

Furthermore, by the close of the initial phase, Nixon realized, as do all Presidents, that his Cabinet was a mixed bag, full of pleasant surprises and serious disappointments. The quiet, calm George Shultz was the biggest surprise. Being Secretary of Labor was not overly taxing, and as in the case of Arthur Goldberg under Kennedy, the Secretary was available for additional assignments. Nixon soon engaged Shultz in such matters as school desegregation policy and welfare reform. On the other hand, Agriculture Secretary Hardin and Treasury Secretary Kennedy did not seem to have the "extra dimension" necessary to be forceful political executives. Finch, who had surrounded himself with assistants considered too liberal by the White House, increasingly appeared ideologically out of phase with his President. And Nixon's ex-Governors were often long-winded and apt to promote their departments' interests beyond what the President felt was reasonable. A system that relied so extensively on face-to-face dealings with these people was highly inefficient.

There was also before Nixon the example of foreign policy de-

25. *Public Papers, 1969*, p. 645.

velopment, free of the internal turmoil that characterized domestic policy-making. Secretary of State Rogers did not make excessive demands;
the staff of the National Security Council reported to Kissinger, and
Kissinger alone reported to the President. Could not a similar orderly
arrangement be devised for the domestic side of government? The President had appointed an Advisory Council on Executive Organization,
under the chairmanship of industrialist Roy L. Ash, and it was being
asked to come up with an answer.[26]

In each year of the Nixon presidency the White House looked different from the year before. To some degree, this is true of every administration. A White House staff is constantly changing, reflecting
the changing abilities and interests of those who leave and those who
join, the rise of favorites and the falls from grace, the new priorities of
the President and new pressures on him. Added to this, at the Nixon
White House there was an endless search "to improve the processes by
which our Nation is governed." It had become clear, the President said
by midpoint of his first year, "that one of the principal requirements is
for new mechanisms."[27] After creating the Council for Urban Affairs
as his first executive order, Nixon went on to establish an Office of Intergovernmental Relations, a Council on Environmental Quality, a
National Goals Research Staff, and a Council for Rural Affairs. Later
he would create an Office of Telecommunications Policy, a Council on
International Economic Policy, and a Special Action Office for Drug
Abuse Prevention.[28] Each new office added to the girth of the presi-

---

26. Chairman Ash was president of Litton Industries. The other members of the
President's Advisory Council on Executive Organization were John B. Connally,
former Governor of Texas; George P. Baker, Dean of the Harvard Graduate School
of Business Administration; Frederick R. Kappel, former Chairman of the Board of
American Telephone and Telegraph; Walter N. Thayer, President of Whitney Communications; and Richard M. Paget, President of Cresap, McCormick, and Paget.
For a useful brief summary of the Ash Council's work, see Harvey C. Mansfield,
"Reorganizing the Federal Executive Branch," *Law and Contemporary Problems*, vol.
35 (Summer 1970), pp. 491–92.

27. *Public Papers, 1969*, p. 511.

28. The Council for Urban Affairs was created by Executive Order 11452, January 23, 1969 (*Public Papers, 1969*, pp. 11–12), and the Office of Intergovernmental Relations by Executive Order 11455, February 14, 1969 (ibid., p. 96). In part the office
was established in an effort to find a substantive role for Vice President Agnew, who
was given supervision of it. The Environmental Quality Council, created by Executive Order 11472, May 29, 1969 (ibid., pp. 422–23), was in part an unsuccessful effort
to forestall the congressional enactment of a President's Council on Environmental
Quality, which the President signed into law on January 1, 1970. The National

dency and each increased the number of people purporting to speak in the President's name. The White House was becoming increasingly compartmentalized, with each office or council operating in isolation. As more and more specialists were added, there was less and less room for generalists.

While the activities around the fringes of the White House often appeared frenetic, at the core there was a growing stillness. The President wanted to be alone. In 1963 in his book on presidential decision-making, Theodore Sorensen wrote: "It is commonly said that our Presidents need more time set aside to do nothing but think" (a view with which he took exception).[29] Now the word went out that the President was scheduling "thinking time." Wednesdays would be reserved for this activity. In part, this need was related to Nixon's overarching interest in foreign policy; great chunks of time were set aside for him to plan and plot disengagement from Vietnam, resumption of relations with the People's Republic of China, and détente with the Soviet Union. In part, it was also related to the way Nixon liked to receive information. Eisenhower found committee meetings congenial; Kennedy preferred small, informal sessions with a few advisers; Johnson would accept any format as long as the information was presented orally. Nixon told an interviewer, "My disposition is to see that the President's time is not frittered away. I've found a way to do it. I'm a

---

Goals Research Staff, created July 12, 1969 (ibid., pp. 510–13), quietly went out of business after issuing its first "Social Report" (July 18, 1970). One reason for its demise was opposition from Ehrlichman and conservatives in the White House, who viewed the operation as a competing staff of liberals. The Council for Rural Affairs, established by Executive Order 11493, November 13, 1969 (ibid., pp. 918–19), did very little and was largely meant as a symbolic counterbalance to the Urban Affairs Council, both groups sharing the same Executive Secretary.

The proposal for an Office of Telecommunications Policy was sent to Congress as Reorganization Plan 1 of 1970 and became effective on April 20, 1970 (*Public Papers, 1970*, pp. 93–95). The office mainly dealt with highly technical questions, such as the assignment of portions of the radio spectrum reserved for government use. Under its Director, Clay T. Whitehead, however, it also became a weapon in Nixon's battles with the TV networks. The Council on International Economic Policy was created by a presidential memorandum dated January 18, 1971 (*Public Papers, 1971*, pp. 40–41), and the Special Action Office for Drug Abuse Prevention by Executive Order 11599, June 17, 1971 (ibid., pp. 739–49). For an excellent case study of the latter, see Mathea Falco and John Pekkanen, "The Abuse of Drug Abuse," *Washington Post*, September 8, 1974.

29. Theodore C. Sorensen, *Decision-Making in the White House* (Columbia University Press, paperback ed., 1963), p. 38.

reader, not a buller. Most of the boys at the Law School had long bull sessions about cases. I studied my cases alone."[30] But the reasons for the President's solitary behavior went deeper. Clues are spread throughout Nixon's memoirs, the most self-revealing book written by an active American politician. *Six Crises*, published in 1962, is organized as a study in crisis management. Each of the six cases suggest to the author a lesson of personal behavior. On his confrontation with Alger Hiss: "The ability to be cool, confident, and decisive in crisis is not an inherited characteristic but is the direct result of how well the individual has prepared himself for the battle." Other "lessons" speak to "the necessary soul-searching of deciding," to "the tension which builds up in a crisis," and to "concentrating completely on how to meet the danger."[31] Solitude for Nixon seems to have been necessary, not only because of the importance he placed on preparation and planning, but also as a method of keeping within the limits of his endurance and of controlling or overcoming other impulses.

This characteristic, more than any other, molded the position of H. R. Haldeman. Initially Haldeman was not a powerful figure, at least in that he had no major voice in policy. He was the staff manager, a neutral—almost pedestrian—assignment. He oiled the machinery of the presidential office, arranging space, transportation, dining room privileges, and the like; he made sure that deadlines were met and that papers reaching the President were adequate for their purposes.

As the President spent less time in meetings with his staff and Cabinet officers, more of the business of the presidency was conducted in writing, and the function of the gatekeeper became more important. The role also grew in direct proportion to the growth of the White House staff. The original staff had been largely transplanted from the campaign organization. Its members' long-standing relations with Nixon could serve to put his wishes in some useful context. The standard complaint about increasing the size of the White House staff is that by exceeding the span of a President's control, aides "go into business for themselves." The concern is not unfounded. Yet in the Nixon White House another type of problem arose. New people moved in, and as one old-timer put it, "They don't know the President intuitively"—so they were likely to accept presidential directives too lit-

30. Theodore H. White, *The Making of the President 1972* (Atheneum, 1973), p. 355.

31. Richard M. Nixon, *Six Crises* (Pocket Books, 1962), pp. 1, 77, 139, 195.

erally.[32] The presidential memo as a form of command—when not supplemented by an opportunity to probe the nuances of the President's intent—can take on a stark, absolutist quality. Communication was still a two-way process, but through Haldeman, and in writing, the process screened out subtleties. Moreover, Haldeman lacked the intuition and instincts of Washington power that might have compensated for the absence of the staff's direct dealings with the President. In some ways, such as his deep suspicion of the press, "a darker side to Haldeman [was] reflective of Nixon's darker side."[33] Thus Haldeman often failed to protect his chief from those impulses that the Nixonian system of solitary confinement were meant to moderate. The White House became an echo chamber, magnifying the voice of the President while losing true pitch.

There was one new person who managed to move into the inner circle past the gatekeeper in 1970. Charles W. Colson, hired in late 1969, was given the modest duties of serving as liaison with nongovernmental lobbying groups. Since 1970 was an election year, Colson, by turning his limited mandate into a theory of a New Nixonian Majority, was able to capture the President's attention. If an election coalition could be built around lower-middle-class ethnics and other aggrieved minorities, then Colson's special interests office was a logical place to start. The operation was to reach sizable dimensions by the 1972 campaign. As one of Colson's assistants testified before the Ervin Committee:

> . . . he had responsibility for all special interest groups such as veterans, the labor, youth, Jewish vote, the ethnic, Catholic, women, elderly, Spanish speaking, black, and I think there were several other groups. All of us had the mandate to develop programs that would best benefit our respective constituencies and within that umbrella was included appointments to high level positions . . . , generating grants and contracts, and . . . trying to publicize all of these accomplishments and achievements under the Nixon administration to our respective constituency.[34]

This was an extension of Johnson's "resident" concept whereby each White House assistant, in addition to his major responsibilities, served

32. John Whitaker, quoted in Allen Drury, *Courage and Hesitation* (Doubleday, 1971), p. 122.

33. Safire, *Before the Fall*, p. 288.

34. Testimony of William H. Marumoto, presidential assistant for coordinating administration efforts on behalf of Spanish-speaking Americans, Ervin Committee, bk. 13, p. 5279.

as liaison with some outside group, usually one with which he shared membership (Italians, blacks, Jews). The Nixon variation, as orchestrated by Colson, was a staff of junior-level people with full-time assignments as White House advocates for definable groups. A worry of Presidents, including Nixon, has been that their departmental appointees would become representatives for special interests. Nixon tried to protect himself by isolation from his Cabinet. Yet, at the same time, he was moving such representation into the White House. Assistants who were expected to be loyal to the President were also being forced to divide their loyalties. As employees of the President, their status would be determined by how successfully they could win victories from the President for their constituents.

Yet if group representation was having the effect of moving White House aides away from the President, over time a counterpull was also developing—a sort of macho theory of staffing, which in a less virulent strain can be found in all administrations. Those who could display their "toughness"—measured by the most unquestioning opposition to those who were thought to be against their President—were most likely to prosper. Magruder identified the "losers" as "those who were seen as 'soft' on the media or on liberals in general." He put Herbert Klein and Robert Finch in this category, while Harlow was " 'soft' in his attitudes toward Congress." The "winners" were Haldeman, Mitchell, and Colson.[35]

The categorization is a little too pat. Burns and Harlow, true conservatives, were also losers. But no matter what characteristics or views caused them to leave, many of the losers were persons of substantial interest and experience in governance; the winners, on the other hand, were largely interested in the techniques of politics and often had had no previous Washington experience. Osborne watched the staff become dominated by nonbelievers. "Moynihan and Burns were believers . . . ," he wrote in 1971, "they fought with each other and for their beliefs, and the likes of them are no longer to be found at the Nixon White House."[36]

The President and his White House loyalists increasingly saw themselves as pursued by three demons—the press, Congress, and the federal bureaucracy. The conclusion drawn from extensive interviews with

35. Magruder, *An American Life*, pp. 55–60, 112. White uses the same terminology in *Breach of Faith*, p. 144: "Klein was 'soft,' Colson was 'tough.' "

36. John Osborne, *The Third Year of the Nixon Watch* (Liveright, 1972), p. 134.

Washington reporters conducted by American University's Department of Communication during the Nixon administration was that
"a majority of the press corps probably votes Democratic" (although it
does not necessarily follow that their stories are slanted).[37] Both houses
of Congress were controlled by the Democrats. Interviews with super-
grade civil servants in the domestic agencies by Joel Aberbach of the
University of Michigan and Bert Rockman of the University of Pittsburgh document "a career bureaucracy with very little Republican
representation . . . a social service bureaucracy dominated by administrators ideologically hostile to many of the directions pursued by
the Nixon administration" (although it does not necessarily follow
that they sabotaged the President).[38] George Christian, Johnson's last
Press Secretary, wrote: "President Nixon inherited a governmental
apparatus that was predominantly Democratic, and there was very
little he could do about it unless he desired to devote his entire time
to the task." (Johnson, according to Christian, recommended that
"Nixon employ a strong loyalty test to those in policy-making roles.")[39]
One might conclude, as do Aberbach and Rockman: "Even paranoids
may have real enemies."[40]

To deal with Congress, Nixon settled on a three-pronged approach.
Rather than try for a policy of conciliation and compromise, he would
take on the legislators frontally, as in his attack on the Senate for being
biased against southerners after it rejected the Supreme Court nominations of Clement Haynsworth and G. Harrold Carswell. He increasingly attempted to accomplish his goals through administrative actions
instead of asking for legislation. And he pushed beyond past interpretations those tools that undergirded the concept of a strong presidency,
such as impoundment, executive privilege, and the war powers of the
Commander in Chief.

The President's response to what he felt was a hostile press was also
multifaceted. The defensive strategy was to minimize the importance
of the Washington news corps. Only twenty-eight presidential news

37. Lewis W. Wolfson and James McCartney, *The Press Covers Government: The
Nixon Years from 1969 to Watergate* (National Press Club, 1973), p. 6.

38. Joel D. Aberbach and Bert A. Rockman, "Clashing Beliefs Within the Executive Branch: The Nixon Administration Bureaucracy," *American Political Science
Review*, vol. 70 (June 1976), pp. 466–67.

39. George Christian, *The President Steps Down* (Macmillan, 1970), p. 258.

40. Aberbach and Rockman, "Clashing Beliefs," p. 467.

conferences were held in the capital in four years. White House reporters were kept occupied with briefings that suited the interests of the
administration. Hagerty had been the first Press Secretary to recognize
that it was possible to adjust the flow of news in a measurable way—
a major breakthrough in the history of news management. (Earlier
Press Secretaries had tried to control the news from time to time by
planting a press conference question or by granting an exclusive interview to a favored reporter.) The genius of Hagerty was to realize that,
all things being equal, White House reporters take the stories they are
given. This technique was expanded by Ziegler so that in the month
of March 1971, for example, there were seven briefings at the White
House that had no direct bearing on the activities of the President,
ranging from the plans for the recreational use of Camp Pendleton
to a visit by the astronauts to college campuses. But the major weapon
in this war with the press was the President's greatly increased use of
television. As James Keogh explained, "Richard Nixon believed . . .
that the best way to communicate with the people was to appear on live
television and speak directly to them. This was, in effect, going over the
heads of the newsmen so that what was said would not be strained
through their political bias."[41] (One New York City cable TV company
devoted twelve *continuous hours* to live coverage of Nixon in China.)

The counteroffensive was a public relations campaign of unprecedented scale. Magruder, a "winner" and a "merchandising type," was
given actual (though not nominal) command over the Office of Communications. Klein was relegated to making speeches, a sort of per-
petual traveling salesman for the Nixon administration. Magruder's
greatly expanded operation used a computer, programmed with 150,000
names, to send presidential statements to groups as differentiated as
"middle-aged black dentists." It also was used to "stimulate letters to
the editor and to members of Congress in support of the President."[42]
A White House aide ran a speakers' bureau. A White House aide lined
up TV appearances for administration spokesmen. A White House aide
wrote speeches for members of Congress. A White House aide named
E. Howard Hunt, directed by Colson, prepared derogatory information
about Daniel Ellsberg's chief counsel, as well as phony State Department cables implicating President Kennedy in the assassination of
South Vietnam's Premier Diem, and these were leaked to newsmen.

41. James Keogh, *President Nixon and the Press* (Funk and Wagnalls, 1972), p. 39.
42. Magruder, *An American Life*, p. 95.

As for Nixon's third demon—the bureaucracy—his New Federalism program had the effect of weakening the control of the permanent government in Washington. Revenue sharing, for example, was meant to transfer federal tax dollars to the states and localities with few strings attached. This was in keeping with traditional Republican doctrine, and the President would have proposed it even if the civil service had been dominated by Nixon enthusiasts. That this was not the case undoubtedly made his proposals even more personally satisfying. Nixon's other serious effort to keep from becoming the hostage of government careerists was to attempt to create—in Richard Nathan's apt language—"a counter-bureaucracy."[43]

The proposals of the Ash Council, incorporated in Nixon's Reorganization Plan 2, March 12, 1970, called for the creation of a Domestic Council and the conversion of the Budget Bureau into the Office of Management and Budget (OMB). "The Domestic Council will be primarily concerned with *what* we do; the Office of Management and Budget will be primarily concerned with *how* we do it, and *how well* we do it."[44]

Nixon described the new council as "a domestic counterpart to the National Security Council." The analogy was strangely correct. Both councils had been approved as Cabinet-level advisory groups to the President. But in fact the NSC under Kissinger had become primarily a White House staff operation, expanded to 132 (50 professionals) by the fifth year of the Nixon administration. The Domestic Council, under its Executive Secretary, John Ehrlichman, was also to serve a comparable staff purpose; Nixon seems never to have meant it as a collegial body.

The first Director of OMB was George Shultz, stepping up from his $60,000-a-year job as Secretary of Labor to a more important assignment at $42,500. (HUD Secretary James Lynn, the fourth OMB Director, was to take the same cut in pay.) Only the federal salary scale had failed to adjust to the flow of power in government. Nixon was reported to have spent about forty hours working on the 1971 budget and to have been bored by the exercise. The appointment of Shultz

43. Richard P. Nathan, *The Plot that Failed: Nixon and the Administrative Presidency* (Wiley, 1975), p. 49.

44. *Public Papers, 1970*, p. 259. The proposal for an OMB was made by Nelson Rockefeller in 1953 and repeated on May 27, 1968, when he was seeking the Republican presidential nomination.

would relieve him of this chore. Traditionally, Cabinet officers have had the right of appeal to the President when negotiating their budgets; now this right was to be denied them. Shultz and Ehrlichman became the final arbiters. Shultz was given an office in the West Wing of the White House, emblematic of his relationship with the President. OMB gained power partly because the inexperienced staff of the Domestic Council had to rely so heavily on OMB's expertise, and more important, because the powers of approving the budget are formidable; the task must be performed, and the vacuum left by Nixon's lack of interest in the process was necessarily filled by the OMB Director and his organization.[45]

When examining the operations of the Domestic Council in 1972, John Kessel of Ohio State University found that there were not substantially less professionals on the staff than there had been in this area during the Johnson administration. Nor were they less qualified according to their educational attainments. "Of 21 Domestic Council staff members, twelve had law degrees, seven had Ph.D. degrees, and the other two had degrees in business administration," Kessel noted.[46] Each of the six Assistant Directors covered a piece of the governmental spectrum; for example, one handled crime and transportation, another energy, environment, and agriculture. There was something akin to an annual process—issues were generally identified in late spring and studies were completed early in the fall so as to be integrated into the budget and the legislative program.[47] An ad hoc "working group" was created to develop each specific program. A representative working group might consist of a member of the Domestic Council staff; an official of OMB, the Council of Economic Advisers, or the Science Adviser's office; and an Assistant Secretary from each of the concerned departments. As Nathan pointed out, "In important ways they were becoming more like Johnson's White House under Joseph Califano, a model that President Nixon at the outset had explicitly rejected."[48] There was, however, an important distinction: Johnson measured his success largely by legislative enactments, while Nixon decidedly did not. The Johnson style was to reach the greatest consensus possible with

45. See Hugh Heclo, "OMB and the Presidency—The Problem of 'Neutral Competence,'" *The Public Interest*, no. 38 (Winter 1975), p. 89.

46. John H. Kessel, *The Domestic Presidency* (Duxbury, 1975), p. 29.

47. See Edwin Harper, "Advising the President: A Panel," *The Bureaucrat*, vol. 3 (April 1974), p. 24.

48. Nathan, *The Plot that Failed*, p. 47.

those whose approval was necessary. The Nixon style—reflected in the composition of the working group—was exclusionary; no outsiders were welcome, not even members of the permanent government. Chester Finn, a member of the White House staff working on education programs, recalled how the group kept civil servants "in an adjoining room during the meetings, summoning them only when their expertise was required. Every time we invited one in, I could sense a certain coolness and reserve descend upon the room. After the presentation, the staffer would be thanked and invited to leave, whereupon the [Working] Group members loosened up and talked frankly once again." Finn concluded, "This is not an administration that relies on outside advice for much of anything."[49] Thus Nixon's proposals had few supporters when support was needed. The one exception was the general revenue-sharing package, which had been negotiated with Mayors and Governors before its introduction in Congress and was the major legislative success of the administration.

The Domestic Council staff increasingly became involved in the most routine departmental operations. One relatively minor matter—making veterans aware of benefit programs—took three or four months of the time of one White House aide. As he recalled: "The Veterans' Administration administered most of the benefit programs; the Defense Department had the best list of discharged servicemen; the Postal Service had to be involved because of the increased work load.... I acted as a go-between with these agencies."[50] More and more department decisions required White House clearance. Presidential assistants worked longer and harder with less to show for their efforts. Cabinet officers became increasingly disgruntled. Interior Secretary Hickel's break with the President probably had less to do with policy differences than with his being locked out of personal contact with Nixon and being forced to take orders from junior White House aides. (Hickel had only two private meetings with Nixon in fifteen months.) By the time Richard Nixon was elected to a second term he recognized that his strategy of creating a counterbureaucracy at the White House had not worked.

Nor had he succeeded in regrouping the executive departments along

49. Chester E. Finn, Jr., "Staffing the Sub-Committee on Education of the Council for Urban Affairs" (Ph.D. dissertation, Harvard Graduate School of Education, 1970; processed), pp. 59 and 92 of "Final Report Abstract."

50. Kessel, *The Domestic Presidency*, pp. 101–02.

functional lines. The President's 1971 State of the Union message, following suggestions made by the Ash Council, proposed merging eight existing domestic departments into four new superagencies—the Departments of Natural Resources, Human Resources, Economic Affairs, and Community Development. It was a plan very similar to the one offered to Johnson in 1967 by the President's Task Force on Government Organization, whose chairman was Ben Heineman.[51] Johnson knew by instinct and Nixon learned the hard way that Congress would have nothing to do with such a drastic reorganization, even after Nixon agreed to keep the Agriculture Department intact. Nixon's only victory was to remove the Post Office Department from the Cabinet, a proposal made by Johnson in his last State of the Union message.[52]

Instantly upon defeating George McGovern, Nixon announced that he planned to overhaul the government. His statement of November 27, 1972, was perhaps the most remarkable pronouncement ever made by a President who had just been reelected. It was a statement of lost confidence in his appointees and in the organizational structure he had constructed to serve him. The White House staff, he said, had "grown like Topsy. . . . It is now time to reverse that growth." A Cabinet member, he said, eventually "becomes an advocate of the status quo; rather than running the bureaucracy, the bureaucracy runs him." Nixon would attempt to reverse the "historical pattern," which is for "an administration to run out of steam after the first 4 years, and then to coast, and usually coast downhill." Nixon did not blame himself. On the contrary, he saw no connection between the administration's operations and the pattern of solitude that had left him physically removed from his appointees and increasingly removed from the seat of government. Speaking from his retreat at Camp David, he said that each President "must work in the way that . . . best fits his own patterns." And for him, said the President, this meant "getting away from the White House. . . . I find that up here on top of a mountain it is easier for me to get on top of the job."[53] The solution would not be to

51. The unpublished Heineman Report of September 15, 1967, proposed domestic departments of Social Services, National Resources and Development, Economic Affairs, and Science and Environmental Preservation. (See note 29, chap. 6.)

52. The creation of the U.S. Postal Service was recommended to President Johnson by his Commission on Postal Organization in June 1968; Nixon proposed it in a special message to the Congress, April 16, 1970, and signed it into law on August 12, 1970. See *Public Papers, 1970*, pp. 359–64 and 666–68.

53. *Public Papers, 1972*, pp. 1148–50.

change his patterns but to make massive changes in personnel and structure.

Between November 28 and December 22, Nixon announced fifty-seven resignations and eighty-seven other personnel decisions. Six new Cabinet officers were nominated. Five White House assistants were to become Under Secretaries, Assistant Secretaries, or agency heads. The Executive Office of the President was to be streamlined by eliminating the Space Council, by shifting the advisory functions of the Office of Science and Technology to the National Science Foundation, and by transferring the duties of the Office of Emergency Preparedness to other agencies. Nixon also sought to abolish the Office of Economic Opportunity. To compensate for the failure of Congress to approve his design for superagencies, Nixon named four of his Cabinet members as Counsellors to the President—Treasury Secretary Shultz, Agriculture Secretary Earl Butz, HEW Secretary Caspar Wineberger, and HUD Secretary Lynn—with overall functional responsibilities respectively for economic affairs, natural resources, human resources, and community development. This meant, for example, that in some areas the Secretary of the Interior would be reporting to the Secretary of Agriculture.

Part of the top-level reorganization was accomplished by internal shifts. The Chairman of the Atomic Energy Commission became the Director of the Central Intelligence Agency; the CIA Director became the Ambassador to Iran; the Deputy Secretary of Defense became the Deputy Secretary of State; the Under Secretary of Commerce became the Secretary of HUD; the Director of OMB became the Secretary of HEW; the Deputy Director of OMB became the Under Secretary of HEW; the Secretary of HEW became the Secretary of Defense, and so forth. This elaborate game of musical chairs reflected the limited number of people who had gained the President's trust. But these circulating executives were also among the most competent of Nixon's first term. Changing assignments is a sensible technique for prolonging the vitality of political appointees. Yet the personnel problem in the Nixon administration was ultimately of a different nature. Consider the experience of Elliot Richardson, possibly the most skilled political executive in the President's inner circle. He served successively as Under Secretary of State, Secretary of HEW, Defense Secretary, and Attorney General. In being moved from HEW to Defense at the beginning of the second term, Richardson was leaving behind an unfinished agenda in a department that would now have its third Secretary in less than three years. During the period 1933–65, the median length of service for Cabinet officials was forty months; during Nixon's presidency it dropped to around eighteen months.

Nor was there always a powerful rationale for bringing some of the new people into government. Efficient managers at Commerce and Labor were dismissed and the Transportation and Commerce portfolios were given to relatively obscure businessmen. The new Secretary of Labor, Peter Brennan, was the head of the building trades union in New York and a political ally of the President's. Nixon apparently had not learned the lesson of Martin Durkin, the ill-fated union leader whom Eisenhower had appointed in the hope of not having to deal directly with the AFL-CIO. George Meany made it clear that he would not be fobbed off on some unionist at the Labor Department and turned Brennan's life into "if not a hell, at least an existence in limbo."[54]

The planned changes in the Nixon Cabinet were completed in September 1973, when Henry Kissinger became Secretary of State without having to relinquish his White House duties. This was one way to reconcile the growing feud between Kissinger and Rogers. As the President told Safire, "I'm sorry about how Henry and Bill go at each other. It's really deep-seated. Henry thinks Bill isn't very deep, and Bill thinks Henry is power-crazy. . . . And in a sense, they're both right."[55] The foreign policy of the first term was based on the Nixon-Kissinger assumption that the most pressing world issues could be best resolved by direct negotiations among the superpowers, each represented by a strong leader. The players were limited, the means were secret. Kissinger, as the President's agent, was the prime operator in the preliminary stages; a series of summit meetings followed. The results in some cases were spectacular. But the system was not without detractors. Congress felt increasingly left out, especially as White House aide Kissinger could not be forced to testify before congressional committees. (Senator William Fulbright even introduced a bill that would have required Kissinger's appearance before his Foreign Relations Committee.) The State Department also felt left out. Senator Stuart Symington complained that Kissinger's ascendancy created "a resultant obvious decline in the prestige and position of the Secretary of State

54. John Herling, "Peter Brennan: Joining the Ambassadorial Ranks?" *Washington Post*, January 29, 1975.
55. Safire, *Before the Fall*, p. 406.

and his department," proving, perhaps, that even the State Department has friends.[56] The two-man system of conducting foreign policy perforce limited the number of issues that could be handled at any one time. During the first term this meant that such questions as U.S. relations with the less-developed world were left simmering on the back burner.[57] Kissinger had once written that "the spirit of policy and that of bureaucracy are diametrically opposed. . . . Good administration thrives on routine, the definition of relationships which can survive mediocrity."[58] Foreign policy during Nixon's first term had "required, to a considerable extent, secret diplomacy . . . conducted on a rather restricted basis." But in the second term, Kissinger implied, the need was for "good administration" that would consolidate gains and build "a structure that we can pass on to succeeding Administrations."[59]

Whether Kissinger's dual responsibilities could lead to conflicts of interest in the internal negotiations of the NSC was not addressed by the President. Eventually, Kissinger's two hats would be attacked by Senator Lloyd Bentsen and others as "dangerously [centralizing] power in the hands of one man."[60] Yet in the short term, as the administration crumbled, the elimination of rivalry between the Secretary of State and the Assistant to the President for National Security Affairs was a fortunate break for the United States.

Nixon's final strategy for taking control of government by shifting proven loyalists to the departments never had a chance to succeed or fail. The last year of his presidency was a fight to survive, not to innovate. The White House was organized around the defense of the President. By the summer of 1974, a team of fifteen lawyers, under James St. Clair, was trying to stave off impeachment. Another group, with Dean Burch and Ken Clawson as its key members, was engaged in a political and public relations counteroffensive. Nixon himself spent longer periods away from Washington. While he was able to concentrate on foreign policy, domestic planning, to the degree that presidential approval is necessary, seemed to come to a standstill. Donald Santarelli, the Director of the Law Enforcement Assistance Administra-

56. Osborne, *Third Year of the Nixon Watch*, pp. 48–49.

57. See I. M. Destler, "The Nixon System, A Further Look," *Foreign Service Journal*, February 1974, pp. 9–14, 28–29.

58. Henry A. Kissinger, *A World Restored: Metternich, Castlereagh, and the Problems of Peace, 1812–22* (Houghton Mifflin, Sentry ed., n.d.), pp. 326–27.

59. Quoted in Marvin and Bernard Kalb, *Kissinger* (Little, Brown, 1974), p. 447.
60. *New York Times*, May 7, 1975.

tion, was quoted as saying, "There is no White House."[61] Yet most of government went on without presidential attention and continued to function properly.

The President brought into the White House a series of advisers of independent stature, wise in the ways of politics and Washington—John Connally, Melvin Laird, Bryce Harlow. But Nixon never told them of the extent of his complicity in the Watergate cover-up, and so their advice was irrelevant and unheeded. Soon he stopped seeing them altogether. After Haldeman and Ehrlichman left, Nixon had even fewer direct contacts with even fewer people. At the end he limited those with whom he regularly met to Alexander Haig and Ron Ziegler.

SOME WERE to blame Nixon's downfall on the people around him. White's epitaph was: "They entered into government, all of them, with no greater knowledge of how power works than the intrigues of the political antechambers and the folklore of advance men—and were quickly off into a dark land."[62]

While the tragedy of Nixon was intimately connected with actions taken by his subordinates, at the same time columnist Joseph Kraft could note: "As the Nixon administration presents its 1974 face to the world, it turns out to be a government by—of all things—professors [who] command among them more influence than intellectuals ever have had in Washington."[63] Kraft cites Shultz, Kissinger, James Schlesinger, and John Dunlop. He could have added, over the life of the administration, such other academicians as Burns, Moynihan, Paul McCracken, Herbert Stein, Lee DuBridge, Murray Weidenbaum, Arnold Weber, and others. Nixon's helpers cannot be simply dismissed as a collection of intellectual ciphers. He had a substantial reservoir of talent at hand. He was inclined to draw on it for specialized and technical advice and then, as with White House working groups, invite his advisers to leave the room. The decisions that ended his career were taken alone.

61. See John Herbers, "President's Grip Found Looser on Bureaucracy," *New York Times*, June 7, 1974.

62. White, *Breach of Faith*, p. 325. A similar observation is made by a former Nixon speechwriter, John R. Coyne, Jr.: "Nixon became the victim of his own system. . . . And part of it, of course, was the men he chose to guard that wall." ("Quit Does: The Story of 'P'," *National Review*, April 25, 1975, p. 466.)

63. Joseph Kraft, "Government by Professor," *Washington Post*, February 7, 1974.

Or take the case of Nixon's relations with Congress. They were as Nixon wanted them to be, despite a liaison staff—Harlow, Clark MacGregor, William Timmons—deeply versed in the sensitivities of Capitol Hill. (In contrast, Kennedy turned to Lawrence O'Brien, who had no congressional experience and admits that initially he had "no real concept of the role" he was to play so well.)[64] Even of Haldeman it was said, "If he didn't exist, Nixon would have had to invent him." [65] And this was true.

The implication should not be left that all of Nixon's actions and organizational concepts were disastrous. Assessments of his administration will be continuously revised. It suffices perhaps to note that Nixon was overwhelmingly reelected in 1972. If he is to be blamed for his shortcomings, equally he deserves credit for the achievements of his presidency.

"He peopled his office himself," Safire wrote, "and was the captive of nobody; he made his fate the extension of his character." [66] The final word belongs to John Osborne. Comparing White House operations under Haldeman and Haig, he wrote in May 1974:

Haig and his predecessor, Bob Haldeman, are very different individuals. Haldeman was secretive, inaccessible, vengeful, a worker in the dark. Haig is open in manner, moderately accessible, much more visible than Haldeman was. Yet the White House with Haig isn't very different from the White House with Haldeman. The reason is obvious. It wasn't Haldeman's White House and it isn't Haig's White House. It was and is Richard Nixon's White House and that is the trouble.[67]

64. Lawrence F. O'Brien, *No Final Victories* (Doubleday, 1974), p. 101.
65. Quoted in *Newsweek*, March 19, 1973, p. 24.
66. Safire, *Before the Fall*, p. 603.
67. John Osborne, *The Last Nixon Watch* (New Republic, 1975), p. 117.

PART TWO

Redefining
the Presidential Task

☆ ☆ ☆ ☆ ☆ ☆ ☆ ☆ ☆ ☆ ☆ ☆ ☆

CHAPTER EIGHT

Toward a More Collegial Presidency

☆ ☆ ☆ ☆ ☆ ☆ ☆ ☆ ☆ ☆ ☆ ☆ ☆

THE Constitution gives and takes away. On the one hand, it vests executive power in the President; on the other hand, it assigns numerous administrative powers to Congress. As early as the Treasury Department Act of 1789, Congress created administrative offices with distinct responsibilities. Since then, except in emergency legislation, Congress has given statutory powers directly to agencies or agency heads instead of to the President. Supreme Court decisions—in 1838 and 1935—upheld this doctrine.[1] Yet the extent to which a President manages the government has been the key element in the continuing struggle for control between the legislative and executive branches and has been the subject of less passionate battles between scholars.

In 1922 Arthur M. Schlesinger, Sr., could distill "the elusive quality of *greatness*" in American Presidents without once referring to managerial talents.[2] James Bryce and Harold Laski, the leading British scholars of the presidency, have not made much of the President as manager either.[3] But an early twentieth century school of public ad-

1. The Supreme Court decisions are *Kendall* v. *U.S.* (1838) and *Humphrey's Executor* v. *U.S.* (1935). See *Watergate: Its Implications for Responsible Government*, A report prepared by a Panel of the National Academy of Public Administration at the request of the Senate Select Committee on Presidential Campaign Activities (March 1974), p. 46.

2. Arthur Meier Schlesinger, *New Viewpoints in American History* (Macmillan, 1922), pp. 123–24.

3. In *The American Commonwealth* (Macmillan, 1922), vol. 1, p. 54, James Bryce stated: "The direct domestic authority of the President is in time of peace small, because the larger part of law and administration belongs to the State governments, and because Federal administration is regulated by statutes which leave little discretion to

ministration, arguing on the basis of "scientific management" rather than constitutional law, made a strong case that the President *should* be the chief manager. As W. F. Willoughby wrote in 1927:

It can be stated without any hesitation that a prime requisite of any proper administrative system is that . . . the chief executive shall be given all the duties and powers of a general manager and be made in fact, as well as in theory, the head of the administration.[4]

By 1974 Peter Drucker would state matter-of-factly, "The President . . . is first of all a manager."

The President dominant over Congress, and an executive fully responsible for the management of the bureaucracy were the major themes of the Brownlow Report of 1937 and President Roosevelt's transmittal message. The latter declared that "the Presidency was established [by the Constitution] as a single strong Chief Executive Office in which was vested the entire executive power of the National Government."[6]

A few scholars, such as Edward S. Corwin and Alfred de Grazia, demurred.[7] The dissenters were either strict constitutionalists or politi-

---

the executive." Harold J. Laski listed fifteen presidential qualities, of which only three could be considered executive, in *The American Presidency* (Harper, 1940), pp. 28–30.

4. W. F. Willoughby, *Principles of Public Administration* (Johns Hopkins Press, 1927), p. 36. As rationale for this arrangement, Willoughby wrote:

Fundamentally these advantages consist in making the administrative branch, both as regards its organization and its practical operations, a single, integrated piece of administrative machinery, one in which its several parts, instead of being disjointed and unrelated, will be brought into adjustment with each other and together make a harmonious whole; one that possesses the capacity of formulating a general program and of subsequently seeing that such program as is formulated is properly carried out; one in which means are provided by which duplication of organization, plant, personnel, or operations may be eliminated, conflicts of jurisdiction avoided or promptly settled, and standardization of methods of procedure secured; and finally, one in which responsibility is definitely located and means for enforcing this responsibility provided. (Ibid., p. 51.)

5. Peter F. Drucker, "How to Make the Presidency Manageable," *Fortune*, November 1974, p. 146.

6. Brownlow Report, p. v.

7. See Edward S. Corwin, *The President, Office and Powers, 1787–1957* (New York University Press, 1957). Commenting on the Brownlow Report, Corwin wrote, "Certainly, to conceive of the President as a potential 'boss of the works' save in situations raising broad issues of policy would be both absurd and calamitous" (p. 98). Also see Alfred de Grazia, "The Myth of the President," in Aaron Wildavsky, ed., *The Presidency* (Little, Brown, 1960), pp. 49–73.

cal conservatives. The vast majority of social scientists were comfortable with the theory of a powerful presidential manager and supportive of the goals for which Presidents wished to apply their power. Not all liberal scholars, however, theorized to fit the convenience of their convictions. Richard E. Neustadt, who had served on Truman's staff and was highly critical of Eisenhower, saw the presidency, not as having inherent powers over the executive branch, but quite the contrary, as an office hemmed in by competing power centers in which the President's success largely depended on his skill at persuasion.[8] And James MacGregor Burns, ever the advocate of presidential government, nevertheless viewed the significance of the presidency in terms of "the ideology of the leadership," separating "management" from "leadership," and placing management in routine and secondary importance.[9]

The growth of presidential powers during the Roosevelt-Nixon period by no means meant that the war between the branches had been resolved in favor of the executive. Beneath the surface, Congress—and particularly its committee chairmen—maintained powerful links to the bureaucracy, which still looked to Capitol Hill for its money. The power to legislate, especially to write the fine print, often was the power to determine the contours of administration. The power to confirm was a reminder to appointees that they owed allegiance not just to the President. The power to investigate was the power to turn a searchlight on the anonymous bureaucracy. Moreover, Congress and the President often seemed to work on a teeter-totter principle with each updown inexorably linked to shifts in public opinion so that in periods of waning presidential esteem, such as Watergate, Congress was able to impose some restrictions on the White House.[10] Then, too, a President's stay in office was far more limited than that of most members of Congress and the bureaucracy.

8. Richard E. Neustadt, *Presidential Power* (Wiley, 1960), especially chap. 3.

9. James MacGregor Burns, *Presidential Government* (Houghton Mifflin, 1966), pp. 194–95.

10. Congressional assertiveness during the period of Watergate included making future appointments of the Director and Deputy Director of the Office of Management and the Budget subject to senatorial confirmation; passing a War Powers Act requiring congressional approval for any new commitment of U.S. troops abroad for periods of more than sixty days; creating a Congressional Budget Office; and levying prohibitions on presidential impoundment. Claims of executive privilege also became subject to court adjudication. See Judith H. Parris, "Congress in the American Presidential System," *Current History*, June 1974, pp. 262–63.

The growth of government over the past four decades made the managerial function infinitely more difficult. It was not merely a matter of scale or that the President had lost control of the power to hire and fire. The question also had to do with what was to be managed. Corporations manage production, and efficiency can be measured in unit costs. But the products of many of the newer domestic programs were far less tangible, such as justice, equality, and participation. Other programs—job training for hard-core unemployables, teaching reading skills to those whom conventional methods had failed—were in fields that were frankly experimental, where there were no certifiable answers. Government was not only doing more, it was doing more difficult tasks. What was to be the measure of efficiency? And was efficiency the correct measurement? Presidents tried to import such corporate tools of control as planning, programming, and budgeting systems (PPBS) and management-by-objectives, always with questionable success.

The problem of Presidents as managers was further complicated because, as I have written elsewhere, "Our Presidents, more often than not, have been atrocious administrators. They often come from an occupation (legislator) and a profession (law) that ill prepares them for management."[11] The people have never been interested in choosing professional managers for President, and professional managers do not run for the office. The presidential selection system is designed to screen politicians, and politicians are rarely trained as managers. Presidents as politicians recognize that management questions—except perhaps calls for "economizing"—have little political appeal and great political risk.

What makes this particularly ironic is that the history of the modern presidency has been one of growing presidential involvement in management. Much of the growth in the presidential establishment relates directly to Presidents' attempts to take over the operation of high priority programs (poverty and drug abuse as examples) or to exercise greater oversight (and eventually control) over the bureaucracy. It is hardly accidental that the Bureau of the Budget has become the Office of *Management* and Budget. All major study groups since the Brownlow Committee have recommended giving the President ad-

11. Stephen Hess, *The Presidential Campaign* (Brookings Institution, 1974), p. 21.

ditional tools for management as a means of increasing his control over the executive branch. But one result of adding to the role of the President as manager is that he spends more and more time doing that which he does badly and, presumably, has less and less time to devote to matters that only the President can handle.

In sum, the role of the President as manager has been distorted in theory and in recent practice, leading the President to become involved in tasks that can be performed better by others.

There are a variety of potential ways out of this dilemma. One solution would be to elect managers to the presidency. If, in fact, the responsibilities of a President were largely managerial, this step would be logical and would only await proper recognition on the part of the electorate. Certainly this is the view of the scientific management school. Thus Drucker could write in 1959, "Today a 'strong' president . . . is not a man of strong policies; he is the man who knows how to make the lions of bureaucracy do his bidding."[12] (H. R. Haldeman was observed reading Drucker and marking passages in colored pencil.) Yet such a view represents a profound misunderstanding: the primary presidential role is to make choices—choices that are ultimately political in nature. *The President is the nation's chief political officer.* He tries to stay astride a process that is quintessentially political, and the political process primarily concerns distribution, not production. It decides who gets how much of what is available, not how to make more available at less cost. A political process cannot be managed in the sense that a corporation is managed, for political decisions are judged according to their fairness, both in the way they are made and in their perceived effect.

Assuming that the bigger the government, the more unmanageable it becomes, a second solution would be for the federal government to do less; or to turn over more of its collected revenues to states and localities to do things that Americans expect government to do (the principle of revenue sharing); or to contract with private parties to perform services that it had previously delivered, as in the case of some educational performance experiments. The proposition then becomes: if the President cannot satisfactorily manage the federal establishment, find ways to decrease what must be managed rather than to increase the managerial ability of the President. These are political decisions,

12. Peter F. Drucker, *The Age of Discontinuity* (Harper, 1969), p. 221.

of course. They could be made if the electorate strongly indicated a desire to move in these directions. They would, however, still leave substantial activities for the federal government to manage.

A third solution would be to reorganize the executive branch so as to reflect a more realistic approach to solving problems and delivering services. Most departments today represent a collection of past answers to yesterday's priority problems, of prior demands on elected officials by important special-interest groups, and of long-forgotten bureaucratic fights for control of program areas. Given the difficulty of changing existing arrangements, Presidents continue to create new agencies and to pull new problems into the White House where their authority is greater. The piecemeal history of recent reorganizations has been that of consolidating related activities, putting all transportation matters in one department, all housing matters in another, and so on. But as housing and transportation, for example, have become increasingly viewed as interconnected, proposals have been made to create a Department of Community Development and similar functional groupings. Such suggestions would result in fewer and larger departments. From the President's standpoint, the advantage would be in reducing the number of officials with whom he has to track. The "lesser" departments, which are apt to be overlooked by Presidents, might be expected to be raised in stature and visibility by consolidation.

While consolidation can equalize the departments' access to the President, the case has not been firmly made that consolidation could avoid creating bureaucratic monstrosities. If the problems of government are partly the result of bigness, are bigger departments the solution? The history of the two giants of the federal bureaucracy—HEW and the Defense Department—suggest that there is such a thing as optimum size. Putting together several small agencies may produce greater efficiency; creating agencies that employ over 100,000 people may produce greater inefficiency and further loss of presidential control. A lesson of the Defense Department reorganization, it seems to me, is that a President had greater control over spending when each military service had to compete before him than he now has when a consolidated department irons out its differences in private and presents him with a common front.

Whether agencies are big or small, however, organization along functional lines makes sense. Government becomes more understandable, no

small consideration in a democratic society, and the prospects of jurisdictional disputes may be lessened. Moreover, functional divisions
should increase agency accountability to the President and Congress.

At the same time, when a President receives his major advice from
those most responsible for its effectuation, there is a higher probability
of achieving results than when policy is imposed by presidential
representatives, usually the White House staff, who are less cognizant
of operational capacity and do not have statutory authority to run
programs.

But the question arises whether reorganizations can long remain in
phase with changing priorities, crises, and fads. What might have been
established as a Department of Environment in 1970 would already
have become an imperfect reflection of national needs by 1974 when
what may have been most desirable would have been a Department of
Energy. The reorganization powers given to Presidents must be flexible
enough to allow government to adjust more quickly to change. Otherwise government will be constantly drifting into dysfunctionality, and
Presidents will continue to rely on distorting ad hoc arrangements. Yet
Presidents must also be aware that there can be problems of excessive
reorganization, as Martha Derthick has pointed out.[13] Constant tinker-
ing takes a toll in the administration of federal programs.

Reorganizing the entire federal government is complicated and outside the scope of this study, but hardly outside the concern of Presidents, who will increasingly turn to reorganization proposals. The
best time to make these proposals is as promptly as possible after assuming office (which, of course, is the time when Presidents are least
qualified to act); and they should be made in such form as to allow
successive Presidents to be able to undo them.

A fourth solution is for Presidents to revert to a pre–New Deal situation of reduced power. Proposals for substantially reducing the presidential role have come from Barbara Tuchman and others who, in the
wake of Vietnam and Watergate, fear the initiatives of a President more
than they are troubled by a President failing to make the lions of bureaucracy do his bidding.[14] Their proposals would assure the continu-

13. See Martha Derthick, *Uncontrollable Spending for Social Services Grants*
(Brookings Institution, 1975), p. 113.
14. See Barbara W. Tuchman, "Should We Abolish the Presidency?" *New York
Times*, February 13, 1973.

ation of federal agencies operating as an independent force, answerable to the President only when they need his support, and of a 535-member legislature assuming a greater role in operational activities. Life without a President may have a fantasy-like attractiveness at certain moments of history, but no society as large and complex as the United States could drift for long on the waning momentum of bureaucracy. The Watergate scandals produced a number of congressional bills to create greater agency autonomy, especially in the Justice Department.[15] Autonomous agencies are certainly preferable to presidential corruption but are no substitute for enlightened presidential leadership. The American people elect Presidents, not civil servants. The problem of how to ensure responsive and humane government performance is real and growing. The question is how it can be achieved within a democratic framework and within the capacities of the types of persons most likely to be elected President.

No PRESIDENT sets out to build the largest White House staff in history, although ultimately each one from 1933 through 1974 earned this distinction. The presidential establishment has grown in four decades from a White House staff of 37 to over 500, with thousands more employed in satellite staffs that also service the presidency. This corresponds to the increased size of the other parts of the national government. There has been a similar growth in Congress, for example, where members' and committee staffs totaled 2,443 in 1947 and now total 10,786.[16]

It is not necessary to impute malevolence or a dictatorial impulse to the growth of the White House. Generally it has reflected a greater participation by the United States in world affairs since World War II; a widened concept of what services government should perform; a vacuum left by the failure of state and local governments to respond to legitimate needs and the shift of services to the federal level; popular support for an increasingly activist concept of the presidency; compli-

15. For proposals on the establishment of an independent Justice Department, see *Removing Politics from the Administration of Justice*, Hearings before the Subcommittee on Separation of Powers of the Senate Judiciary Committee, 93 Cong. 2 sess. (Government Printing Office, 1974).

16. See Harrison W. Fox, Jr., and Susan Webb Hammond, "The Growth of Congressional Staffs," in Harvey C. Mansfield, Sr., ed., *Congress Against the President*, Proceedings of The Academy of Political Science, vol. 32, no. 1 (1975), p. 115.

cated interrelationships between government programs; and new offices imposed on the White House by Congress. Other growth relates to the failure of existing federal agencies to do an adequate job, in which case Presidents have tried to fill the void by creating new White House offices.

White House expansion also mirrors the Presidents' accedence to demands for group representation on their staffs and to the law of propinquity. Presidents turn to those around them to do what is uppermost on their minds; the harried first-echelon White House aide responds to demand by adding a second echelon to assist him. Expansion follows the bureaucratic imperative as the White House takes on the characteristics of a bureaucracy. Presidents also have been inclined to use the White House as a dumping ground (or face-saving device) for high officials who have failed them elsewhere.

These types of White House growth reflect a certain permissiveness on the part of Presidents. Faced with difficult choices relating to programs and personnel, they have followed the course of least political resistance, encouraged by a generation of social scientists nurtured in the glow of the New Deal. Each President lives with the permissiveness of his predecessor. Until recently the consequences of bringing people and programs into the White House have not been spelled out or necessarily recognized as being counterproductive. Possibly it has been made too easy for Presidents to "solve" their problems in this way.

But is the size of the White House staff the reason why the present presidential system does not work very well? After all, even the bloated White House of today is no bigger than the central office of a major corporation. There is waste in the White House undoubtedly, as there is in other large enterprises, but the savings from its elimination would be measured in the thousands out of a nearly $400 billion annual federal budget. Rather, and perhaps paradoxically, the centralization of responsibilities in the person of the President has lessened his ability to perform the duties of the office. This is the cause. Substantial presidential staffs are the effect of the way Presidents have chosen to view themselves in the operation of the government.

Any reorganization of the way government is conducted must begin by defining the appropriate role of the President. Without meaning to minimize the centrality of presidential leadership in the U.S. government, over time Americans—and their Presidents—have inflated the rhetoric of the presidential job description. The basic functions to be performed by a President, generally with the concurrence of Congress, consist of:

—Devising policy to ensure the security of the country, with special attention to those situations that could involve the nation in war.

—Formulating a legislative program that presents recommendations for new initiatives, presumably ordering them in terms of priority.

—Preparing the annual budget, which recommends changes in the size of existing programs.

—Sharing responsibility for government adjustments of the economy.

—Selecting noncareer government personnel.

—Informing the people and their representatives in Congress of actions taken or proposed and presenting assessments of the state of the nation and of U.S. world involvements.

—Resolving conflicts between departments and seeking coordination of departmental policies.

—Overseeing the executive branch with some shared authority for promoting efficient and humane services and for ferreting out corruption.

—Such other duties as laws require.

Many of the duties of the White House staff do not relate directly to these functions. Other White House operations were once performed by people outside the White House and could be again. A President now has a substantial information (some would say propaganda) arm in the White House. Political operatives, who once were employed by a President's national party, now work out of the White House. Congressional lobbying, which even under Roosevelt and Truman was primarily a responsibility of the departments, is increasingly done by White House assistants.

In some important instances the chief reason why Presidents have turned to personal assistants is that they have not trusted those who otherwise would have performed these services. Nixon's distrust of the FBI caused him to create the "plumbers' unit." Thus, at its extreme, the concentration of responsibilities in the White House relates to the psychological makeup of Presidents.

The White House staff is first of all a service unit to assist Presidents in their daily routine, to help schedule their time, to aid them in preparing speeches and correspondence, and to assist them with travel plans and relations with the press. But beyond this, Presidents have come to rely on staff for primary advice in performing the nine major tasks of office, and White House aids also have increasingly assumed operational responsibilities for government programs. In recent years a presidential assistant, not the Secretary of State, has been the chief adviser on foreign policy. It is therefore the functions assumed by the White House that have created the basic problems of the presidential system—the size of the staff merely reflects these functions.

Operating in a much shorter time frame than that of the rest of the executive branch, Presidents have viewed the bureaucracy as too slow to respond to their leadership, too unimaginative in proposing policy change, too unwilling to accept political direction, too closely allied with special interests. They turn, often in desperation, to those closest at hand, their personal assistants. Yet the White House staff is not a sufficient fulcrum to move the weight of the federal establishment. It can never be large enough to do the job.

The Presidents' solution—salvation-by-staff—is self-defeating. An enlarged White House staff overprotects Presidents in a political environment where their greatest need is the need to know. Sycophancy can replace independent judgment. By extending the chain of command, Presidents have built additional delay and distortion into the system. Tensions between White House staff and Cabinet officers become inevitable. In the game of "who saw the President last," the department heads are badly positioned. Their exclusion from the inner circle creates a vicious cycle—the loss of power generating the further loss of power. Morale declines in the departments. Thus the careerists who ultimately must implement presidential policy no longer have as much of a stake in its success. They need only wait long enough and there will be another President.

But Presidents cannot wait. Indeed the pressure of time often pushes them to try to overwhelm or end-run the bureaucracy and Congress. For future Presidents, the lesson to be learned from Johnson and Nixon, both of whose careers were cut short, may be in the futility of this approach. The processes of persuasion and negotiation are painfully slow, and for these purposes Presidents need colleagues. White House aides generally are not colleagues; they are extensions who can be lent presidential powers but who rarely have additional resources to throw into battle on the President's behalf. Among the limited number of people who are in varying degrees beholden to the President, Cabinet members are the best bet to extend the reach and effectiveness of presidential leadership.

The chief conclusion of this study is that effective presidential leadership in the immediate future is likely to result only from creating more nearly collegial administrations in which Presidents rely on their Cabinet officers as the principal sources of advice and hold them personally accountable—in the British sense of "the doctrine of ministerial responsibility"—for the operations of the different segments of government.

Trimming the White House staff is a relatively simple matter for Presidents, if there is the will. The political risks are modest. The authority exists. It is a logical place to begin the process of striking a new balance in government. Of much greater difficulty will be the effort to create a presidential reliance on the Cabinet, to devise mechanisms of support for such an undertaking, and to remove obstacles that historically have worked to build a wedge between Presidents and their department heads.

The proposals for creating a more collegial government that follow in the next three chapters are meant to keep Presidents out of matters that are not presidential in nature, to remove the dangers of an overextended White House staff, to guide Presidents in the direction of seeking advice from those who will be most responsible for policy implementation, and to further the responsiveness of the bureaucracy to the wishes of the electorate by increasing the leverage of department officials whose fate depends on public mandate. Such a design, however, is no guarantee that there will be no Vietnams and no Watergates.

The conclusion reached in chapter 6, which reviewed the wide variety of advice Lyndon Johnson received against escalating the war, was that, as Larry O'Brien put it, Johnson "knew the problem. Nonetheless, he went ahead and pursued the war policy that he believed to be the right one."[17] There can be no assurance that a President will always act wisely, that he will always get good advice, or that he will accept good advice when it is offered. What is to be learned from Vietnam relates more to the powers of the presidency and to the competing powers of other institutional forces than to the machinery of presidential decisionmaking.

The history of Watergate, reviewed in chapter 7, argues that the cover-up, the act for which Richard Nixon was forced to resign, was a decision made by the President, not the product of a faulty advice system. Watergate, of course, does reflect on the moral character of those

17. Lawrence F. O'Brien, *No Final Victories* (Doubleday, 1974), p. 190.

staff members who assisted Nixon in the cover-up, but in the end it is the President who sets the moral tone of his administration. What is to be learned from Watergate, then, has most to do with the personal qualities that are necessary in Presidents.

BEFORE MAKING specific suggestions on how to reach the goal of collegial government, it is necessary to state five general propositions that are the boundaries of what follows.

1. A President is elected on the basis of certain expectations as to his ability to honor commitments that he has made to the voters and to perform the duties of his office within a constitutional framework. The people have a right to expect that he will be able to be as effective a leader as his abilities permit. This means that he deserves the best advice that is available and the most useful organizational structure that can assist him in the performance of his responsibilities.

2. For the purposes of the proposals that are made in succeeding chapters, it is unnecessary to deal with the President's role as tone-setter for the nation. ("Moral leader" strikes me as rather too grand for an elected politician.) This is not meant to deny the importance of having a President who can help provide effective reassurances and exhortations in difficult periods, or give a heightened sense of national purpose, or put before the citizenry a vision of a better society. But such abilities are most affected by the people's trust in a President based on his past record, his personal conduct, his forensic skills, situational factors such as being in office during a "just" war, and other matters that are not closely correlated with a President's methods of organizing his administration.

3. My proposals also do not involve the ceremonial functions of a President. Some have viewed these functions as frivolous, as a waste of valuable presidential time, and have suggested that they be turned over to the Vice President or that a "ceremonial" head of state be created in addition to a "working" head of government.[18] (In fact, many of these duties are currently performed by the President's wife and children.)[19] Without belaboring the point, I contend that the President's ceremonial duties, which are adjustable to fit the time he is

18. See Michael Novak, *Choosing Our King* (Macmillan, 1974), pp. 262–64.

19. For an interesting account of the degree to which the First Lady has become the ceremonial head of state, see Lady Bird Johnson, *A White House Diary* (Dell, 1971).

willing to expend, can serve a highly useful purpose in keeping him in touch with the people, in helping to create a sense of national unity, and in endorsing worthwhile undertakings. On the other hand, giving such responsibilities to someone other than the President and his family could have divisive consequences that cannot now be calculated.

4. Much that goes on at the White House is done in the President's name—reports to Congress, greetings and routine letters, proclamations, appointments to honorific positions, and so forth. A book published in 1970 devotes 166 pages to listing just those activities that are a President's legal responsibilities, such as annexing any rock, island, or key not belonging to another government and on which a deposit of guano is found.[20] But most of these duties do not require more of a President's time than the incessant signing of his name, which even under Truman occurred more than 400 times a day. The distinction between responsibilities that need a President's personal attention and those that do not is well illustrated by the experiences of government during the months before Nixon's resignation. The apparent paralysis of the presidency, in fact, affected little of the routine functioning of government. The presidency that concerns me here relates only to those activities in which the active participation of the President makes a difference.

5. In suggesting a different way that a President might choose to organize his presidency, I am guided by an overriding bias: whatever format is easiest to change, reverse, or abolish is best in the long run. Changes that can be made informally or by executive order are preferable to those that are formal and statutory, just as changes that can be made by statute are to be preferred to those that necessitate constitutional amendment. There is a logic in proposing flexibility. The White House is peculiarly idiosyncratic. It must and will reflect the habits of its occupant. The needs and desires of the people also change, and the government should be able to adjust. Then, too, existing systems resist change. I propose changes that have the best chance of winning acceptance, although some will feel that such expectations are overly optimistic.

Little of what follows would leave a consenting President bloody and alone at the barricades. Yet there is much that is different from the

20. See Aspen Systems Corporation, *The Powers and Responsibilities of the President* (Pittsburgh: ASC, 1970).

present system and much that would be difficult to put into practice, especially given the limited public enthusiasm for matters of government organization. These proposals are considered best only for *now*. They may very well be inappropriate at some point in the future but would permit future Presidents to undo them.

☆ ☆ ☆ ☆ ☆ ☆ ☆ ☆ ☆ ☆ ☆ ☆ ☆

CHAPTER NINE

The White House Staff

☆ ☆ ☆ ☆ ☆ ☆ ☆ ☆ ☆ ☆ ☆ ☆ ☆

THE ORGANIZATION of the White House depends largely on the style of Presidents, which obviously changes from one administration to another. But important guidelines can be established concerning the size and configuration of the White House—which functions belong there and which do not—as well as the types of people who should be selected as presidential assistants and what a President should have a right to expect from various kinds of advisory systems. In this chapter I propose such guidelines and discuss the lessons that can be learned from the techniques and organizational arrangements of past Presidents.

Ever since the Brownlow Committee concluded that "the President needs help,"[1] there has been an unremitting effort to help him by increasing the size of his staff. If he followed sound management principles, there seemed to be no reason why a President, like any other executive, could not be measurably assisted through a sensible delegation of his work load to an enlarged body of intelligent and loyal assistants.

That something went wrong is hardly in dispute. The risks of imposing a large staff between the President and the departments are greater than in other types of large organizations. Presidents as political executives must bear special responsibilities for the actions of those who work for them. More important from a management standpoint is the vast potential for distortion as the wishes of a President are passed along an extended chain of command. Presidential command takes on the characteristics of the children's game of "telephone." As each par-

1. Brownlow Report, p. 5.

ticipant whispers the President's message into the ear of the next person, the message loses definition until the last relay (presumably to the person who must carry out the command) may be substantially different from the original message. Simple messages have the best chance of surviving intact. But presidential messages are rarely simple. The expanded staff fails to compensate for the complexity and nuances of presidential decisionmaking.

The problem of a White House staff grown beyond the personal attention of a President was well illustrated by the testimony of John Dean before the Ervin Committee. Although Dean held the exalted title of Counsel to the President, he revealed that he had had no direct contact with Nixon for nearly two years after his appointment. Yet during that period he dealt with others in and out of government in the name of the President.

Control-by-staff is premised on a naiveté about power in Washington: that a President has a greater chance of taking charge if there are enough "President's men" to act on his behalf. But recent experiences suggest that a President's reach cannot be extended beyond a certain point through White House surrogates; beyond a certain number, White House aides become counterproductive. Certain types of problems cannot be properly handled at the White House level and should not be.

Enlarging the White House staff beyond a certain point ensures that more problems are drawn to the White House for resolution, decreases the problems that can be resolved below the White House level, cuts the time that a President can give to any one problem, forces him to spend more time on the care and feeding of his staff, increases the potential for aides to misspeak in his name, and builds pressure to further expand the White House staff.

There is a snowballing effect to the growth of the White House. Each group that is rewarded with representation on the staff—whether youth, the aged, or labor—sets a precedent for the next group to apply for similar recognition. Each new presidential assistant, in keeping with the bureaucratic imperative, measures his own importance by the size of his staff. Each new staff member finds ways to keep busy. A President agrees to additional group representation because there are no political benefits to be derived from denying such requests. Special-interest representatives at the White House often come from the ranks of those interests and can be expected to eventually return to their previous line of employment. "Having chosen men because of their affiliations with particular constituencies," wrote Roger Hilsman, "a president can hardly be surprised if they speak for that constituency in the internal policy debate."[2] Yet a President expects an aide to be his representative *to* a client and is surprised to find that his aide has become a representative *for* outside clients. Outside interests discover that they can end-run the departments and take their demands directly to their representative at the White House. This affects morale in the departments.

While the original theory was that each new Special Assistant relieves the President of some responsibilities and shields him from some outside demands, in practice each Special Assistant bargains for a portion of the President's time. In effect, he lures the President into accepting additional responsibilities and adds to the demands made on the President. As the White House takes on the characteristics of a bureaucracy, the President's time increasingly is allotted on the basis of internal bureaucratic politicking and trade-offs between staff members that do not necessarily reflect the relative importance of issues.

Presidents can increase their effectiveness by shortening the chain of command, thus eliminating some of the filters that now cause delay and distortion, by attempting to limit the number of White House aides to those who can be kept reasonably apprised of their intentions, and by keeping their personal staff out of the operating end of government. Ultimately, reducing the size of the White House establishment is the surest guarantee that Presidents will be forced to rely on department and agency heads for advice and follow-through.

Government designed around group representation has been seriously questioned by Theodore Lowi and others.[3] Yet government, and particularly the President, must be made aware of the hopes and frustrations of different segments of society. Especially the least powerful should have a right to expect that a President as the only elected official with the whole nation as his constituency has an understanding of their concerns. The clash of interests is healthy if all interests are adequately represented. Still, there is a wide variety of ways to be heard other than through a permanent spokesman at the White House.

Although there is still a hazy distinction between White House per-

2. Roger Hilsman, "Improving Foreign Policy 'Machinery'," in Thomas E. Cronin and Sanford D. Greenberg, eds., *The Presidential Advisory System* (Harper and Row, 1969), p. 278.

3. See Theodore Lowi, *The End of Liberalism* (Norton, 1969).

sonnel and those in the Executive Office of the President, the entire presidential complex can be pictured as two concentric circles, the Chief Executive at the center. The circle closest to him is the Inner Staff; on the perimeter is the Outer Staff whose assignments require little personal attention by the President or deal with subjects in which his political stakes are modest. Sometimes they have been placed in the presidential orbit only because of congressional enactment, as in the cases of the Office of Telecommunications Policy and the Office of the Special Representative for Trade Negotiations. Other Outer Staff units often reflect accommodations that have little to do with the proper functioning of the presidential office, such as solving a sticky personnel problem (Chester Bowles in the Kennedy administration) or conferring status on an important constituent group (creating a Special Assistant for the Aged in the Nixon administration). As a rule of thumb, presidential assistants who rarely see the President should not be on the White House staff. Almost all Outer Staff offices could easily be relocated elsewhere in the government.

Inner Staff assistants are those who perform personal services for the President, those who are engaged in areas of high presidential involvement (such as national security and economics), and those whose opinions are sought or who are given assignments on a wide variety of subjects, especially in areas where they are not expert. Occasionally Inner Staff people, such as Robert Kennedy, are not even located in the White House Executive Office. Then, too, titles can be deceptive: Theodore Sorensen as Special Counsel was Inner Staff; John Dean as Special Counsel was not until he was given responsibility for the Watergate cover-up. The problem of the Inner Staff is not in the function it performs, but rather that it often consists of the wrong people to have been placed in such close proximity to a President.

Generally a common denominator of Inner Staff people is that they have known the President for a long time. Unlike the process of Cabinet selection, the choice of Inner Staff personnel will be determined primarily by the circle of friends a President has gathered on the way to the presidency. Since he usually has had a career in elective politics founded on a state base, the press will quickly categorize his staff as the Missouri, Massachusetts, Texas, California, or Michigan Mafia. (Eisenhower, whose career was otherwise, escaped such shorthand.) If the President is a former Senator or House member, he will bring with him the small staff that he accumulated in the legislature, and some of its members will find that they are out of their depth in the White House. Often the staff will have been through a presidential election together; this, of course, will not be the situation in the case of a President-by-accident.

Choosing presidential assistants from the campaign organization has a certain superficial logic aside from being a matter of obligation. Some campaign duties of a personal service character, such as scheduling and press relations, are also necessary in the White House. Once in the White House, however, these aides become drawn into governance, and the skills required for campaigning and governing are often quite different. The freewheeling mind-set useful on the campaign trail can be dangerous when transplanted to the seat of power; witness the involvement of Nixon's Appointments Secretary, Dwight Chapin, in setting up a "dirty tricks" operation directed against Democratic candidates in 1972.

While the excessive loyalty of the Nixon men was often faulted in postmortems of Watergate, it is neither surprising nor exceptional that Presidents want to surround themselves with persons who are dedicated to them and who have proved their trustworthiness. As Pierre Salinger said of the Kennedy staff, "What we had in common . . . was our salary . . . and our commitment to the President, which was total. . . . Our faith in him and in what he was trying to do was absolute."[4] The problem is really definitional: loyalty must be to more than the person who is President. It also must be to the presidency and to a system of political democracy, civil liberties, and government through the competition of balanced institutions. Therefore, in picking Inner Staff assistants, the easy choice is often the wrong one since campaign workers may lack the necessary qualities for governance, and the judgment of friends may be skewed by personal loyalty.

"Presidential staff members," wrote Charles M. Hardin, "rarely if ever argue vehemently with him [the President] and probably never attack him with scorn and derision, hammering the table and telling him that if he persists in a course of action he is a fool."[5] Edward Weisband and Thomas M. Franck agree: "The rule against ruffling Presidential feathers is virtually absolute."[6] It is true that people in

4. Pierre Salinger, *With Kennedy* (Doubleday, 1966), p. 63.
5. Charles M. Hardin, *Presidential Power and Accountability* (University of Chicago Press, 1974), p. 25.
6. Edward Weisband and Thomas M. Franck, *Resignation in Protest* (Grossman, 1975), p. 137.

government—and even critics who are invited to the White House—are civil when addressing the President of the United States. Yet the picture of a President surrounded by yes-men is grossly overdrawn, as should have been obvious from the battles between the Clifford and Steelman forces in the Truman White House, the struggle between Moynihan and Burns in the Nixon White House, or the dissent over Vietnam policy by Moyers and McPherson in the Johnson White House. The absence of protest resignations should not be mistaken for the absence of internal conflict.

The danger is rather that dissent grows dimmer the longer a President stays in office, and a President must then make an extra effort to keep in touch with differing opinion. Outside opposition generally forces internal consensus as administration officials begin to huddle together for comfort. And a President, feeling increasingly threatened, turns more and more to those who give him the most loyal support. A form of Gresham's law takes over as the loyalists gain the ascendancy over those whose loyalty to the President is less single-minded. The "losers" are not disloyal, but they may have other loyalties as well—to certain ideas and principles, to wife and children. This is not a question of ideology. In the Nixon White House conservatives got expelled along with liberals. What may then happen is that the President is left without the necessary internal checks and balances, which are nearly as important as the checks and balances built into the Constitution.

In the end, unless the President is constantly alert, he may become isolated and overprotected by sycophants. He no longer has a desirable panoply of judgment on call, and if he is particularly unfortunate, he can be brought down by scandal or bad advice.

Verdicts on past White House staffs are mixed. George Reedy has issued a blanket indictment: to him they form a "conspiracy of mediocrity—that all too frequently successful collection of the untalented, the unpassionate, and the insincere."[7] On the other hand, Patrick Anderson concluded, "For the most part, the Presidents have brought men of outstanding ability onto their staffs ... [who have] often perform[ed] admirably, even heroically, rendering genuine, little-known services to the country."[8] The truth, as usual, lies somewhere in between.

7. George E. Reedy, *The Twilight of the Presidency* (New American Library, Mentor, 1970), p. xiv.
8. Patrick Anderson, *The Presidents' Men* (Doubleday, 1968), p. 398.

Generally, White House service has been the high point of most public careers. Occasionally, a Clark Clifford, a Nelson Rockefeller, or an Averell Harriman will go on to high elective office or a Cabinet post. But most former presidential assistants have failed when subsequently they ran for office. And a substantial number used their White House contacts and knowledge to later enrich themselves as lawyer-lobbyists.

It is extremely hazardous to generalize about the people who have served on White House staffs. They have been notable for diversity. They came to Washington from all sections of the country, from backgrounds in law, journalism, the military, academics, politics, even theology. Some presidential assistants have been members of the nation's moneyed aristocracy; others have worked their way out of poverty.

They are usually younger than Cabinet officers, which has caused problems. The trend toward youth has been a fallout of the activist presidency and reflects the supposed need for stamina as the White House has become more operational. The energy of the young presidential aide often draws operational matters into the White House. The confluence of loyalty and ambition, when unchecked by experience and public scrutiny, caused unacceptable conduct in the matters of Watergate and possibly in earlier situations. Two of the most talented young assistants in the Nixon White House, Egil Krogh and Edward Morgan, went to prison for doing things that they thought their President wished to be done. There is no reason to expect the very young to be wise or crafty in the ways of Washington—or even humble in the exercise of the powers they have been given. What is remarkable is that there have been some very young presidential assistants who must have been born wise, crafty, and at least outwardly humble, for surely they did not have time to acquire these traits.

There is much to recommend having potential presidential aides step down, rather than up, to White House service. For example, Clarence Randall under Eisenhower and Peter Peterson under Nixon, both former chief executives of major corporations, had little incentive to limit their advice to what might comfort the President and were not overawed in his presence. Ironically, however, persons of substantial achievement, unless they are too old, are often made department secretaries rather than presidential assistants. The irony is twofold. The successful executive's experience may have limited applicability or may even prove counterproductive in running a department. (To para-

phrase Charles Wilson: what works for General Motors will not necessarily work at the Department of Defense.) On the other hand, the energy-laden young White House aides may sometimes be exactly what is needed in the departments to make the lions of bureaucracy do the President's bidding. Stamina gives department executives an important advantage that presidential counselors do not need in the same abundance. Loyalty is necessary in political executives who head departments, where centrifugal forces work to pull an appointee away from the President; wisdom is the necessary quality at the White House, where counselors will be the last barrier between a President and a possibly ill-advised decision. Thus under the present system the President may have the wrong people in the wrong jobs at both ends, White House and departments.

Another problem for the President is how long to retain the services of a White House aide. As Clark Clifford has pointed out, after a while presidential assistants encounter automatic resistance from certain quarters in the administration, either for policy or personality reasons. Moreover, since the work load in government is so unevenly distributed, principal aides are apt to burn themselves out. Often, however, the problem will solve itself as the White House aide is attracted to a higher paying job in the private sector or finds a more prestigious job in a department. (White House staffers in the personnel office are particularly well positioned to find themselves such assignments, a situation that has the added advantage of bringing new blood into the personnel operation, where the personal networks of each recruiter expands the talent available to the President.)

Those who have excelled at the White House, even the young ones, almost always have had some previous experience and a feel for Washington and the power equations of government. The obverse is almost always equally true—the failures have often been newcomers who flouted the conventions of doing business in a complex milieu where stakes are high and there are people—such as columnists—who make their living by shooting down the mighty. Frederic Malek, on leaving government after five years in the Nixon administration, commented, "I used to believe that the highly intelligent, highly capable guy could go in anywhere. You didn't have to worry about his lack of experience. He would adapt. I don't buy that any more. Maybe the guy with the brilliant mind and no experience can do the job, but now I'd say, don't

bet on it. I'll take the proven commodity every time, the guy with experience, who has shown he can work in Washington."[9] First-hand
knowledge of how government looks from the points of implementation
can be particularly useful to White House aides who advise Presidents
on personnel selection.

It would be highly unusual to find a radical of any stripe on the
White House staff. But it would be equally remarkable for the American people to elect a radical President. Occasionally a President will
choose an assistant of somewhat different philosophy, as when Nixon
picked Moynihan as his urban affairs adviser. Yet such decisions and
their potential consequences should be most carefully weighed. Patrick
Buchanan of the Nixon staff has recounted how "the newly installed
President was not an inattentive student to the engaging Dr. Moynihan.
. . . And so, the President made a conscious decision to shift leftward on
domestic and social policy."[10] Conflict, up to a point, is healthy on a
White House staff, but ultimately a President is expected to pick aides
who reflect his values.

What the better White House aides have *not* had, with some notable
exceptions, has been "a passion for anonymity"—that classic definition
of the White House assistant. It has been impossible for them to
remain anonymous since the media have decreed that their actions
and lives are news. Nor should they remain anonymous. Their potential
influence is too important to the workings of government to allow them
to stay hidden. This hardly argues for the adoption of White House
"sunshine" laws. The concept of confidentiality is vital to the proper
functioning of the White House. Indeed competition within the White
House—which appears to be absent only to those who have never been
there—would be seriously limited if internal struggle were constantly
exposed to public view. But the principle of executive privilege cannot
be used to shield acts of criminality, as Nixon attempted to do. Clearly
the modern White House aide should have the ability to work grace-
fully in the limelight, while recognizing always that his powers are
derivative.

Some recent studies have stressed the growing institutional character
of the presidency. This emphasis can leave the impression that a Presi-

9. Quoted in Alan L. Otten, "Politics and People," *Wall Street Journal*, September 5, 1974.

10. Patrick J. Buchanan, *Conservative Votes, Liberal Victories* (Quadrangle, 1975),
p. 17.

dent is increasingly locked in by form, his options severely limited by the machinery of the White House. The case histories in chapters 2 through 7, however, indicate that Presidents disregard the system at will. It makes no difference if an office is congressionally mandated or whether it is part of the presidential establishment by tradition. Nixon, for example, abolished the Science Adviser post, kept away from the Council on Environmental Quality, listened to one Chairman of the Council of Economic Advisers but not to another, and delegated the budget responsibility to a subordinate. Presidents also may create offices as a way of sloughing off unpleasant duties—a factor in Eisenhower's establishing a congressional relations staff.

The history of the Council of Economic Advisers, reviewed at length in the Truman chapter, is instructive in what it says about the Presidents' uses of a statutory office. The CEA was created by Congress in 1946 to force Presidents to accept economic advice in a particular form. Yet they have chosen to use or not use the CEA largely on the basis of whether they preferred working with an individual council chairman to receiving economic advice from other sources. It is convenient to have economists close at hand, but primarily this is because there has been a marked increase in the responsibility Presidents have had to take for the management of the domestic economy, and not because Congress invented an institution whose form was innately correct.

The statutory National Security Council is another case in point. Created in 1947, and modified in 1949, its membership indicated which officials Congress expected Presidents to consult. Yet Truman did not regularly meet with the NSC until after the outbreak of the Korean war and did not seek the advice of the NSC as a body on whether he should send troops to Korea. Eisenhower, who placed great emphasis on the NSC, made his decision to send troops to Lebanon outside the NSC chambers. Kennedy dismantled much of the NSC machinery and created Ex Comm, supposedly an Executive Committee of the NSC, to advise him during the Cuban missile crisis. This allowed him to turn to those statutory NSC members who had gained his trust, to exclude others, and to add outsiders to his inner circle. In planning Vietnam strategy, Johnson narrowed his advisory group to a body of six, two of whom were on the White House staff, and met with them at lunch on Tuesdays, creating in fact (if not in name) a War Cabinet. The NSC's greatest value to Nixon was in providing him with a vehicle for building a personal staff in the national security area. Thus Congress gave

Presidents a mechanism they could use if they so desired but was unable to decree that it must be used. The operations of the NSC should give pause to those who wish to impose mandatory advisory machinery on Presidents. Congress can give the President advisers, but it cannot make him listen. The NSC has often served the presidency well, particularly by presenting a flow of more routine matters in an orderly manner. But if Congress had not established a National Security Council, Presidents would still seek the advice of the Secretaries of State and Defense and other concerned agency heads in some form.

The White House Office of Science and Technology, created by Congress in 1976, forces Presidents to have some scientists on their staffs —just as the CEA created permanent presidential economists. But it will be easier for Presidents to ignore a science council than to ignore either the CEA or the NSC. When compared with the economy and national security, science policy is less apt to be seen by Presidents as central to their role. They are also more likely to suspect scientists as special pleaders (after all, the federal government spends $18 billion annually on scientific research and development), and most of the men who have attained the presidency have not been keenly interested in science. (The three exceptions were Jefferson, John Quincy Adams, and Theodore Roosevelt.)[11] White House councils are always of limited value if they deal with subject areas that are not perceived by Presidents as central to their responsibilities.

This would be the problem for a long-range planning office of the sort proposed by Wassily Leontief and others. The two similar planning experiments under Roosevelt and Nixon were disasters. Presidents will continue to think in terms of four-year cycles and will seek professional advice that helps them to meet immediate and near-term needs. The success of the CEA has been maintained by the council's recognition that advice must be presidentially useful—during the President's time in office. Government leaves too much to chance, but this will continue to be the case until long-range planning is built into the regular processes of running the federal government; it cannot be corrected by putting another box on the organizational chart of the Executive Office that Presidents can and will ignore with impunity. Advisers in

11. A case for a science adviser in the White House is made by G. B. Kistiakowsky, "Presidential Science Advising," *Science*, April 5, 1974, pp. 38–42. Also see Eugene B. Skolnikoff and Harvey Brooks, "Science Advice in the White House? Continuation of a Debate," *Science*, January 10, 1975, pp. 35–41.

the White House can expect attention only if they operate within the same time frame as the President.

The sum of experience in this area is that congressional attempts to mandate presidential advice systems have cluttered the White House without necessarily serving the intended purposes. Presidents, too, have contributed to this process by proposing statutory White House offices that are eventually inherited by their successors. There should be little expectation that future Presidents will not continue to ignore unwanted statutory advisers or will not distort the mechanisms they have been given to serve other ends. There would be less manipulation and more efficiency in White House operations if Presidents had a freer hand in arranging the internal machinery of their office.

The presidential establishment, of course, consists of more than the White House staff. Besides the Cabinet (discussed in the next two chapters), a President relies to varying degrees on his Vice President, friends, family, and outside commissions and task forces. Each has a place, but it is equally important for a President to recognize their limitations.

The degree to which a President makes use of his Vice President depends on the depth of their personal relationship, which is apt to weaken over time for a variety of reasons. My colleague, Hugh Heclo, who worked on a Vice President's staff, told me that Presidents feel uncomfortable around Vice Presidents, whom they do not like to see sitting at the table day after day, waiting. Roosevelt did not even tell Truman the secret of the atomic bomb, although FDR was the first President to give overseas and domestic operating assignments to a Vice President (Henry Wallace). Most Vice Presidents have filled their days chairing advisory committees, which prompted Nixon to comment on the risk of turning the Vice President "into merely another bureaucrat—and a 'Secretary of Catch-All Affairs' at that."[12]

Eisenhower also used Nixon as his political surrogate and had him assume most of the burdens of campaigning during the midterm elections. This partly resolved the dilemma of how a President could be "chief magistrate of all the people" and "chief party leader" at the same time. Commenting on the use of Agnew as a campaigner, Ross Baker called it "the Mario Puzo Theory of the vice-presidency. . . . The President is the Godfather and the Vice President is his 'button man.' The Vice President is sent to knife, cosh and garotte the oppo-

12. Richard M. Nixon, "The Second Office," *The 1964 World Book Year Book* (Field Enterprises, 1964), pp. 93–94.

nents; after which the President turns up at the memorial services for the victim wearing a carnation."[13]

Many observers have proposed substantially increasing the administrative duties of the Vice President (and even creating multiple Vice Presidents).[14] A problem with such suggestions was illustrated by the struggle between Vice President Henry Wallace, when he headed the Board of Economic Warfare, and Commerce Secretary Jesse Jones. Ultimately, Roosevelt had to relieve both of their responsibilities. More recently Vice President Rockefeller's initial mandate to advise the President on domestic affairs proved an embarrassment to Ford when he found he could not always accept the advice. A President should not be forced into the position of having to reject the Vice President, which is almost inevitable when a Vice President has operational duties. Eugene McCarthy has stated: "A Vice President in office should be treated much as a crown prince is treated in a monarchy. He should be trained in the arts of government. He should not be used in the temporary and transient affairs of state."[15] The reasoning is sound. Presidents, under the present system, would be ill-advised to use their Vice Presidents for other than bureaucratically marginal or symbolic chores on the fringes of the administration.

Few Presidents have made much use of individuals outside government for advice on a regular basis, although here too their practices have been different. Roosevelt, immobilized by polio, brought a steady stream of outsiders to him—if not primarily to solicit their advice, at least to receive their impressions. Ford in his first year in office arranged for different groups of intellectuals to discuss a specified topic on the average of once every six weeks and met about as often with a group of

13. Ross K. Baker, "Spiro Agnew," Society, September–October 1973, p. 88.

14. Rexford G. Tugwell proposed two Vice Presidents, for "internal affairs" and "general affairs" (The Emerging Constitution [Harper's Magazine Press, 1974], p. 604). Herman Finer proposed the election of eleven Vice Presidents to serve as the President's Cabinet (The Presidency: Crisis and Regeneration [University of Chicago Press, 1960], pp. 303–06 and 313). Milton Eisenhower proposed two Executive Vice Presidents—one for international affairs, one for domestic affairs (Johns Hopkins Magazine, November 1974, pp. 23–24). Donald E. Graham proposed that the President appoint the Vice President to head "one of the major Cabinet departments" ("The Vice Presidency: What It Is, What It Could Be," Washington Post, September 18, 1972).

15. Eugene J. McCarthy, "The Crown Prince," New York Times, August 17, 1972.

old friends, mostly former Congressmen and lobbyists. Johnson made the greatest use of outsiders of any post–World War II President. Their purpose was described by one member of this select circle: "I don't think he really expects answers from his friends most of the time. He uses his friends as sounding boards, letting his thoughts come out and bounce off them. He doesn't put things on paper, pro and con, like a lawyer. He talks things out. The chief function of his friends is to let him talk"[16]

Another value of presidential friends is to serve as entertainers. The Court Jester has a long history. At best, as in Shakespearean plays, he presents the king with wise comments disguised as foolishness. One should not underestimate the need of Presidents to have people around with the ability to amuse them. The urge to be solemn in the presence of Presidents can be overpowering. On the other hand, a President's cronies can be politically embarrassing if given positions of responsibility, as was the case in the Truman administration.

The notion of a "Kitchen Cabinet," a group of outsiders to whom Presidents turn first for advice, is the vestige of another era, kept alive by mass media eager for any scrap of information about presidential associates. While the Kitchen Cabinet may have existed when White House staffs consisted of one secretary, the speed, secrecy and complexity of modern presidential decisionmaking usually preclude the serious involvement of those who are not deeply immersed in each situation. Colonel House, President Wilson's foreign policy adviser, today would have had to be on the White House staff or be Secretary of State to have comparable influence.

Lucky are the Presidents who can rely on the advice of their families. Milton Eisenhower, Robert Kennedy, Lady Bird Johnson, and Betty Ford could be expected to balance total loyalty with independent judgment—a rare combination. Eleanor Roosevelt's role was more as an advocate, but one of considerable importance in maintaining the liberalism of the New Deal.

In one respect Presidents turn to outsiders more than ever. This is done through the form of collective advice known as the commission. The appointment of citizen commissions started with George Washing-

16. Quoted in Ben H. Bagdikian, "The 'Inner, Inner Circle' Around Johnson," *New York Times Magazine*, February 28, 1965 (reprinted in Nelson W. Polsby, ed., *The Modern Presidency* [Random House, 1973], p. 184).

ton and accelerated under Theodore and Franklin Roosevelt. In a perceptive and only slightly cynical article published in 1968, Elizabeth Drew listed eight reasons why Presidents turn to this system of advice.

> To obtain the blessing of distinguished men for something you want to do anyway. . . . To postpone action, yet be justified in insisting that you are at work on the problem. . . . To act as a lightning rod, drawing political heat away from the White House. . . . To conduct an extensive study of something you do need to know more about before you act, in case you do. . . . To investigate, lay to rest rumors, and convince the public of the validity of one particular set of facts. . . . To educate the commissioners, or get them aboard on something you want to do. . . . Because you cannot think of anything else to do. . . . To change the hearts and minds of men.[17]

These reasons are not necessarily trivial. The Brownlow Committee, for example, was designed by Roosevelt to tell him what he wanted to hear and to give him support in getting it from Congress. Nor was it unimportant to him that appointing a committee might defuse a political issue that could have been used against him in his bid for reelection. Although commissions can buy some time for a President, increasingly their internal dynamics produce recommendations that the President cannot honor. Thus, as a former commission member noted, "The gap between what he is held responsible for and what he can actually do, which he sought to close by resorting to a commission, ultimately is widened by it."[18] The lesson drawn from the experiences of the three most visible recent commissions—the Commission on Civil Disorders, the Commission on the Causes and Prevention of Violence, and the Commission on Campus Unrest—is that, in the opinion of Chester Finn, "large sudden manifestations of problems with deep-seated causes and no ready remedy . . . are not the sort of thing commissions handle well."[19]

When Presidents seek collective advice on near-term concerns, such

17. Elizabeth B. Drew, "On Giving Oneself a Hotfoot: Government by Commission," *Atlantic*, May 1968, pp. 45–46. For a much more sanguine assessment, see Thomas B. Wolanin, *Presidential Advisory Commissions* (University of Wisconsin Press, 1975).

18. Martha Derthick, "On Commissionship—Presidential Variety," *Public Policy*, vol. 19 (Fall 1971), p. 635. Derthick was a member of President Nixon's Commission on Campus Unrest in 1970. For another useful opinion by a former commissioner, see Daniel Bell, "Government by Commission," *The Public Interest*, no. 3 (Spring 1966), pp. 3–9.

19. Chester E. Finn, Jr., "Advising the President," *Commentary*, February 1976, p. 88.

as formulating a legislative package, they use the task force format, which usually differs from commissions in size (they are apt to be smaller), time frame (they generally issue a report quicker), composition (they are more likely to include some members from inside the government), and often secrecy of deliberations. The fewer members on an advisory group, the more likely its recommendations will be "actionable" (precise, practical, and geared to available resources). Yet as Kissinger has noted, "Committees are consumers and sometimes sterilizers of ideas, rarely creators of them."[20] They act as vacuum cleaners, sucking up existing proposals that are scattered about the landscape. At best, they bring in some suggestions that may have escaped the apparatus of the permanent government. As in the case of Johnson's task forces, to be useful to the President the recommendations then have to be sorted out by those around him who have a better feel for his objectives and style.

Very large advisory bodies, such as White House conferences, are least able to produce immediately useful proposals for Presidents. Their purposes are more likely to include providing a safety valve for the frustrations of various special interests, broadening participation in government, moving ideas from germination to public approval, and providing support and a rationale for actions that Presidents want to take. White House conferences now meet on the average of once a year. Presidents are required to convene some of these, such as the one on children that has a long history of decennial gatherings. But Presidents often call optional conferences without fully understanding that recommendations will result that cannot be accepted, if only because of budgetary constraints.

Outside advisers, singly or collectively, then, can serve certain useful purposes, but they are only tangentially connected to the continuing problems of running the government. While the art is to know which outside advice system is most useful for which purpose, ultimately Presidents will conclude that such systems are supplemental and that they must receive major advice from White House staff, heads of agencies, or some combination of the two.

Compared with the rest of government, the White House barely qualifies as an organization at all, if "organization" implies a fixed plan that is likely to look about the same tomorrow as it did yesterday. The

20. Henry A. Kissinger, "The Policymaker and the Intellectual," in Cronin and Greenberg, *The Presidential Advisory System*, p. 160.

very vibrations of the place are markedly different depending on the personality of the President. This is best illustrated when a Vice President is thrust into the presidency. For a while at least he will keep many of his predecessor's assistants, yet there will be a perceptible change in atmosphere and results.

Despite repeated reports to the contrary, there have been no Svengalis on the White House staff. Even under the most pyramidal arrangements, those of Eisenhower and Nixon, the persons who were placed at the top were serving purposes of presidential design. Both Sherman Adams and H. R. Haldeman were replaced by men of considerably different mien, without measurably changing the direction of the two presidencies.

There are no immutable designs for organizing the presidency—schemes that usefully transcend a particular administration. For each President has his own way of doing things and he is usually too old to change; each President has his own objectives and goals that may be better served by one form of organization than by another. Roosevelt would have felt hemmed in by Eisenhower's system, and Eisenhower would have been befuddled by the chaos of Roosevelt's. Roosevelt's chief objective, coaxing new solutions out of government to respond to a lingering depression, might have been less forthcoming from Eisenhower's system of noncompetitive jurisdictions; Eisenhower's chief objective, restoring a sense of tranquility to a buffeted society, might have been more difficult to achieve under Roosevelt's highly competitive manner of structuring his administration. Each would have had to find ways to ignore the system of the other if it had been mandated by law.

In the final analysis, it is the President's style—his work habits, the way he likes to receive information, the sort of people he prefers to have around him, the manner in which he makes up his mind—that will be the key to how the White House is organized.

The extremes of presidential organization are attributed to Roosevelt and Eisenhower. The Rooseveltian model is described as a circle. The President is in the middle surrounded by a collection of generalists of no fixed assignment competing for his favor. At its best, the President rubs two aides together and lights a fire of creativity. At its worst, the result is petty quarreling, with the President forced to get rid of one or both of the combatants. The Eisenhower model is viewed as a pyramid. The system is a series of filters through which options move up to the top in an orderly fashion and in which each aide, usually a specialist, is given a carefully prescribed territory. At its worst, decisions fall between the cracks on the organization chart or have been too diluted by the time they reach the President. At its best, the President is presented with information in a timely fashion and his decisions are more likely to have the support of all parties because all feel that the process has given them a fair hearing. The organization that is more fluid is likely to produce more policy innovation; the organization that is more structured is likely to give more guidance to the permanent government.

The two models of presidential staffing, however, are not nearly as discrete as they are usually presented. This is partly because Presidents are always making exceptions; even Eisenhower put several White House offices to work on foreign policy questions in competition with Secretary of State Dulles. And it is partly because the Presidents' needs and perceptions change over time, and they make adjustments as they go along. Both Roosevelt and Nixon found that aides of greater creativity were most needed in the formative period; aides with skills in congressional lobbying and in coordinating departments were more necessary after policies were agreed upon. As Presidents have discovered, they must usually turn to different people for different talents. Then, too, it is a characteristic of the types of people who are apt to be on White House staffs to be highly competitive. Louis Koenig noted that successful Presidents have always been served "by personal advisers whose talent for the *diabolique* was definitely major league."[21] Such people are inclined to manipulate organizational patterns and job assignments to fit their talents and ambitions. Moreover, routine systems of decisionmaking have a way of being ignored when Presidents are under extreme pressure; elaborate procedures prove to be too slow moving and subject to leaks. The more important a decision, the more likely it is that established channels will break down and be replaced by informal, ad hoc arrangements.

The problem of the Nixon White House was not so much that it had a structured staff system, which had served Eisenhower well, but that this was the wrong system for Richard Nixon. Eisenhower knew from long experience how to bend such an organizational arrangement to meet his needs; Nixon did not. Of even more importance, a President so given to isolation should have guarded against choosing a system that permitted him to become remote from the other players and forces

21. Louis W. Koenig, *The Invisible Presidency* (Rinehart, 1960), p. 24.

that a President must be in continuous contact with in order to govern effectively. The greatest danger in organizing the White House can come from a President choosing to isolate himself.

The type of personnel as well as the staffing patterns at the White House may be affected by whether the President is a Democrat or a Republican. While all Presidents rely heavily on people trained in the law, Democratic Presidents usually turn to "political" lawyers and Republicans more to "business" lawyers. Republicans often select more structured organizations, perhaps because of the corporate base of party support, and Democrats often select more fluid structures, perhaps because of the greater reliance on staff with broad political experience, politics being an occupation that relies on temporary and informal arrangements. It may also be that these differences reflect a greater stress on administration in a Republican White House and on policy innovation under Democrats.

There are trade-offs involved in whatever techniques a President employs. Johnson, for example, invested heavily in group meetings. The advantages of such meetings include ego-massage for the participants, a certain understanding by the President of the nuances of those with whom he meets, a useful way for the President to directly convey a message, and the symbolic cue to the public that the President cares about a certain group. Group meetings, however, are an inefficient way for Presidents to get information. They are extremely time-consuming and can cause embarrassment in that the President's control over content and sometimes even decorum is limited. On the other hand, a system that relies heavily on paper work may de-emphasize the political and overemphasize the technical. Political implications are important to Presidents in balancing competing objectives, yet they are less likely to be committed to paper than they are to be whispered. Presidents always pay a price for the techniques they choose.

Presidents have a way of creating a theory of governance out of the techniques they choose for the conduct of their business. Scholars then debate the competing claims of Presidents. An emphasis of the case histories in this study has been on illustrating that presidential techniques of running the presidency often have nothing to do with theory. Of greater importance, for instance, may have been that Kennedy had a bad back. It must have been physically painful for him to sit through Cabinet meetings. He was also a relatively young man, boundlessly energetic. Indeed most reports of Kennedy in meetings comment on his inability to sit still. Eisenhower, by contrast, was the nation's oldest President and had spent a lifetime training himself to sit through meetings. But Kennedy's rationale for virtually abolishing the Cabinet as a collective body was that members of the domestic Cabinet had nothing to contribute to members of the national security Cabinet and vice versa. And Eisenhower built a case for the importance of the Cabinet meeting even though many of the matters discussed were of no more significance than the architectural plans for Dulles Airport. An analysis of the place of the Cabinet in the Eisenhower and Kennedy governments leads to the conclusion that these Presidents were motivated, perhaps subconsciously, by their respective rates of metabolism.

Presidential organization of the White House can be likened to an artist's exercise in free form. It is a Calder, not a Rodin; a De Kooning rather than a Rembrandt. Trying to create useful structure becomes an attempt to nail currant jelly to the wall, as Theodore Roosevelt once said in another context. Yet it is an undertaking worth the effort, given the similar patterns of dysfunctionality that keep recurring in the nation's experience with recent Presidents.

Assuming that Presidents can substantially accept or reject the organizations they inherit, that neither law nor tradition has a binding effect on those who wish to recast their own staffs and their relations with the public executives they appoint and can fire, and assuming moreover that this is not an unsensible arrangement, a plan that proposes a way Presidents may find useful in organizing their presidencies must be general enough to suggest that any President, an Eisenhower or a Roosevelt, would be able to fit comfortably into such a design.

Furthermore, "a plan" suggests that all Presidents have common problems even though they have very different personalities and work habits. The evidence strongly supports such an assumption. Presidents as different as Kennedy and Nixon became equally convinced that the bureaucracy was thwarting presidential initiatives. Truman and Nixon engaged in similar and bitter assessments of the White House press corps. Johnson and Nixon created similar systems for formulating domestic policy at the White House after each had vowed to work through the Cabinet. And each learned some of the same lessons over time. The differences between them were most pronounced at the beginning of their administrations. Their attitudes began to converge as outside forces and adversity limited their options. They started from different bases to centralize control in the White House, and moved at different speeds, but each moved in the *same direction*, and each ended his term with more staff and more operational assignments residing in the White House than when he took office.

☆ ☆ ☆ ☆ ☆ ☆ ☆ ☆ ☆ ☆ ☆ ☆ ☆

CHAPTER TEN

The Cabinet:

Personnel

☆ ☆ ☆ ☆ ☆ ☆ ☆ ☆ ☆ ☆ ☆ ☆ ☆

THE OVERBLOWN presidential staff, I have argued, has become counterproductive to the purposes of Presidents. Among the more glaring
deficiencies of a White House–centered system is that it increasingly
draws no-win problems into the Oval Office; this in turn contributes to
undermining public trust in Presidents. Outsiders, I have also argued,
can be of only peripheral utility to a President in decisionmaking, less
so in management. This leaves, if by a process of elimination, the department and agency heads as the likely candidates to buttress the
presidential role.

Aaron Wildavsky has concluded that "the more prominent a President's Cabinet is, the less of a target he becomes."[1] Over time this
proposition should become more obvious to Presidents. And when they
begin to equate their political survival and renewed public confidence
in the presidency with greater Cabinet responsibility, the conditions
for the introduction of collegial government will have arrived.

There are good reasons why it will be difficult to breathe life into
the Cabinet, but one basic cause relates to the quality of people who
have traditionally been department secretaries. In this chapter I first
argue that a series of recent changes in political institutions now allow
Presidents a previously unthinkable freedom in the selection of Cabinet
officers, although recent Presidents have been slow to realize how the
present differs from the past. Confronting the need for a higher caliber
of leadership in the Cabinet, Presidents are faced with two serious

1. Aaron Wildavsky, "The Past and Future Presidency," *The Public Interest*, no.
41 (Fall 1975), p. 73.

questions: what are the qualities they should look for and where in our society should they look to find them? These are the subsequent concerns of this chapter.

A certain romance has slipped into the history of past Cabinets. Arthur Schlesinger, Jr., wrote: "Genuinely strong Presidents are not afraid to surround themselves with genuinely strong men [in the Cabinet]."[2] Past Presidents, in fact, rarely have had more than one or two significant department heads at the same time. While Schlesinger mentioned six "strong men" in the Roosevelt Cabinet, he was referring to a period of over twelve years, and the six never served simultaneously. Time, too, blurs shortcomings. Schlesinger cited Secretary of State Cordell Hull among his examples; yet Dean Acheson recalled that "Secretary Hull was intimidated by President Roosevelt, who was, in turn, bored by the Secretary."[3]

Historically, Presidents have selected their Cabinets on the basis of traditions, trade-offs, and obligations (as distinct from commitments, which are rarely given before the election). As examples, the Secretary of the Interior was expected to be a westerner, and the party chairman was rewarded with the position of Postmaster General. Once the "obligations" were fitted into appropriate slots, "balances" had to be made. Protestants had to be appointed if there were too many Catholics, northerners to balance southerners, and so forth. The end result was often that a new President found himself surrounded with some people of less than inspiring ability, personalities that were incompatible, and even some Cabinet members of questionable loyalty.

In very recent years, however, the following subtle changes have occurred in the party system, Congress, and the way Presidents get nominated and elected:

—State primaries as the means of selecting delegates to presidential nominating conventions have replaced the caucus system in thirty states. Candidates must make their appeals directly to the party rank and file. No longer are powerful state leaders the key to winning presidential nominations. Thus there is not the same obligation to reward political leaders for early support, as was the case when President Ken-

2. Arthur Schlesinger, Jr., "Presidential War," *New York Times Magazine*, January 7, 1973, p. 28.

3. Dean Acheson, "The President and the Secretary of State," in Don K. Price, ed., *The Secretary of State* (Prentice-Hall, 1960), p. 38.

nedy appointed Governor Abraham Ribicoff of Connecticut to the secretaryship of HEW.

—Public financing of candidates for presidential nominations and in the general election, in effect for the first time in 1976, also lessens the influence of fund raisers and "fat cats," another type of obligation that was sometimes rewarded through Cabinet appointment, such as when President Nixon made Maurice Stans his Secretary of Commerce.

—Television has become the primary means of appealing to the voters. This, too, is a break with the past when the presidential candidates relied on and rewarded their prominent campaigners for electioneering services. The case of William Jennings Bryan and Woodrow Wilson is a notable example. Television is one reason, though not the only one, for the gradual disintegration of parties as the loci of political action, clearly manifested in the steep increase in the number of voters who call themselves "independents." Nixon in 1972 entirely divorced his campaign from his party's organization. Since Presidents now owe less to their parties, they are under less obligation to choose Cabinet members on the basis of party label.

—Finally, there has been the diffusion of power in Congress. The passing of such leaders as Lyndon Johnson and Sam Rayburn, which is very possibly a permanent condition, means that Congress will no longer exert the same influence over Cabinet selection, as, for instance, when President Eisenhower gave veto power to Senator Robert Taft in 1952.

These developments have lessened traditional constraints on selecting the Cabinet. Presidents will still incur obligations on the way to the White House, but more than ever before they will be free to choose their department heads on the basis of ability.

Some of President Ford's Cabinet appointees did reflect a diminution of partisan influence in the selection process. Although Ford was not an elected President, such choices as Attorney General Edward Levi, Secretary of Labor John Dunlop, Transportation Secretary William Coleman, HUD Secretary Carla Hills, HEW Secretary F. David Mathews, and UN Ambassador Daniel P. Moynihan were not responses to party demands. Most were not Republicans and none had previously obligated the President. In several instances, however, such considerations may have been replaced by increased concern for group representation. (The appointments of a black and a woman, for example.) Still, the high quality of these officials suggests that broadening the types of people who serve in the Cabinet need not restrict a President's options.

This does not mean that Presidents necessarily will make better selections in the future, merely that they will have a larger pool of talent to draw on, or put another way, that they will have to recognize fewer limiting factors.

This point must not be underestimated in considering a President's capacity to create a proper role for the Cabinet. Despite the constant habit of recent Presidents to ignore department heads and to transfer decisionmaking to their White House staffs, there have been enough examples of strong Cabinet officers during this period of strong White House control to suggest firmly that an appropriate system is possible if the right people are put in the Cabinet. Certainly this was true in the Kennedy administration in the cases of the Justice, Defense, and Labor Departments—at Justice because of the President's implicit faith in his brother; at Defense because of Robert McNamara's self-confident, articulate, and assertive posture as a manager; and at Labor because the President's high regard for Arthur Goldberg was combined with his relatively low interest in the work of the department. During the Nixon administration, when White House control was the most centralized, such Cabinet officers as George Shultz and John Connally still were able to run their departments with the enthusiastic approval of the President. Even Joseph Califano, a leading advocate of a dominant White House government, agrees that "strong men will run their departments" and that "the question of more or less independence [for department heads] is going to depend on the strength of the people involved and their relationship with the President."[4]

The right people in the Cabinet do make a difference and can draw responsibility to the departments. Moreover, perhaps ironically, Congress has given Cabinet Secretaries more reorganization authority than it has given the President.

The experience of Richard Nixon in choosing his first Cabinet illustrates some problems that confront all nonincumbent Presidents-elect. In theory, new Presidents have at least ten weeks before inauguration to complete the selection of the Cabinet. In practice, they wish to move more quickly so as to give the designated Cabinet members a chance

4. Joseph A. Califano, Jr., "The White House Staff: How Many Speak for the President?" in Charles Roberts, ed., *Has the President Too Much Power?* (Harper's Magazine Press, 1975), p. 159.

to wind up their current duties and to have time to pick subordinates and learn some of the details of their new positions before taking office. Nixon was elected on November 12 and announced the Cabinet on December 11; Eisenhower completed picking his Cabinet by December 1; Kennedy by December 17.

Nixon made a useful change in the technique of Cabinet selection when he withheld all names until the full slate was completed. While this forfeits some learning time for Cabinet members, there are offsetting advantages for Presidents. Putting together the Cabinet is a complicated crossword puzzle, the choices intersect as do the "downs" and "acrosses." The process is made more difficult when a prospective appointee is unavailable or when Presidents wish to switch persons from one slot to another. Seriatim selection can become like filling the blanks in ink. Presidents-elect unnecessarily narrow their options if they make announcements before all Cabinet members have been picked. The rush to select the Cabinet, often a psychological need for a new President, must be tempered with an understanding that these appointees will both shape and mortgage the future of his administration.

Often a President's second-round Cabinet choices are of higher caliber. This was true of Truman and in a majority of cases under Roosevelt. Some of the second Cabinet come from within the administration where they have proved themselves to the President. Promotions generally are made from the ranks of Under Secretaries, occasionally from the White House staff.

It is a stark fact of political life that those who seek the presidency are consumed by the demands of campaigning. They will not usually assign valuable staff members to think about the post-election needs of policy, organization, and personnel. To do so, they may feel, would make it look as though they were taking the voters for granted. Moreover, in the course of running for office they are seldom involved with the sorts of people who make superior Cabinet members. Past Presidents have not had to start from ground zero on questions of policy and organization. The Office of Management and Budget keeps track of the candidates' policy commitments, and reports are prepared by candidate-appointed task forces. Eisenhower in 1952 commissioned a transition study from a management consulting firm; in 1960 the Brookings Institution did a study with the cooperation of both Kennedy and Nixon. But doing pre-election work on personnel selection is far more difficult, both because it is likely to have a divisive effect on the campaign staff, encouraging jockeying for position, and because personnel selection depends so heavily on the personal chemistry between appointer and appointee so that even the most preliminary work can only be done by people who have very close ties to the candidate. Yet preparation for the presidency must include more serious attention to the personnel needs of an administration. Awareness of this problem would be a first step toward a more rational system.

Time pressures often force Presidents-elect to turn to old friends and total strangers for their Cabinets. Whether they are better served by friends or strangers is an interesting question. Nixon's strangers proved a mixed blessing; his friends proved even less useful. Of the strangers, George Shultz (Labor) worked out well and was subsequently reassigned to two more important Cabinet-level posts (OMB, Treasury), while David Kennedy (Treasury) and Clifford Hardin (Agriculture) were disappointments and did not survive the first term in the Cabinet. Nixon's three closest friends in the Cabinet were Attorney General John Mitchell, HEW Secretary Robert Finch, and Secretary of State William Rogers. Mitchell, as shown in the Watergate case, probably made decisions or kept knowledge of decisions from Nixon that should have been made by or made known to the President. Finch felt constrained from pressing for certain actions because of his closeness to Nixon—a sort of bend-over-backwards attempt to avoid exploiting an old friendship. And Rogers was often shunted aside, which Nixon could do without fearing the usual threats of resignation and leaks or the usual pressures of having to give each Cabinet member some real or symbolic victories. These were not questions of cronyism—of appointing unqualified persons strictly on the basis of personal relations. Rather, the choosing of old friends suggests certain potential dangers of misplaced loyalty, which in different cases can work to either restrain or aggrandize the appropriate behavior of a Cabinet officer.

"Representativeness," of course, is not irrelevant in making Cabinet appointments in that it can provide powerful symbols of presidential intent to reach out to all segments of society. Presidents may decide that the best interests of the nation are served by picking public executives from certain minority groups, as when for the first time Roosevelt chose a woman and Johnson chose a black. It is to be hoped, however, that the same criteria of competence will apply. "Economic representativeness"—choosing businessmen, union leaders, and farmers respectively to head the Departments of Commerce, Labor, and Agriculture—on the other hand, underscores the "special pleader" nature of those agencies.

In the past, Presidents have picked members of their political party or those with compatible views unless there were very good reasons to do otherwise. Roosevelt brought two Republicans into his Cabinet as a sign of World War II bipartisanship. Kennedy turned to a Republican for the Treasury portfolio to allay Wall Street uneasiness. The Democrats, as the majority party, have a greater choice of elected officials—national, state, and local—to draw on for their administrations. Business executives are more apt to turn up in Republican administrations. But in a system of only two major parties, there are no serious limitations on available talent.

The personnel efforts of Presidents will continue to reflect the American establishment, regardless of party. Presidents pick from among those who have been successful in some pursuit. High federal office is an inappropriate place for on-the-job training. This usually means that those with wealth have certain advantages: the ability to buy a good education, the leisure to concern themselves with public affairs, and helpful contacts. Wealth, however, does not buy political appointment, except for certain ambassadorial positions. It does—depending on how it is acquired and how it is used—become part of the matrix in which success is measured.

Paradoxically, perhaps, members of the establishment are more likely to be called on for public service in Democratic administrations, despite the party's greater appeal to the less advantaged. The Truman administration, for example, relied heavily on such Cabinet officers as Dean Acheson, James Forrestal, Robert Lovett, and Averell Harriman. This elite was not merely correlated with wealth but more importantly with long-held wealth, social standing, and identification with certain institutions. Eisenhower and Nixon turned more frequently to self-made men and representatives of those newer centers of wealth that are away from the East Coast.

Choosing the successful or even the rich need not significantly narrow the range of ideology available to a President—at least within the centrist limits that are acceptable to the nation at large. The editor of the *National Review* and the publisher of the *New York Review of Books* are both listed in the *Social Register*, which is not a recommendation but merely some indication of the range of beliefs within our class structure.

Presidents should carefully assess the ideological commitments that a potential nominee will bring to government. The single-mindedness of the ideologue is often the best guarantee of getting something accomplished. But for Presidents, this also can be akin to grabbing the tail of a tiger with glue on their hands. It is doubtful that Nixon understood the journey he would be undertaking when he appointed Daniel P. Moynihan as his urban affairs adviser or that Eisenhower recognized the policy implications of making Ezra Taft Benson his Secretary of Agriculture. In choosing one adviser, of course, Presidents always have the option of also appointing a competing adviser.

Presidents should consider how much policy diversity they wish in their Cabinets. This they rarely do. Eisenhower was an exception. He deliberately sought like-minded department heads save for his Secretary of Labor, who resigned after nine months. While there is always the possibility that Cabinet members of sharply different views will be unable to work together, a strong countertendency soon begins to operate, closing the gap between administration officials as adversity and outside pressures create an atmosphere of "us against them." Bill Moyers and Henry Graff have both noted how this affected Johnson's advisers during the Vietnam period.[5] Other than the competition for scarce resources, serious clashes in past Cabinets have resulted more from personality factors than from policy disagreements.

The Cabinet system, which has no constitutional limitations on who can serve, permits unusual opportunity to attract superior people to government service and to broaden the "representative" base of an administration. While Presidents have often appointed Cabinet officers with prominent records in elective politics (and such backgrounds can contribute to their usefulness), a unique aspect of the presidential system that distinguishes it from a parliamentary form of government is its ability to draw people into public service who have not run for office. Whereas parliamentary Prime Ministers must usually, by custom, pick their Cabinets from among those members of their party in the legislature, American Presidents are without such restraints. Thus the various proposals to move in the direction of a parliamentary cabinet would severely limit the supply of potential department heads.[6] This

5. See Bill Moyers, "The White House vs. the Cabinet," *Washington Monthly*, February 1969, p. 3; and Henry F. Graff, *The Tuesday Cabinet* (Prentice-Hall, 1970), p. 6.

6. In *The President: Office and Powers, 1787–1957* (New York University Press,

strength of the presidency should be exploited. A system that does not rely on previous election as a condition for Cabinet service has special possibilities for reaching out to people of diverse achievement.

A President on assuming office is usually prepared to delegate to and hold responsible his Cabinet officers. What often happens, however, is that he holds them responsible for functions over which they may have little control or gives them assignments that prove to be impossible to perform under congressional statute or civil service regulation. A proper understanding of these constraints would indicate to Presidents that sometimes a Cabinet member's best or only available strategy is to make incremental change while continuing to push Congress and the permanent government in the desired direction. The popular notion of Cabinet officers as "the natural enemies of the President"—a quotation from Charles Dawes[7]—rarely reflects the true situation, which is that generally Cabinet officers are less able than willing to follow their President's dictates.

Frustrated Presidents quickly assume that they have picked a weak Cabinet officer or that the Cabinet officer has become a turncoat or a captive of the bureaucracy, Congress, or the special interests. Sometimes, of course, the wrong people are picked, in which case Presidents should promptly correct their errors and fire the low-performance or offending department heads. Roosevelt compounded confusion by dealing directly with an Assistant Secretary rather than removing the Secretary of War. Nixon created additional problems for himself by allowing the Secretary of the Interior to remain in office after he had lost the President's confidence. Johnson, in retrospect, believed that retaining Kennedy's Cabinet had been a lingering mistake. Only Truman and Ford of the modern Presidents have moved expeditiously when they felt they needed to make changes.

McGeorge Bundy, after serving in the Kennedy and Johnson White House, became a forceful proponent of strengthening the control of Cabinet officers as the only means of providing an effective presidential presence within the executive branch. He argued that to do this Presi-

---

1957), p. 297, Edward S. Corwin proposed "that the President should construct his Cabinet from a joint Legislative Council to be created by the two houses of Congress and to contain its leading members." Also see Robert M. Hutchins and Harvey Wheeler, "The Constitution Under Strain," *The Center Magazine*, March-April 1974, pp. 47–48.

7. Quoted in Harold Seidman, *Politics, Position, and Power* (Oxford University Press, 1970), p. 72.

dents must give their Cabinet officers the right to select their own second and third level executives.[8] Too often Presidents have inserted people at the Under Secretary and Assistant Secretary echelons who have proved to be incompatible with the department heads. The White House is a bad vantage point from which to choose the sub-Cabinet. Rarely will a President fully understand the needs, responsibilities, and nuances of Assistant Secretary posts. When the White House views appointments at this level primarily as patronage, it is starting from the wrong end—seeking to place people (party workers, campaign contributors, friends of the President) rather than beginning with the qualities necessary for a particular job. If Cabinet officers are to be held accountable by the President, they must have the power to hire and fire in order to ensure, in turn, that their own staffs fill their needs.

One approach to analyzing what qualities are desirable in a department Secretary is to look at the record of past Cabinet members. But how is performance to be measured? All department heads are more successful in managing some aspects of their jobs than others. Few people have an opportunity to observe public officials in all facets of their work. Judgments will depend on vantage points and points-of-view. Reporters may rate Cabinet officers on their openness and the images they project; civil servants may judge them first as administrators. What applies to Cabinet officers should apply equally to other public executives with the exception of those who fill positions of a highly technical nature, such as the Comptroller of the Defense Department.

The mix of qualities will differ somewhat among Cabinet jobs, and Presidents should be aware of these distinctions. The Secretary of HEW must work with many more congressional committees than the Secretary of Defense. The Secretary of State spends more time in negotiations than does the Secretary of the Interior. Some departments resemble integrated enterprises and others look like holding companies; some deal more with ideas, others more with products. Moreover, Presidents should be aware that different talents are often needed at different times in a department. As Joseph Califano pointed out, the primary need in a Secretary of HEW in 1964 and early 1965 "when the bulk of . . . controversial and far-reaching health and education proposals was working its way through Congress" was a person "who knew how to

8. See McGeorge Bundy, *The Strength of Government* (Harvard University Press, 1968), pp. 39–40.

lobby" (Anthony Celebrezze). After the legislation was passed, the need was for a Secretary "who could add a special prestige to service in the department and who could attract . . . brilliant and imaginative talent" (John Gardner).[9]

Certain executive talents are self-evident, whether employment is public or private. Every executive should keep his word, for example, and should have the ability to pick able assistants and draw the most from them. Every executive should be loyal to his superior, the President in this case, while offering his best independent judgment. Yet there are clear distinctions—seldom recognized when Presidents begin to construct their administrations—between the duties of the public executive and those of his counterpart in the private sector:

—Cabinet officers deal extensively with individuals and groups outside their organizations. It is probable that they spend two-thirds of their time on external relations—testifying before Congress, meeting with individual legislators, and preparing for congressional appearances; participating in press conferences, interviews, television performances, and other encounters with the media; maintaining relations with the department's constituencies through speeches, travel, and meetings; and engaging in symbolic and political activities, especially if they have elective backgrounds.

—Cabinet officers work in organizations that are both larger and less homogeneous than those that are likely to be found in the private sector. They must rely on many different kinds of people—whose interests and priorities sometimes clash with those of the Cabinet officers—for information, ideas, and implementation. The federal departments compensate for the lack of close and longstanding personal relationships by placing heavy emphasis on procedure and routine. The safeguard against dishonesty is red tape.

—Cabinet officers hold their positions, even at best, for relatively brief periods. They must learn their jobs faster than in nongovernmental employment, and if they wish to accomplish anything, they must work faster.

—Cabinet officers are employed by the public. The "shareholders" to whom they are ultimately responsible are many, different, and unseen and cannot take their trade elsewhere.

In trying to learn from the backgrounds of past Cabinet officers, I have attempted two "cuts"—one across time, looking collectively at

9. Joseph A. Califano, Jr., *A Presidential Nation* (Norton, 1975), pp. 195–96.

all past Secretaries of Defense; and the other across an administration, looking collectively at all those who served in Nixon's Cabinet during his first term.

Probably no Cabinet office has been as consistently filled by men of high quality as that of Secretary of Defense. Of the twelve men who headed the department from its creation in 1947 until mid-1975, only two or three performed below the level that the public has a right to expect.

Despite the size and complexity of the Defense establishment, it is actually an easier post in which to achieve success than some of the domestic agencies. Except for the last years of the Vietnam war, the nation has been highly united in support of the department's mission, and the appropriate members of Congress to whom the Secretary reports, particularly the committee chairmen, have been supportive to a degree unknown in the relations of the legislature with other departments.

Defense Secretaries also may have been superior on the whole to their counterparts in the domestic departments because Presidents have selected them more carefully and have been less influenced by demographic or political considerations. Although at least two persons have declined to serve as Secretary of Defense, it is probable that Presidents have found it easier to attract talented persons to this post than to some other Cabinet offices.

In 1957, reviewing the qualities most needed in a Defense Secretary, Samuel Huntington stated:

First, he should be a man of experience, possessing some familiarity with the problems with which he will be dealing. . . . Second, the Secretary should be a man of respect, commanding the admiration of informed public opinion. . . . Third, he should be a man of dedication, acting and thinking purely in terms of the needs of the office. . . . Finally, the Secretary must be a man of policy. His greatest needs are breadth, wisdom, insight, and, above all, judgment. He is neither operator, administrator, nor commander. But he is policy maker.[10]

In comparing this scholar's expectations with actual Pentagon leadership during the past four decades, it is possible to conclude that while all Secretaries have not been household names when appointed, their careers generally have inspired public confidence, particularly in the

10. Samuel P. Huntington, *The Soldier and the State* (Harvard University Press, 1957), pp. 453–55.

cases of James V. Forrestal, George C. Marshall, Robert A. Lovett, Elliot L. Richardson, Charles Wilson, Neil McElroy, and Robert McNamara—the last three because they had already run giant corporations. Others, such as Clark Clifford, Melvin Laird, and James Schlesinger, had reputations that created respect in more elite groups. Their record of being familiar with the problems of their department probably surpassed that of other Cabinet officers over the same period. Five of these Defense Secretaries had had prior experience in high-level Pentagon posts; four had had other service that related to national security (Clifford at the White House, Laird in Congress, Richardson at the State Department, and Schlesinger as Director of the Central Intelligence Agency). Only the three corporate presidents—Wilson (General Motors), McElroy (Procter and Gamble) and McNamara (Ford)—lacked extensive Washington experience. Being "a man of dedication" is harder to measure, but none have been seriously accused of being otherwise. Some, however, have not notably been "men of policy."

They came from various professions or occupations: six from the business world, the last being McNamara (1961–68); three from the law; and one each from the military, the legislature, and the academy. Different Presidents have had different preferences. Truman chose all his secretaries with Pentagon backgrounds, Eisenhower chose all businessmen, and Nixon's secretaries did not fit a pattern. Those who probably were least "men of policy" were Eisenhower's businessmen, who tried more than most to function primarily on the administrative level. Indeed Secretary of State Dulles had more to do with defense policy than did the Defense Secretaries. Nixon, who chose no businessmen, made sure that the Under Secretary slot was filled by a corporate executive.

What made the Defense Secretaries unique, and possibly most effective, were the multidimensional aspects of many of their careers. Marshall had been Secretary of State before returning to the Pentagon. Richardson had been Secretary of Health, Education, and Welfare, Under Secretary of State, and Lieutenant Governor and Attorney General of Massachusetts. Schlesinger had already headed two major government agencies, the Atomic Energy Commission and the CIA. Clifford had been the chief domestic adviser on the White House staff under Truman. Forrestal also had served as a White House assistant. Even McNamara, whose career had been almost entirely with the Ford

Motor Company, had spent three years on the Harvard faculty. Judging from the record of Defense Secretaries, "breadth, wisdom, insight" are more apt to be found in Cabinet officers whose careers display diversity, usually gained through job mobility, than in those who have hewed to a steady pattern—even when rising to the top—within a single organization.[11]

In early September 1971, *Wall Street Journal* reporters interviewed scores of people in the Washington community to assess the performance of Nixon's Cabinet. The findings suggest some possibilities in measuring the effectiveness of department heads, as well as the difficulties of constructing a scorecard.[12] (At the time, seven of the President's original eleven department heads were in office.)

—In five instances Cabinet officers were judged by comparing them with their predecessors. Elliot Richardson (HEW) and Rogers Morton (Interior) earned high marks partly because of the records of Robert Finch and Walter Hickel, while James Hodgson (Labor) was found wanting as the successor to George Shultz.

—Most Cabinet officers (nine out of eleven) were rated on their relations with Congress. Those who fared well, such as Melvin Laird and Morton, had served in Congress, or as in the cases of Rogers and Richardson, had had considerable experience in dealing with Congress. Those who did poorly, particularly Mitchell and Hardin, were new to Washington.

—Cabinet officers' relations with those in their departments were used as a criterion for judgment in seven cases. No pattern emerged, but those who were popularly perceived as being close to the President received the highest marks. Commerce Secretary Stans, for instance, was credited with giving "some small boost to [department] morale." The exception was Attorney General Mitchell.

—Relations with outside groups were mentioned seven times. Department heads with political backgrounds generally did best in this

11. For an opposite view, see Douglas Hallett, "The President's Men: Mistaken Identities," *Washington Post*, June 23, 1974. He felt that high mobility is not desirable in public executives. Citing one White House aide who subsequently went to prison for his part in Watergate, Hallett wrote: "He made it as far as the White House precisely because the one special quality he did have was a willingness at each stage to leave behind his past, to abandon his home and friends, and reach for the next brass ring."

12. See Alan L. Otten, "The Scorecard: President's Cabinet Gets Mixed Reviews for Efforts to Date," *Wall Street Journal*, September 8, 1971.

regard. For example, HUD Secretary George Romney was cited for getting "along well with the mayors."

—Ability as an administrator was only mentioned twice, and there was no emphasis on how well a department was run on a day-by-day basis or on the quality of a Cabinet officer's subordinates. Few past Cabinet officers have concentrated on administering their departments, although Presidents have often picked them for this reason. The standard practice is for Cabinet members to leave administrative detail and the running of internal operations largely to their Under Secretaries.

It would thus appear that Washington experience is particularly valuable in working with Congress, political backgrounds are most useful in dealing with constituent groups, and administrative ability is not a quality that rates high in judging Cabinet officers.

In one sense, no matter how successful individual Cabinet officers were, the collective Nixon Cabinet had a dysfunctional turnover rate, indicating errors in selection and in the President's use of his department heads. Public executives must stay in office long enough to learn their jobs and to put their knowledge to work. It took even the experienced Richardson over two years to put together his plan for reorganizing HEW. This suggests that effective Cabinet members should serve at least three years. Some people familiar with the high turnover in the upper reaches of government estimate that one-half to two-thirds of all public executives leave because they initially made only a short-term commitment.[13]

Rotating Cabinet members is a useful means of prolonging the effectiveness of superior executives in a two-term administration. This is a well-developed technique in Great Britain. Nixon made more use of rotation than any of his predecessors, but rarely kept his people in place long enough to make maximum use of their talents. Motion in this case usually created one problem by solving another.

It has sometimes appeared that Presidents have shied away from strong candidates for the Cabinet because of fear of being overshadowed. History indicates—for example, in Lincoln's appointment of William H. Seward, Harrison's of James G. Blaine, or Wilson's of William Jennings Bryan—that such a fear is without foundation. Cabinet members cannot successfully compete with a President, regardless of their past standing.

13. See Marver H. Bernstein, *The Job of the Federal Executive* (Brookings Institution, 1958), p. 162.

While the notion of a Cabinet "type" can be overdrawn, there are qualities that Presidents should look for in public executives. These include:

Persuasiveness. This is necessary in large, hierarchical organizations where leaders have limited control over personnel and where the tug of inertia may be considerable. It involves the ability to engender excitement for programs and proposals, as well as the type of quiet persuasion that is effective with legislators and elite groups.

Personal stability. Cabinet jobs involve disruption of family life, a great amount of traveling, and many flattering perquisites. This calls for a sturdy internal gyroscope, stamina, and the ability to work under pressure. Having a sense of humor helps, although some have survived without the ability to laugh at themselves.

Broad-gauged intelligence. Cabinet officers need not be intellectuals, but they should have the ability to conceptualize, to see the policy implications and consequences of their actions. They will have to keep many balls in the air and move easily from subject to subject. They deal mainly with crisis and policy change—always quickly. Being a quick study, able to absorb masses of data in short periods, is highly useful.

Flexibility. Although they are extensions of the President, Cabinet officers also are answerable in different ways and at different times to Congress, the bureaucracy, the media, constituent groups, and the public. Thus they may often have to change course. They must do so without losing sight of the President's ultimate goals. They must know what is an advantageous compromise. There are times, however, when tenacity, as in the case of Harold Ickes, can be an advantage.

A sense of duty. Cabinet officers cannot forget that they are engaged in a public calling. Yet unlike the President and members of Congress, they are not elected. This means, paradoxically, that they must have an even sharper sense of responsibility than an elected official—for they are public officials who are not directly answerable to the public.

A thick skin. Cabinet officers should be lightning rods for public unhappiness and, if they are doing their jobs properly, they will deflect from the President as much criticism as possible.

Patience and impatience. Cabinet officers deal with endless procedures, repeated congressional hearings, and careful negotiating, both within government and between government and outside parties—all of which calls for considerable equanimity. Yet at the same time they must prod their subordinates to do better and must use their impatience with the status quo as a constructive tool of management.

Even a more complete distillation of the qualities necessary for high Cabinet performance would not assure that qualified individuals could be easily located. The United States has neither a vocational school for Cabinet training nor a shadow Cabinet. Perhaps the closest approach to the latter was party chairman Paul Butler's Democratic Advisory Council in the 1950s. It is a constructive enterprise in a democratic society to have individuals who belong to the party that is out of power assigned to tracking the work of the departments. Undoubtedly this can contribute to creating considerable talent with substantive policy familiarity. Yet this is just one piece of the Cabinet job description. Richard Fenno has pointed out: "As requisites to successful departmental administration, the two most important personal qualifications would seem to be administrative experience in a political environment and some acquaintance with the substantive policy problems of the department involved."[14] The problem, as Marver Bernstein correctly states it, is that "we have developed no theory that explains how professionalized administration is made compatible with the politics of democracy. An agency head is expected to be both political executive and administrative manager; yet the two capacities seldom go together well."[15]

Social scientists have provided little guidance. Recent Presidents sometimes have turned to personnel management consultants whose experiences have been outside the political environment. Such efforts often produce nonpolitical managers. Generally, however, Presidents fall back on traditional Old Boy Networks, which emphasize political experience. Such efforts often produce political nonmanagers.

One technique of discovery would be to review the sources of supply. What follows, therefore, is an attempt to examine skills required in certain occupational categories that can be considered relevant to a political administrative environment as well. No claim is made to special insights into the working worlds of businessmen, lawyers, union officials, and so forth, and some of the generalizations may be based on

14. Richard F. Fenno, Jr., *The President's Cabinet* (Harvard University Press, 1959), p. 224.
15. Marver H. Bernstein, "The Presidency and Management Improvement," *Law and Contemporary Problems*, vol. 35 (Summer 1970), pp. 517–18.

popular misconceptions or even misinformation, but they will serve a purpose if they generate more precise thinking and underscore the need for more systematic study. Virtually every occupation or profession has produced outstanding public executives at some time. Here, consideration of tendencies or probabilities is based on the belief that pools of talent for the Cabinet may be deeper in some places than in others.

The law. Noting the substantial number of his partners who had joined the Kennedy administration, Adlai Stevenson is reported to have said, "I regret that I have but one law firm to give to my country."[16] There were no lawyers in Sir Thomas More's *Utopia*, but American public life has always been overpopulated with them, and one can be sure that this condition will continue. There are, of course, reasons for this other than tradition. These have to do with economics (public service is a good way for a lawyer to get ahead), sociology (successful lawyers come from the social class most susceptible to public life), training (the tools of thought, method, and facts that are taught in law schools can be most useful in public life), the nature of public policy (it has a great deal to do with the law), the working conditions of the profession (it provides flexibility and contacts), a sense of service (lawyers probably contribute more time to civic enterprises than other professionals), and supply (there are more lawyers per capita in the United States than in other countries).[17]

Lawyers are generally involved in three sorts of activities—litigating, counseling, and negotiating. As professional counselors, it is hardly surprising that they are called on for advice by Presidents. As professional negotiators, it is equally unexceptional that they are often appointed Secretary of State. The Attorney General, by definition the government's chief law officer, is always a lawyer. But since lawyers also have served in recent administrations as the heads of every department, they are obviously thought to have other qualities that make them superior Cabinet members. It cannot be their managerial skills, although many lawyers have successfully moved into business enterprises. The typical practicing lawyer works on his own or in a firm whose personnel rarely exceeds 150, and the management techniques of even

16. Quoted in Erwin O. Smigel, *The Wall Street Lawyer* (Indiana University Press, 1969), p. 10.

17. See Donald R. Matthews, *U.S. Senators and Their World* (Vintage, 1960), pp. 33–35, for an interesting review of why so many lawyers are in public life.

major law offices are rudimentary by corporate and government standards. Probably what makes a lawyer most valuable as a public executive is his ability to deal in complexities and ambiguities, as well as his habit of moving quickly from subject to subject since his schedule is determined by an array of clients.

Given the great diversity within the legal profession, there are at least three things that provide clues to a lawyer's potential as a public executive: the size of his firm, his standing in his firm, and the nature of his practice.

Erwin Smigel suggested that the smaller the law firm, the more likely it is to deal with people; the larger the firm, the more likely it is to deal with policy, power, and institutions. Lawyers in solo practice are most likely to see themselves as defenders of the poor and needy. Lawyers in small firms are apt to be more active in local political life, and lawyers in larger firms usually are more active in professional associations. The larger the firm, the greater the stress on teamwork and conformity.[18]

All lawyers in large firms, however, are not equal nor do they spend their time in similar activities. Smigel compared the career pattern of a lawyer in a large firm to an hourglass.

The practice of the beginning lawyer is broad because he works on a great many matters in a wide variety of fields. If he stays with the firm he becomes more and more specialized, although he now has increasing opportunity to see more of the large picture. If he is made a partner, he begins to broaden again. This time the broadening does not involve research on a number of problems, but advising about these problems. Both advising and responsibility increase as the lawyer grows into a senior partnership.[19]

The younger the lawyer, the more he deals with details; the more senior the lawyer, the more he deals with policy implications. Yet Dean Acheson, who thought highly of his profession's ability to produce outstanding public executives, warned: "Lawyers, who are habituated to having their main choices made for them by the necessities of their clients, are often at a loss, when, as in government, for instance, they have wide latitude in a choice of policy."[20]

There are differences in the types of law practice. For example,

18. See Smigel, *The Wall Street Lawyer*, pp. 25, 173, 201, 322.
19. Ibid., p. 160.
20. Dean Acheson, *Fragments of My Fleece* (Norton, 1971), p. 129.

Martin Mayer quoted one lawyer as claiming that "tax law is immutable, inflexible and immoral."[21] It is also extremely complicated. Those who work in real estate and banking law, according to Smigel, have to be especially methodical, prudent, and disciplined. Comparing different sections within a large firm, he wrote, "There probably is more argument and debate in the litigation department than in the corporate section."[22] Trial judges, in Mayer's opinion, combine independence, concentration, patience, decisiveness, and efficiency. "Brilliance is an almost impossible burden for a trial judge," he said.[23]

Even from such scattershot generalizations, it should be evident that close scrutiny of the legal profession, sorting out variables that relate to types of law, size of firms, and seniority, could more sharply focus the search for the qualities necessary in public executives. Assuming the need for generalists of high persuasive ability, for example, Nixon might have concluded that a specialist in municipal bonds would not make an ideal Attorney General. Likewise, it might be concluded that lawyers from smaller firms may have an aptitude for running "people" departments.

Business. When filling Cabinet offices, Presidents often choose businessmen on the basis of their experience in running enterprises of great size. The analogy between a giant corporation and a federal department immediately comes to mind. If a President's objective is to cut back on federal operations, as was the case with Nixon, he is especially likely to seek the managerial skills of the corporate world.

The assumption underlying this choice is that a corporation executive is judged and promoted because of his ability to maximize profits. Yet Robert A. Gordon contended that a corporate executive's prestige is most closely linked to the size of an enterprise and not necessarily to its profitability.[24] This helps explain the corporate urge to expand, even at the expense of profit, and the hesitancy to liquidate unsuccessful operations. It also may explain why some corporate executives, after entering government, have become strong advocates for the growth of their agencies, although they may claim to be ideologically opposed to

21. Martin Mayer, *The Lawyers* (Harper and Row, 1967), p. 405. See also pp. 494, 498.

22. Smigel, *The Wall Street Lawyer*, p. 327.

23. Mayer, *The Lawyers*, p. 498.

24. In this section, I rely heavily on Robert A. Gordon, *Business Leadership in the Large Corporation* (University of California Press, 1961), pp. 306–11, 328, 264, 97.

"big government." When John Ehrlichman accused Cabinet members of "going native"—the implication being that they were "captured" by clever, expansionist bureaucrats and outside interest groups—he may have misread the forces at work. For example, George Romney, who as President of American Motors had been an eloquent opponent of bigness, quickly became a tenacious fighter against moves to cut HUD programs once he became its Secretary. It is less probable that Romney was captured by the bureaucracy than that he was following well-defined corporate practices.

The President who wants programs reduced may have to choose a different sort of executive than the President who wants programs to expand. He will have to look for an executive whose career, such as law or management consulting, has depended less on growth as a measure of success. He also may find that owner-managers are more tied to profit-efficiency motives than are executives employed by large corporations.

A problem with picking public executives from small businesses, usually owned by an individual or a family, is that they are used to operating in a more authoritative fashion, with fewer controls from outsiders—directors or stockholders—than the executives of large corporations are. It is not the size so much as the absolute authority vested in management that makes small business operations less analogous to running a government department.

In making other comparisons between big and small businesses, Gordon believed that the larger the business, the less venturesome its executives might be. The strong desire for security that an executive of a large corporation has would appear to be a liability in the high risk world of the Cabinet officer. On the other hand, Gordon saw large-scale business leadership as concentrating more on long-term strategic considerations, a perspective that could be important to bring to government, where most pressures on a Cabinet officer are in the direction of doing what is feasible in the short run. Gordon also found that more original decisionmaking is delegated in larger firms. Certainly the inability to delegate, if it is more prevalent in the executives of small businesses, would be a serious handicap in Washington.

The pattern of a business career may have an effect on how an executive will perform in public service. At least Averell Harriman thought so. "People have to be given big jobs when they are young, or else their minds become permanently closed," he said. "The men who

work their way step by step to the top in business are no good for anything big in government. They have acquired too many bad habits
along the way."[25] The corporate president who has a legal background
appears to concern himself with those functions of his business that
are most similar to the duties of a Cabinet officer, that is, "matters of
finance, organization, public relations, and relations with government."[26] According to Gordon, he is apt to delegate the responsibility
for operations. Then, too, there may be significant differences between
businesses that are government regulated and those that are not. Presidents of railroads and public utilities are most likely to involve themselves in their companies' public relations. It would be instructive to
know more about differences that might relate to the proportion of a
corporation's sales to government, about producers of consumer items
versus basic industries, about businesses that have a closely related line
of products and those that are broadly diversified, about centralized
and decentralized corporate structure, and about companies of an
international character—all variables that can be factored into assessing
executive potential for high appointive office.

Questions of age and compensation may have a constraining effect
on a President's ability to recruit corporate executives. The greatest
difficulty is in attracting those whose services are most desirable—energetic executives in their middle years who are about to reach the highest echelon and feel that they cannot risk a prolonged absence from
their companies. Also, of course, the pay scale at the top of government
cannot compete with private enterprise at a comparable level. In many
cases, the difference is primarily a matter of compensation deferred
since an executive is usually worth more to a private employer after
having held a position of prominence in government. The attractiveness of government service will fluctuate with the state of the economy;
when times are good, the public sector becomes less competitive. Recruitment, however, generally does not become a problem until late in
an administration. In the beginning, the excitement of a new regime
will create a buyer's market for the President.

Many businessmen, regardless of the size or nature of their enterprise, have common problems in public employment. They are often
uneasy with news media and congressional scrutiny. Controversy that

25. Quoted in Arthur M. Schlesinger, Jr., *A Thousand Days* (Fawcett, 1967),
p. 144.
26. Gordon, *Business Leadership in the Larger Corporation*, p. 264.

impugns their motives or their morality will be quite different from what they are accustomed to. In the words of Robert Stevens, an Army Secretary who was forced to tangle with Senator Joseph McCarthy in the early 1950s, "The security of a family textile business is not good training for an alley fight."[27] They will be frustrated by the pace of government, by its inability to devise quantitative measurements of performance standards, and even by the failure of government to measure the utility and acceptability of its product.[28]

A person in the private sector, whether in business or another calling, can acquire some of the skills necessary for high Cabinet performance in activities outside his principal employment, of course. An executive's record of serious substantive involvement in public policy issues, such as participation in the Committee for Economic Development, as well as election or appointment to positions that make him responsible to various constituent groups (school boards and local legislative bodies) may be more indicative of his potential for a career in Washington than the attainment of some corporate positions may be.

Labor unions. Union leaders represent a largely untapped source of supply for public executives. Few have been given high-level appointments outside the Department of Labor, which, ironically, may not be the best location for their talents. Martin Durkin and Peter Brennan, two union officials appointed by Republican Presidents to serve as Secretary of Labor, were not notable successes. Each was torn between loyalties to the competing objectives of his union and his administration. Moreover, while Nixon felt that the appointment of Brennan would cement labor support, George Meany viewed Brennan as an unneeded layer between himself and the White House. Even Kennedy's appointment of Arthur Goldberg, the respected General Counsel of the AFL-CIO, was initially opposed by the building trades unions. Apparently the top leadership of the union movement would prefer a sympathetic outsider to someone who has taken sides in its internal management.

Two factors suggest that union leaders have the potential to be superior public executives. The first has to do with how they arrived at union leadership; the second with the nature of leadership at the top.

27. Quoted in Bernstein, *The Job of the Federal Executive*, p. 211.

28. Note the frustration of former Under Secretary of Commerce Joseph W. Bartlett in Bartlett and Douglas N. Jones, "Managing a Cabinet Agency: Problems of Performance at Commerce," *Public Administration Review*, vol. 34 (January-February 1974), pp. 62–70.

Almost all labor leaders have come up through the ranks. Their career pattern is a progression of winning successively higher elective offices within their unions. By the time they have reached national leadership, they have become deeply versed in political skills. Presumably they have become highly sensitive to the concerns of their constituents and expert at the compromises necessary to construct a majority.

Once at the top, they have relatively little authority over their member unions. As Derek Bok and John Dunlop pointed out, "The AFL was founded with the explicit understanding that the affiliated unions would retain their authority. Throughout its history, the federation had to rely, with mixed success, on persuasion and conciliation instead of exercising formal powers or sanctions."[29] This accent on persuasion without power corresponds to the running of a federal department.

On the other hand, the national union executive has had limited experience in managing large and complex organizations. As Jack Barbash commented: "Considering the magnitude of membership and finances, the headquarters organization of the national union is not only simple . . . but is also on the modest side."[30] There are exceptions, such as the United Auto Workers, whose technical and administrative departments include community relations, education, international affairs, legislation, legal, research, and others.

A more detailed breakdown of union patterns as they relate to the skills necessary in a public executive would include the differences between craft and mass production unions. Craft unions have generally been led by better-educated men. Some of the mass-production unions have been noted for more creative leadership.

The biggest obstacle to transferring union skills to public administration may be style. The sharp edges of a lifetime in the adversary business of collective bargaining may produce a manner that is too brittle to fit successfully into the more low-key negotiations within the bureaucracy and with the White House and Congress.

Higher education. Although politicians have a certain disdain for eggheads, no job in the private sector comes quite as close to that of running a Cabinet department as does a college presidency. Michael E.

29. Derek C. Bok and John T. Dunlop, *Labor and the American Community* (Simon and Schuster, 1970), p. 52.

30. Jack Barbash, *American Unions: Structure, Government, and Politics* (Random House, 1967), p. 86.

Cohen and James G. March described colleges as "organized anarchies" and running them as exercises in "the ambiguity of power."[31] Indeed, like a Cabinet officer, a college president has more responsibility than he has authority. Both must learn to live with and use power that is not quite there. The corporate executive sees ambiguity as a liability. But the ambiguousness of power can serve the public executive. It can be a reason for not doing something that he does not want to do as well as for doing something that he is not clearly empowered to do. One criterion for the selection of a public executive might be phrased, "What has a candidate accomplished without formal authority?" It is not always a grand accomplishment to do something that one has been given the power to do.

Interestingly, college presidents see their jobs as "political." Moreover, their work patterns closely resemble those of the Cabinet officer: a great deal of travel; long hours; much time spent in meetings; considerable emphasis on the verbal; and perhaps most important, direct responsibility to a large number of constituencies (trustees, faculty, students, administrators, alumni, community, and in the case of public institutions, legislative bodies).

While there are differences between institutions, such as size, wealth, and public-private control, that must be considered in more sophisticated analyses, one factor that often cuts across these distinctions is the "availability" of college presidents. This is because they are usually appointed at a relatively young age. The typical college president is selected when in his mid-forties, and the average age of college presidents is fifty-three. Thus they may have between fifteen and twenty-five years before normal retirement. According to one survey, college presidents list their party affiliations as 41 percent Democratic, 37 percent Republican, and 22 percent "none" or "other."

In recent years, college administrators (presidents or deans) have headed HEW, Agriculture, Treasury, Labor, and Justice. College professors (who were not primarily administrators) have headed State, Defense, and HEW. The professor as Cabinet officer reflects the growing dependence of government on specialized knowledge. In addition, almost all presidential science and economic advisers have been professors, as a growing number of the more influential ambassadors have

31. Unless otherwise noted, data in this section come from Michael D. Cohen and James G. March, *Leadership and Ambiguity: The American College President* (McGraw-Hill, 1974).

been. Yet the work patterns of professors and public executives are quite dissimilar. There are, of course, all manner of academics: research professors and teaching professors, professors of economics and professors of Greek. But in general, professors have extended vacations and flexible work schedules, place heavy emphasis on working alone, have few constituents (especially if tenured), often produce a written product (research), and have modest ceremonial duties. As I. M. Destler has written, "Life in the [nonadministrative] academic world requires, at least for the man who has made his reputation, considerably less attunement to the needs and the feelings of one's colleagues and subordinates than life in most other modern organizations."[32] The academic may bring to government a strong ideological bent. In speaking of the forces that fueled U.S. commitment to Vietnam involvement, James C. Thomson of Harvard mentioned the social scientists in the Kennedy-Johnson administrations "who had developed theories of counter-guerrilla warfare and were eager to see them put to the test."[33]

A related source of Cabinet talent is the philanthropic foundations. Two important department heads (Dean Rusk and John Gardner) were foundation presidents, but less than a dozen foundations have enough professional staff to furnish public executives on a regular basis. Unlike colleges, foundations can hardly be considered to have constituents. What a foundation does have in ample supply is supplicants. The foundation official is in the business of giving out money. He must guard it as if it were his own and use it to achieve maximum leverage. He is also expected to learn to say no with taste and courtesy. Thus there are some obvious parallels with certain government agencies that are primarily involved in making grants.

James Schlesinger was the first Cabinet officer to have come (indirectly, at least) from the world of "think tanks," having served as Director of Strategic Studies at the RAND Corporation. The research-for-hire institutions primarily have been suppliers of public executives in the Defense Department, but as they become increasingly involved in domestic matters it is likely that they will provide Cabinet members in other fields as well.

Other sources. There are other sources of talent available to fill

32. I. M. Destler, *Presidents, Bureaucrats, and Foreign Policy* (Princeton University Press, 1972), p. 145.

33. James C. Thomson, Jr., "How Could Vietnam Happen?" *Atlantic*, April 1968, p. 48. See also Theodore Draper in "No More Vietnams?" ibid., November 1968, pp. 102–04.

Cabinet posts, and they too deserve consideration. Only once in recent years has a President picked a Cabinet officer from local government (Anthony Celebrezze, a Mayor of Cleveland, who was an HEW Secretary under Kennedy); on occasion a President has turned to the civil service (Postmaster General Jesse Donaldson under Truman); and from time to time a President has chosen someone from the media, always a newspaper publisher (Frank Knox under Roosevelt; Oveta Culp Hobby and Fred Seaton under Eisenhower). George Marshall proved that a "political general" could be an outstanding Cabinet officer, although Presidents turn to the military only in rare instances. A fertile field that has been tapped recently is the House of Representatives (Stewart Udall, Melvin Laird, Rogers Morton, and Donald Rumsfeld). Those with an elective background are usually strong on skills that involve persuasion, sometimes less strong on the administrative side.

The multiple skills necessary for high Cabinet performance may suggest that those who have successfully mastered several occupations— law and business, university administration and law, business and university administration, politics and another pursuit—would be the best prospects for service as a public executive.

IF, AS I HAVE ASSUMED in this and the preceding chapter, it is possible for a President to trim the size of the White House staff, to identify persons of Cabinet quality, to attract them to government service, and to give them the backing necessary to make them an effective extension of the presidential presence within the executive branch, there still remains the related matter of whether it is also possible to assure the collective functioning of the Cabinet as a President's chief advisory system. This I discuss in the final chapter.

☆ ☆ ☆ ☆ ☆ ☆ ☆ ☆ ☆ ☆ ☆ ☆ ☆

CHAPTER ELEVEN

The Cabinet: Advisory Functions

☆ ☆ ☆ ☆ ☆ ☆ ☆ ☆ ☆ ☆ ☆ ☆ ☆

THERE IS LITTLE in American history to create a sense of optimism about the Cabinet becoming a viable collective body that Presidents can rely on as the prime supplier of advice. The Constitution does not require a Cabinet, and no laws can force Presidents to make use of one. The Cabinet served a purpose for Eisenhower, none at all for Kennedy, and something in between for Truman, who used it often at first and seldom at the end. It is difficult—some would say impossible—to get the department heads to advise Presidents beyond the jurisdictions of their agencies. They see themselves in competition for the same resources and do not take kindly to second-guessing by their Cabinet colleagues. If left to their own devices, they will present only the most trivial matters for peer review, saving questions of real substance for private meetings in the Oval Office. In the words of Jesse Jones, Roosevelt's Commerce Secretary: "My principal reason for not having a great deal to say at Cabinet meetings was that there was no one at the table who could be of help to me except the President, and when I needed to consult him, I did not choose a Cabinet meeting to do so."[1]

From the perspective of Presidents, Cabinet meetings soon appear as a platform for the least able. Yet these meetings can play a highly useful role in giving a President's chief political officers a continuing sense of the overall direction of the administration and in providing an opportunity for a President to set the tone of government. At a minimum, they can serve as briefing and pep rally. If Presidents cannot inform and enthuse their Cabinets, what success can they expect

1. Quoted in Robert J. Sickels, *Presidential Transactions* (Prentice-Hall, 1974), p. 31.

to have with the bureaucracy, Congress, or the electorate? Unfortunately, Presidents learn only slowly the degree to which they must proselytize their own appointees, and underestimating this need, they are apt to underestimate the importance of Cabinet meetings. The result, as Daniel Patrick Moynihan once noted, is that presidential initiatives are "rarely followed up with a sustained, reasoned, reliable second and third order of advocacy."[2]

But more important, if future Presidents would appoint superior persons to the Cabinet, they would find that no comparable body of advisers could bring as valuable insights to the formulation of policy. Outsiders can be of only tangential value in the telescoped world of government problem-solving. White House staffs, as a rule, are personal services assistants who are often sucked into matters of governance, are too involved in the needs of the Presidents to provide disinterested judgment, and are often too young to have acquired much useful experience or wisdom. Cabinet officers, on the other hand, collectively define what is doable in the executive branch, have the major responsibility for the implementation of presidential policy, provide a secondary level of advocacy that does not exist on the White House staff, and have power bases of their own to commit to the President's battles.

Indeed it is the need to narrow the separation of advice from implementation that is the most essential reason for an invigorated Cabinet system. Presidents have no difficulty obtaining advice. They need only ask. But those around Presidents who can implement administration policies are extremely few in number. Government policies can be implemented only by government officials. The history of the modern presidency indicates that the White House staff is not an effective implementer. This leaves the Cabinet. Yet a President is bound to receive less enthusiastic support from Cabinet implementers if they are left out of the decisionmaking and are expected to enforce policies that have been formulated behind their backs. In this case, implementation rests on unquestioning loyalty or coercion, hardly ingredients designed to ensure the success of presidential administrations.

The argument against the utility of the Cabinet as a collective body usually boils down to, "What does the Secretary of Labor have to con-

2. Daniel Patrick Moynihan, "The Middle of the Journey," speech delivered at the White House, December 21, 1970, in Waldo W. Braden, ed., *Representative American Speeches: 1970–1971* (Wilson, 1971), p. 35.

tribute to a discussion of international monetary reform?" A partial response is that the affairs of government are becoming increasingly interrelated and inseparable. At present, for example, more than twenty agencies and departments have some jurisdiction over energy policy. An even more satisfactory response is that if a Secretary of Labor has wisdom, then he has something important to contribute. What can make his advice of special value is its detachment. The problem is rather that he may adopt an attitude of refraining from "sticking his nose in other people's business" so as to keep other people out of his business. The challenge is how to turn a Cabinet officer into a participant on matters beyond his immediate purview.

This suggests that the effort, no matter how difficult, deserves to be made to remove roadblocks to the effectiveness of the collective Cabinet—a statement that should not be interpreted as an argument for a Cabinet system of the British type. The President is not the leader of equals in an administration. He is the only one at the table who has been elected. Ultimately, decisions must be his.

The purpose of this section is to point the way to a more satisfactory system of advising Presidents. What follows in these concluding pages is a series of stratagems available to Presidents to reach this goal. If they were adopted, the functions of the White House staff would again be to assist Presidents in their personal needs and to service the Cabinet as the prime vehicle of a presidential presence throughout the executive branch.

1. *The makeup of the Cabinet must be reconstituted to reflect the President's need for advice.*

The Cabinet by tradition has been defined as consisting of the heads of those federal agencies that are called departments. A problem, of course, is that all departments are not equal and that some agencies that are not departments are more important than other agencies that are.

The first step in working toward a useful Cabinet collectivity is to adjust the membership to fit more accurately the power base and responsibilities of the executive branch. When Presidents look around the Cabinet table they must see those who have been given the principal assignments for assisting them in the nine basic presidential functions outlined earlier.

One of these functions is the preparation of the annual budget.

Thus the Director of the Office of Management and Budget should be a member of the President's Cabinet.

Another responsibility is the formulation of a legislative program. Thus the leaders of the President's party in the Senate and the House of Representatives should be members of the Cabinet. The addition of these legislators also might have the salutary effect of easing tensions between the two branches. The Cabinet, however, must remain a presidential advisory system, not a joint undertaking of the executive and legislative arms of government. This proposal differs from those made by Edward Corwin and Thomas Finletter in that the Cabinet would include only a very small minority of legislators and no congressional representatives of the opposition party.[3]

A third presidential responsibility is for maintaining the health of the economy, which suggests a Cabinet seat for the Chairman of the Council of Economic Advisers. In effect this would put him on a par with the Secretary of the Treasury, a move that could create friction— but perhaps of the creative variety, which certainly might make for more interesting Cabinet meetings.

In situations of extreme urgency, such as the energy crisis, the government official with primary responsibility should be added to the Cabinet. Having the Secretary of the Interior in the Cabinet, but not the head of the Federal Energy Administration, violates the rule that the body must reflect the areas of major presidential concern. If Presidents and Congress continue to create new agencies to deal with the most pressing domestic problems, as has been their habit since the depression, it becomes imperative for the Cabinet to stay in phase through a process of constant adjustment. Bestowing Cabinet status, however, must be done sparingly and must be rescinded when circumstances warrant.

The President also, as in Great Britain, should be able to nominate several ministers without portfolio. They might be elder statesmen, chosen for the detached wisdom they could bring to the consideration of government affairs.[4] The addition of elder statesmen would build a

3. See Edward S. Corwin, *The President: Office and Powers, 1787–1957* (New York University Press, 1957), p. 297; and Thomas K. Finletter, *Can Representative Government Do the Job?* (Reynal and Hitchcock, 1945), pp. 88–89.

4. Eisenhower proposed the addition of "several distinguished elder statesmen" to the National Security Council during the 1952 campaign but took no action after his election. (See Laurin L. Henry, *Presidential Transitions* [Brookings Institution,

historical memory into the system, given the high probability that many department heads will be new to government. Choosing some members solely on the basis of acquired wisdom also would upgrade the Cabinet, a form of prestige-by-association, and could help promote public trust in government by legitimizing presidential decisions. Yet including persons without functional responsibility would run counter to the natural impatience of Presidents and their penchant for the immediately practicable. Ultimately, such an action must depend on the Presidents' respect for this sort of advice, on their recognition that it may otherwise be absent in government, and as a matter of self-interest, on their belief that it may prevent them from making crippling mistakes. The temptation to give assorted operational duties to these people—as such duties are given to the Vice President—should be kept under control. Their value would be as presidential advisers who, because they have been taken into government, would not have to operate under the handicaps that limit the usefulness of outsiders.

Congress should permit all designated Cabinet members to be paid at the rate of department secretaries, which is not now the case. Other ways should be sought to equalize status among Cabinet members. One minor example might be to drop protocol in the assignment of seats around the Cabinet table with members simply sitting in any available chair.

2. *The size of the Cabinet must be strictly limited.*

This is not inconsistent with the previous suggestions for additions to the Cabinet. The question of size and composition is only loosely related, for over the years Presidents have been adding second-class Cabinet members (nondepartment heads, paid at a lower rate) for a variety of not very good reasons.

Starting with Eisenhower, for instance, the chief U.S. Representative to the United Nations has been given Cabinet rank. Otherwise, he resides well below the Secretary of State in the foreign policy hierarchy. In this case, Cabinet rank is meant to symbolize the country's willingness to view the UN as important to its interests. But particularly in appointing Henry Cabot Lodge and Adlai Stevenson, the bestowing of

1960], p. 616.) Benjamin V. Cohen recommended the creation of "a small Executive Council [to advise the President] of not less than five or more than eight persons of highest public standing." ("Presidential Responsibility and American Democracy," Royer Lectures, University of California at Berkeley, May 23, 1974; processed.)

Cabinet rank was meant to "correct" the embarrassing fact that their past achievements exceeded their present position. Likewise, it solved other problems for Presidents Eisenhower and Kennedy. Lodge was suitably rewarded for his early support of Eisenhower's presidential candidacy; Kennedy passed over Stevenson for Secretary of State without appreciable loss of face by either party.

More recently, Nixon established a Cabinet-level post on the White House staff, the first formal recognition that White House assistants could be at least as important as department heads. His initial appointee was the distinguished economist Arthur Burns. Ultimately, however, Nixon succumbed to the temptation of proliferating such honorific Cabinet positions. In this way he was able to remove Robert Finch from the position of HEW Secretary by the subterfuge of making him a presidential counselor and was able to elevate Anne Armstrong, a White House assistant with modest duties, in lieu of appointing a woman to a "real" Cabinet post.

Presidents should not use Cabinet membership to solve tricky political and personnel problems, although this is difficult advice to practice. Its best chance of achievement probably depends on Congress strictly limiting the number of persons who can hold Cabinet rank and requiring Senate confirmation of all appointees, as is now the case with department secretaries.

The reorganization of the executive branch along the functional lines proposed by commissions under two administrations would reduce the number of department heads and ensure that representatives of anachronistic agencies were not included in the Cabinet.

The swelling of the Cabinet has the effect of making it an even less viable body for collective advice-giving. Robert Cutler correctly noted the correlation between size and frank discussion. At some point a group is transformed into a town meeting. "Once this invisible line is passed, people do not debate; they remain silent or talk for the record."[5]

Recent Cabinet meetings have resembled a Geneva disarmament conference, with each department-nation represented by a delegation, in addition to a myriad of White House aides. One commonsensical suggestion would be to remove all the chairs from around the perimeter of the Cabinet Room. No staff—neither departmental nor White House

5. Robert Cutler, *No Time for Rest* (Little, Brown, 1966), p. 298.

—should be in attendance, except for the Cabinet Secretary, who would take notes and later brief others on relevant parts of the discussion.

The British system again suggests possibilities for more intimate conduct of meetings: "If a Minister is absent through illness or travel abroad his views are left out of account. . . . An absent Minister may be represented by a junior Minister; but he would be entitled to speak only on specific departmental matters."[6]

3. *Cabinet meetings should be held frequently on a regular schedule.*

The time of department heads must be engaged significantly in the work of the Cabinet. Only in this way will Cabinet members be encouraged to take on a presidential perspective, to see their purpose and role beyond the confines of their departments, and to become more willing to offer advice that does not relate directly to their specialized jurisdictions. This will not happen if, as under the present system, they spend only 5 percent or so of their time on Cabinet matters.

Increasing the frequency and the regularity of Cabinet meetings can work to the advantage of Presidents as a way of countering the forces that move department heads away from them, and to the advantage of department heads, who must be assured of greater presidential attention.

One hypothetical schedule of Cabinet meetings might include:

—Weekly meetings (perhaps every Thursday) to consider events anticipated for the next week. Cabinet members, for example, could report on actions scheduled in Congress that affect their departments, outlining proposed positions to be taken, prospects, and tactics; and review upcoming speeches or press conferences, indicating points they wish to make or questions they expect.

—Biweekly meetings on policy formulation devoted primarily to discussing proposals made in Cabinet subcommittee reports and also used for reviews of government programs and informational items.

—Quarterly meetings on political matters, with presentations from the national chairman, House and Senate campaign committee chairmen, and representatives of the party's Governors and Mayors.

—Semiannual meetings with outsiders. Some of these could be planned as mind-stretching exercises, presentations that have practical application or that identify long-range concerns. Other meetings might be with major special-interest group leaders.

6. Patrick Gordon Walker, *The Cabinet* (Basic Books, 1970), p. 102.

—An annual meeting on the state of the nation with the leading public opinion survey people and others who would report on and interpret polling data and trends.

Such a schedule, of course, would have to change over time to reflect the normal life cycle of an administration. Policy formulation, for example, is of prime importance during the first year; then attention turns to the enactment of legislation and later to the oversight of programs.

4. *An effective Cabinet requires a skillful secretariat in the White House.*

Even adjusting membership to suit the Presidents' needs, limiting membership to a manageable number, and scheduling frequent meetings will not ensure the success of the Cabinet. There must be a staff at work to counter the inherent lethargy of committees, to subtly correct imbalances between Cabinet members, and to prod participants into airing matters that they would prefer to keep off the agenda.

A skillful Cabinet secretariat should know how to keep meetings interesting. This is particularly important when the ultimate utility of the Cabinet as a presidential advice system depends on keeping Presidents engaged in the deliberations. While boredom is a characteristic that is seldom mentioned in discussions of the presidency, it is a key factor in determining who gets to see Presidents and how they choose to receive information. The Cabinet secretariat must create agendas, including the juxtapositioning of items that will guarantee presidential attendance. It must understand the need for selectivity, ensuring that meetings are not dominated by trivia, yet sometimes it may choose to bring up minor problems that involve major principles or conflicts between departments. It must know the proper length for a meeting. It must help speakers make their presentations cogently and succinctly. It must brief Presidents on angles that may be kept from view. It must be able to insist that certain matters are placed on the agenda. It must strictly enforce the injunction on excess staff at meetings. It must keep the rest of government informed on decisions taken. It must constantly remind Cabinet officers of their obligations to implement presidential directives. It must schedule follow-up reports at reasonable intervals.

It must do all this at all times without playing favorites, with procedures that are considered fair by all parties, and with deference to the

Cabinet members. The secretariat would consist of staff. It should not be in the business of advising Presidents. It must be firm when carrying out presidential wishes, but it should know its place.

5. *Cabinet members should be the primary spokesmen for the administration.*

In recent years, more and more first-line advocacy and defense of policy has come from presidential Press Secretaries and other White House officials. The White House press office now routinely makes announcements that have only the slightest bearing on the personal activities of Presidents. The release of information relating to the economy is an important case in point. The Nixon White House became the source of monthly data that once emanated from the Departments of Labor, Commerce, and Treasury.

From the vantage point of Presidents, making their Cabinet officers the principal spokesmen for administration policy builds useful buffers into the system. No longer need Presidents be out front on all matters of government concern. At the same time, promoting the visibility of Cabinet members is another way of increasing their status and their control over their departments.

6. *The Cabinet must become the focal point of the White House machinery.*

If the Cabinet is to be the President's main provider of advice, the White House must be reorganized to reflect this reality. This means the adoption of a substantially different staff hierarchy and a substantially different pattern of how information flows to the President.

The person who heads the Cabinet secretariat should be the highest ranking member of the White House staff. He would be administratively responsible for the machinery that links the President to his chief operating officers and his chief policy advisers. Placing the Cabinet Secretary closest to the President in the organization of the White House is meant to be more than symbolic, although the symbolism is not insignificant in attempting to move from a position of White House staff dominance to one of collegial government.

The Cabinet Secretary, however, should not be a member of the Cabinet. This is a staff job, without line authority. He should not direct department officials. Cabinet members should have direct access to the President and should not have to become supplicants to a member of the White House staff.

It might even be useful to select a Cabinet Secretary from the ranks of the permanent government. Over the years there have been out-standing persons in the Budget Bureau, for example, who have proved that civil servants can be totally dedicated to Presidents. The two Executive Secretaries of the NSC under Truman were careerists, as were Eisenhower's two Staff Secretaries. It then might be possible for the Cabinet Secretary to remain beyond the life of an administration (as has been the case with the Executive Clerk of the White House), or given the rigors of the job, to train a successor.

Most White House advisory systems should be subgroups of the Cabinet. The functions of the National Security Council, the Domestic Council, and the Council on Environmental Quality should be per-formed by clearly delineated Cabinet subcommittees. Their staffs should be part of the Cabinet secretariat; presumably each would be serviced by a Deputy Cabinet Secretary. The Council on International Economic Policy and the Economic Policy Board might be placed either under the Cabinet secretariat or the Council of Economic Ad-visers. If the latter format is chosen, one of the three CEA members should be an expert in international economics with primary responsi-bility for the operation of what is now the Council on International Economic Policy.

Such subgroups would prepare policy papers and propose options. In many cases relating to minor or technical questions, it would be unnecessary to seek full-dress Cabinet review. But issues of major im-portance should be debated by the Cabinet.

This system was specifically rejected by the Commission on the Organization of the Government for the Conduct of Foreign Policy, chaired by Robert D. Murphy, in its report of June 1975. The Murphy Commission viewed an overall policy council as "cumbersome and inefficient." It felt that there are issues "so distinctively 'foreign' or 'domestic' as to put an unnecessary burden on those many members of the Cabinet . . . who would take no interest in them, and whose pres-ence might inhibit free discussion among those more directly in-volved."[7]

The collegial model, by a process of trial and error, would eventually have to sort out the inconsequential from the significant. The time of Cabinet members is limited. But the system's basic strength, in my judgment, is what the Murphy Commission seems to feel is its greatest

7. *Commission on the Organization of the Government for the Conduct of Foreign Policy*, Report (Government Printing Office, 1975), p. 36.

weakness. Namely, a collegial system is designed to give a President the advice of superior persons who may not be directly involved, who bring a sense of detachment to bear, and who may even approach problems from fresh or oblique angles.

This could be of particular value in the conduct of foreign policy. As I. M. Destler pointed out, "[The] misreading of domestic politics— or failure to take it very seriously—can be disastrously counter-productive in terms of the goals of foreign policy. . . . The effective integration of domestic political and foreign policy advice becomes a matter of some urgency."[8] The headlong pursuit of involvement in Vietnam might have been slowed down if President Johnson had chosen to consider policy in a forum that gave greater weight to public opinion and congressional concerns. Placing the NSC under the Cabinet secretariat would be a move in this direction.

The present system resembles a tree with too many limbs sapping strength from the trunk. A minutely detailed chart of President Ford's White House staff organization, published in December 1974, contained seventy-two boxes (including "The President").[9] The scope of this organizational chart would be considerably reduced by the changes I propose. The suggested White House staff discussed in chapter 9 would have no special-interest representation offices or offices with programmatic operational responsibilities. It also would be reduced in size to eliminate some of the causes for delay and distortion in the present system.

7. *Above all, the President must want the Cabinet to be an effective instrument of advice.*

Presidents have been disinclined to commit themselves to a mode of operation that can be time-consuming, irritating, and potentially challenging. The benefits of an advisory system that raises doubts and represents diverse perspectives have been less obvious. Yet it is time for the skeptic to be honored in presidential councils, rather than merely tolerated. If some of the ineffective ways the Cabinet has functioned in the past could be removed, and if its value could be understood by Presidents, then there are many techniques available to a

8. I. M. Destler, "National Security Advice to Presidents" (paper prepared for the Conference on Advising the President, Princeton University, November 1, 1975; processed), pp. 45, 46.

9. See *The National Journal*, December 28, 1974, pp. 1956–57.

President to encourage constructive collective advice. Some of these techniques have been suggested by Irving Janis and Alexander George.[10] Janis, for example, believes that a President can make better use of advisory sessions if he remains "impartial instead of stating preferences and expectations at the outset."[11] A President who first gives his own views surely will get them parroted back to him by loyal subordinates. At times Truman and Kennedy chose to absent themselves from certain meetings in order to facilitate debate; at other times Eisenhower and Kennedy set up competing teams to work out different options.

The skill of a President in drawing the best advice from his Cabinet and the positive reinforcement that a President can give to a system of collegial government ultimately will be of greater importance than all mechanical adjustments combined.

ORGANIZATIONAL arrangements are static only on paper. In practice, they are constantly drifting as sand responds to tide. People come and go. Relations between officials change. New problems arise. Unfortunately, Presidents usually pay attention to the processes through which they govern only when they are first elected. They quickly become consumed by day-to-day matters. Certainly a lesson that emerges from studying the organization of the presidency is the need for the Presidents' continuous attention to the procedures of governance.

Still, Stephen K. Bailey was right when he said that "there are no organizational gimmicks capable of overcoming the enormous centrifuge of governance in our pluralistic society."[12] The proposals set forth here should not be viewed as a series of gimmicks but as a different way to consider the workings of government. If the recognition is shared that greater collegiality is needed in governing a democratic society, these proposals suggest an appropriate organizational framework.

"Good people cannot do good things with bad mechanisms," Richard Nixon once said. "No, the major cause of the ineffectiveness of government is not a matter of men or of money. It is primarily a matter

10. See Irving L. Janis, *Victims of Groupthink* (Houghton Mifflin, 1972); and Alexander L. George, "The Case for Multiple Advocacy in Making Foreign Policy," *American Political Science Review*, vol. 66 (September 1972), p. 764.

11. Janis, *Victims of Groupthink*, pp. 209–10.

12. Stephen K. Bailey, "Managing the Federal Government," in Kermit Gordon, ed., *Agenda for the Nation* (Brookings Institution, 1968), p. 304.

of machinery." [13] Yet good people often can overcome the handicap of bad machinery and bad people can corrupt good machinery. Faith in machinery is faith misplaced. The machinery proposed in this study is designed merely to *support* Presidents who choose to move away from a system of White House dominance and vestigial Cabinet power.

The implementation of these proposals would not automatically produce creative, humane, efficient, balanced democratic government. Collegial government would not untie the invisible strings that connect congressional committee chairmen to powerful special interests and the chairmen to bureau chiefs. It would not negate the institutional interests of government agencies or the rivalries between them. What collegial government could do is pull department heads and the sub-Cabinet more firmly into the presidential orbit, giving Presidents considerably greater outreach than they have under a centralized system while providing them with a broader base of advice and support. Presidential leadership will be more effective when it is rooted in shared responsibility.

13. *Public Papers of the Presidents, Richard Nixon, 1971* (Government Printing Office, 1972), p. 473.

Index